W9-CCU-757

Ex Libris
© APCo

special plants

special plants

over 500 outstanding plants for the enthusiastic gardener

Jane Taylor

with photographs by Marijke Heuff

Quadrille

PAGE ONE *Few plants are as subtly coloured as* Aquilegia viridiflora, *with its alabaster wings and chocolate spurs.*

PAGE TWO *Low, late summer sun lights up pink Japanese anemones and* Rosa *'Astrid Lingrun'.*

RIGHT *On the thread-fine smoke of a dark-leaved* Cotinus coggygria, *drops of rain gleam like crystal beads.*

First published in 1998 by Quadrille Publishing Limited

Alhambra House, 27–31 Charing Cross Road, London WC2H 0LS

Art Editor • Françoise Dietrich

Design Assistant • Sara Jane Glynn

Editorial Assistant • Katherine Seely

Picture Researcher • Nadine Bazar

Indexer • Antonia Johnson

Production Manager • Candida Lane

British Library Cataloguing-in-Publication Data

A catalogue record for this book is available from the British Library.

ISBN 1 899988 51 3

Printed and bound in Singapore

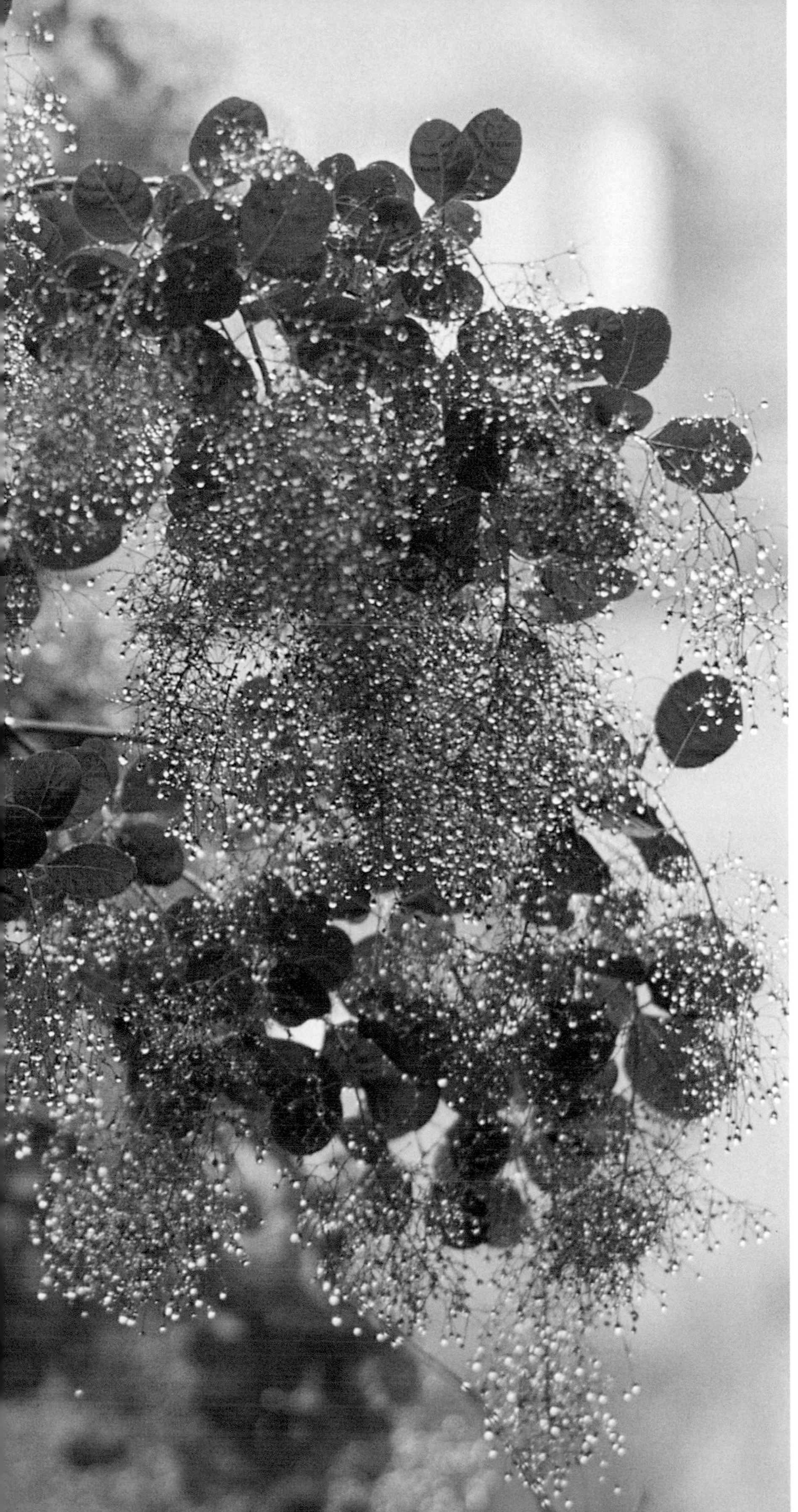

contents

introduction

This book is intended for the discerning gardener who is not content with the current fashion in plants, or who aspires to more than the 'garden centre one hundred' of plants that are easy to produce and to sell. It is a personal selection, with all the idiosyncracies that implies, of plants familiar and plants not so well known. What unites them is that they have all, in one way or another, captured my heart, by their beauty, their strokeability, their evocative fragrance, their bravery in the face of winter's intemperance, their silken frailty or their muscular robustness. Often it has been hard to choose from among the thousands of plants I have grown. Some of those with which I am most besotted are hardly available commercially, and I have reluctantly omitted them. Some are widely available, while others you may have to search for; I hope, when you track them down, you will find them as irresistible as I do.

The selection begins with the trees and shrubs that have sufficient structure to form the framework, or backbone of the garden. Trees to provide grateful shade

Dark-veined foliage sets off the modestly-nodding blooms of Helleborus torquatus *'Little Black', their sombre petals framing ivory stamens.*

and trees to wipe your eye with colour of flower or foliage or fruit; trees of discreet grace and trees of bold outline; evergreen trees and deciduous trees that may be as beautiful in their winter tracery as in their summer livery: the choice is wide. Accompanying them are the characterful shrubs that have presence for much or all of the year. The smaller the space at your disposition, the more important is the year-round aspect of your trees and shrubs; those that have two or even three seasons of beauty must take precedence.

It is perfectly possible to make a beautiful garden with only trees and shrubs, set off by grass or stone. But most of us want more, and so I move next to the vertical dimension, with a selection of climbers to tempt you. Climbers can link house and garden; add colour in little space as they adorn walls or scale trees; or add an extra season's beauty to a host shrub. Thus it is that your borders, even, may be home to climbers. True aficionados of climbing plants will scrutinize each tree and shrub, not only for its beauty or its utility but with the question: How would this look with a climber adorning its branches? Once this habit of mind is acquired, even a comparatively new garden will prove to have many

The winter foliage of Bergenia *'Sunningdale', just touched with crimson or, where the full light of the sun touches the leaves, richly claret-flushed, is rimmed with hoar frost.*

possibilities of growing climbers beyond the obvious house walls or boundary fence.

But the mainstay of the border are the plants that make sweeps and drifts of colour, whether of leaf or of flower; the plants that are the equivalent of the watercolourist's broadbrush, full with washes of colour. These are plants to grow in quantity, not in ones or twos; even the smallest garden is the better for some generous plantings, chosen with due care so they do not leave a great gap once their principle season is ended. Among the candidates for broadbrush effects in the border I count also the plants often described as 'architectural': those with strong lines of spear leaves or bold paddle-foliage, or with an infloresence in which outline is as visually compelling as colour.

It is perfectly possible to design a border for a single concentrated season of impact, with broad sweeps of colour, and to ignore its dull or derelict appearance at other times of the year. But most gardeners, especially those of an experimental or acquisitive bent and with limited space at their disposal, want their borders to look at least respectable, and preferably alluring, all year. At their service are the plants that I categorize as fleeting: bulbs that drift among shrubs or spear up between clumps of perennials to waken the spring border, add summer colour while taking the minimum space, or prolong the season into autumn; annuals and biennials with which to ring the changes of colour and outline with far less effort than if a whole perennial grouping were to be altered and renewed; and tender perennials and subshrubs that need renewing each year, but repay that small effort manyfold.

Some of the loveliest plants in the lexicon are those that need the shade and shelter of woodland, or that thrive in grassy meadows. Many of them are species, or very near to species' wildling grace; in the main, highly bred plants belong not in such spaces but in the more formal setting of the border. The classic woodland shrub is the rhododendron, with camellias closely rivalling them, but even gardeners with the lime-rich soils that are death to rhododendrons can make beautiful woodlands in miniature, and they will find much to tempt them in the chapter on woodland and orchard.

So handsome are many of the plants that thrive in damp or boggy soils that keen gardeners will contrive artificial bogs, using plastic liners to retain moisture. There is, of course, nothing like the real thing; a natural stream with, here and there, agreeably soggy banks where moisture-loving plants can grow to their full, jungly character. Since many lusty weeds also thrive in damp

soils, it is as well that plenty of bog plants have handsome and weed-excluding foliage among which incidents of flower come and go.

There is no perfect way to order a book, any more than there is the perfect garden. Nor is even the most personal choice of plants, captured within the pages of a book, necessarily the same as the plants that the writer would choose when presented with a given plot of land to decorate with a living palette. The discerning gardener, then, will read this book with – I hope – interest and even excitement, but also with scepticism, regarding it not as a recipe book nor as a catalogue but as the gateway to a world of possibilities, some to be seized, some sought, some rejected. Even the best of plants, wrongly placed, will not achieve its potential; and the best of plants merit the best of treatment. From the inspiration this book may provide, gardens may be created that are framed and decorated with fine plants, chosen with a critical eye for their intrinsic beauty and their suitability for the place they fill. For it is in this dual perspective, not in simply following another's choice, that the faculty of discernment most fully manifests itself.

Bold drifts of foliage – the velvet-soft, silvered carpet of Stachys byzantina, *mounds of pale* Santolina chamaecyparissus, *and* Pinus strobus *'Nana', with a tan-felted rhododendron – frame the proud spires of a single bold clump of* Acanthus mollis *Latifolius Group.*

framework plants

trees & shrubs with character

The cloudy 'smoke' of Cotinus coggygria *'Royal Purple' is frozen into blanched immobility by winter's grip, with just a few lingering, reddish leaves to recall the glowing colours of summer. From spring, when the young foliage expands as lucent as rubies, through summer's rich garb, to the incandescence of autumn's dying leaves, this is a shrub for all seasons.*

Trees are the soul and shrubs the structure of a garden. The trunks of trees stand stately and solid or gothically gnarled, clad in ghostly white bark or gleaming mahogany, sinuously striped or roughly flaked. Their branches soar upwards as the ribs of a cathedral arch, or dip amiably towards us to display their blossom – spring-fresh or summer-opulent – and the rich harvest of their fruits. Autumn is marked by the surrender of living green foliage to a vivid death, mirrored in carpets of fallen leaves beneath and honoured by the stalwart evergreens. And all the while they cast shadows, dappled and flickering with sunlight, passing imperceptibly, inexorably across lawns and borders and paths. Beneath and among them, firmly grounded, stand the shrubs which give backbone to our plantings. Flaunting or retiring, their foliage and flowers and fruits mark the passage of the seasons, filling winter's cold air or summer's sultry days with fragrance.

framework plants

The delicate blooms of standard-trained Rosa *'Ballerina' float above the rounded heads of foliage, while the vertical lines of rose stems are echoed in the spikes of lavender – violet-blue 'Hidcote' and pale 'Loddon Pink' – that half-conceal them. Beyond are coral-pink* Alstroemeria ligtu *hybrids.*

Advancing into our consciousness or retreating into obscurity after their floraison, growing from babyhood to maturity and lapsing into senescence, trees and shrubs are never static as time works its transformations upon them, yet they give the garden its sense of timelessness.

People plant trees for all sorts of reasons; for trees appeal to us in a diversity of ways. The aesthetic impulse is of course strong. Many trees are beautiful, a precious few of them all year round, many more at one or two seasons when their flowers, or foliage, or fruits, or bark are at their most alluring. We are highly visual animals, so the look of a tree is what first catches our attention; but as we live with them, we come to appreciate the perfume of their flowers, the texture of their bark, and the sound of their leaves either whispering in the summer breeze or pattering down in autumn.

It should go without saying that trees have a major role to play in design, framing or dominating the garden scene. They give welcome shade in summer and, at a more mundane level, can hide an ugly view, or help to reduce noise from the road or the neighbours. For some people, such aesthetic and utilitarian considerations are almost irrelevant: for them, planting a tree is a statement of

'Charles de Mills' is a fine old gallica rose with blooms which when fully open recall nothing so much as the underside of a mature field mushroom, so regular and intricately-pleated are the wine-crimson and maroon-red petals.

More usually seen as a spreading, free-growing tree, here the Judas tree (Cercis siliquastrum) *has been trained over a pergola, which it decks in spring with its shocking pink flowers, erupting from the branches and twigs as the rounded leaves unfurl.*

The pleasurable melancholy of autumn, heightened by the misty sunlight that hints of winter's chill to come, is captured in this scene of leaf-strewn grass. The glowing colours of Acer palmatum *are enhanced by the sombre tones of the gracefully weeping branches of* Picea breweriana *beyond.*

defiance against our mortality; it is a dynastic act. And many of us, though we may be inarticulate about it, feel almost mystical about trees: we seem to sense the soul that inhabits them, each one with its own personality, slowly unfolding over the years as they grow from babyhood to maturity.

The aesthetic appeal of trees is very diverse. The majesty of a mature oak is entirely different from the slender weeping outline of a Mount Etna broom, or the airy tracery of a birch. Some trees – including many of the most popular for today's small gardens – appeal above all because of their flowers, even if they have little to offer outside their season: Japanese cherries (though some colour brightly in autumn) are the classic of this type. Others appeal solely or mainly because of their elegant foliage; Japanese maples (which have the bonus of incandescent autumn tints), *Gleditsia triacanthos*, the lucent green *Ligustrum lucidum*, Brewer's spruce and the long-needled pines, for example. Coloured foliage is another lure: the silver of *Elaeagnus angustifolia*, the dusty blue-grey of the Arizona cypress, even – if you must – the heavy purple of certain crabs or *Prunus cerasifera* cultivars. Some trees offer a double season of value with flowers in spring and fruit in autumn: several dogwoods, and many *Sorbus*, both rowans and whitebeams; other double-barrelled trees are *Amelanchier canadensis* and *Amelanchier lamarckii*. Yet other trees have such beautiful flowers, allied perhaps to foliage that is handsome or dainty, that they earn their keep for many months each year: magnolias, of course, for opulence, the Judas trees and redbuds for their rich colouring and profusion, or *Styrax japonicus*, for grace and charm of flower, leaf and outline.

Other trees have different attractions: the foliage of *Cercidiphyllum japonicum*, is attractive enough, but its glory is its autumn colour and aroma; and the snake-bark and paper-bark maples,

Hydrangea macrophylla *'Générale Vicomtesse de Vibraye', one of the most popular of mophead hydrangeas, is a grand old cultivar, achieving these vibrant blue tones in soil that is both acid and high in aluminium salts (in alkaline soil it bears bright pink flowers). Here it grows in the shade of hornbeams* (Carpinus betulus) *that have been pleached into a hedge on stilts, their trunks framed by the hydrangea blooms.*

too, are glorious in the fall. These maples have another quality which is often much under-rated: beautiful bark. It is, of course, above all for their bark that birches are planted; but *Arbutus* × *andrachnoides*, *Eucalyptus pauciflora* subsp. *niphophila*, and the stewartias also have bark worthy of the foliage. Such bark is not only lovely to behold; it invites the discerning gardener to run an appreciative hand along the trunk and limbs.

However strongly they appeal to our aesthetic sense, few if any shrubs quite have the other-worldly, soulful quality of trees. I find it helpful, when making a garden, to think of shrubs that are solid or structural enough in character to form part of the framework of the garden and, on the other hand, those that are more flimsy or evanescent in their appeal. The first will have a firm framework of branches, or grow into strong, rounded or tiered or pyramidal outlines; the flimsies, making their impact more usually in flower or leaf than in form, are to be found in the chapter on borders. As always, when making a garden in the English idiom, one is working in four dimensions: spatial and temporal. A shrub that has the capacity to fill all four dimensions, though it may do so in changing ways at different seasons, has another value in the garden from one that hardly impinges on our consciousness except when in flower or fruit.

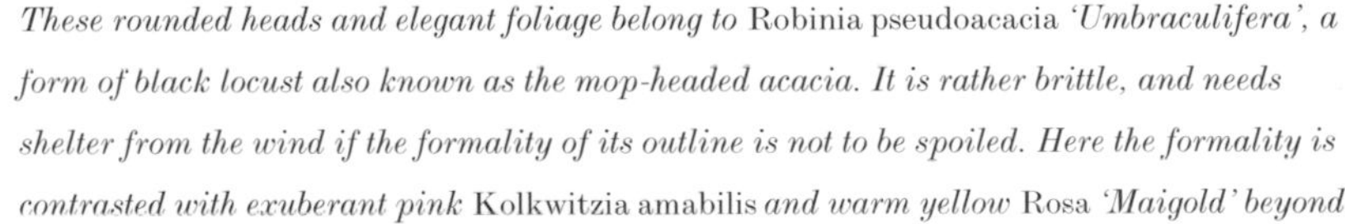

These rounded heads and elegant foliage belong to Robinia pseudoacacia *'Umbraculifera', a form of black locust also known as the mop-headed acacia. It is rather brittle, and needs shelter from the wind if the formality of its outline is not to be spoiled. Here the formality is contrasted with exuberant pink* Kolkwitzia amabilis *and warm yellow* Rosa *'Maigold' beyond.*

The snowball tree, Viburnum opulus *'Roseum', is a form of the guelder rose in which all the florets are sterile, producing – in the same way as mophead hydrangeas – a rounded head of flower rather than the lacy inflorescence of the wild species.*

The white lacecap heads on tiered branches of Viburnum plicatum *'Mariesii' are spread beneath a white-trunked silver birch. Overhead, the leaves of a copper beech* (Fagus sylvatica *Atropurpurea Group) are touched to garnet translucence by the sun.*

framework plants

At the height of its autumn incandescence the Japanese full moon maple, Acer shirasawanum *'Aureum', begins to reveal its winter tracery to come, as the fiery leaves fall to carpet the ground beneath its spreading branches.*

Whereas a tree bare of leaves retains its character and has its own beauty in the tracery of branch and twig, few deciduous shrubs, once stripped for winter, have much to offer. Evergreens, on the other hand, give a sense of enduring stability against which more ephemeral incidents are heightened. Not that evergreens are unchanging, mere backdrops for colourful flowers or fruit. They too produce new growths and shed old leaves; it is the rhythm with which they do it that differs. They display a contrast, in spring and summer, between bright or pale new shoots and the darker, harder-textured old leaves; and they may take on purple or mahogany or metallic tones with the onset of winter. Among the evergreen shrubs of character that I have selected are *Choisya ternata, Fatsia japonica, Itea ilicifolia, Photinia × fraseri, Osmanthus heterophyllus* and some viburnums, together with camellias, ceanothus, and – of course – rhododendrons, shrubs with beautiful flowers as well as handsome foliage. Along with the smaller rhododendrons there are, among low-growing shrubs for year-round good looks, *Bupleurum fruticosum*, and the shrub that, more than any other, I should never wish to be without: *Daphne pontica*.

These are dense enough to count as ground-cover, or rather as a comely clothing for bare soil (ground-cover is such a utilitarian phrase). So too are sun roses and their allies, the deckle-edged, grey-leaved *Brachyglottis monroi*, and most evergreen azaleas (with the further advantage of being portable, so you can plant closely and then spread them out or start a new group elsewhere as they expand). Winter-flowering sarcococcas and the lower-growing skimmias, with their bright berries or colourful winter buds, almost belong in this category too. And that brings me to the precious shrubs that flower in winter: witch hazel and some viburnums among them. We are now moving into a category of shrubs that are more decor than framework, taking centre stage when in flower or fruit and discreetly merging into the background once their season has passed. The winter-flowering shrubs are followed in early spring by corylopsis and Japanese quince, and soon by brooms, tree peonies, and yet more viburnums, leading to the high summer pleasures of buddlejas, hydrangeas, and *Aesculus parviflora*.

The honeyed perfume of buddlejas is part of summer as much as the butterflies that dance around their arching spikes of flower. Fragrance is one of the most potent and yet elusive qualities of plants: impossible to describe, sometimes fickle, always evocative. Think of mock orange (*Philadelphus*), roses, myrtle, the dwarf lilac, *Pittosporum tobira* and – yet again – viburnums; the best one can do is to liken their fragrance to that of something else, for there is no other vocabulary for scent beyond the feeble 'spicy', 'rich', 'sweet' and the like. These are for the most part shrubs that belong in domesticated settings; many make good border components, or serve to link the wilder parts of the garden with the more formal, near the house.

However they are used, what is certain is that a garden without shrubs is a garden less than half-clothed; and one without trees is hardly a garden at all.

With the onset of cold weather the slender, pointed leaves of this Viburnum nudum *'Pink Beauty' flush with rich tones, enhanced by the clusters of pale berries.*

The purple foliage of Prunus cerasifera *'Pissardii', and the brooding Austrian pine* (Pinus nigra) *behind it, are lightened by the silvery leaves of* Elaeagnus angustifolia. *Together with the dark, mounded shrubs in the background, they lend solidity to the insubstantial grasses:* Miscanthus sinensis *'Strictus'*, M. s. *'Silberfeder' and* M. s. *'Malepartus'*, Molinia *'Transparent'*, Deschampsia cespitosa *'Goldschleier' and* Panicum virgatum *'Rehbraun'*.

The flowers of Abutilon vitifolium *have all the tissue-fine quality typical of mallow flowers, their glacier-pale colouring enhanced by the rich orange stamens at their heart.*

Abies koreana

evergreen conifer H 3m/10ft S 3m/10ft
summer to autumn Z 4–8

At all seasons this silver fir is a neat, pyramid-shaped conifer with needles dark green above and white beneath. It is the cones, however, which are its chief appeal. Appearing even on baby specimens hardly higher than your knee, they stand up proudly on the branches, and are as long as a finger but considerably stouter, of intense indigo-violet. There are other silver firs with similar deep blue cones; but this is the only one that is compact and slow-growing enough to find a place in small gardens. It is not the easiest plant to place, needing companions that are low enough not to mask its characteristic pyramidal outline and discreet enough not to compete with its subtle colouring. Avoid the tritely obvious heathers, which have become such a cliché with conifers; try instead *Epimedium* × *youngianum* with its purple-tinted young foliage, or *Mahonia nervosa* for its foliage of almost metallic texture. Such combinations bring out the best in conifers, which if chosen with discernment have much to offer.

Abies koreana needs a deep, moist soil to give its best. The only pruning that is normally needed is to remove any dead wood.

Abutilon vitifolium

deciduous shrub H 4.5m/15ft S 3m/10ft
early to mid summer Z 8–10

The softly downy, vine-shaped leaves of this Chilean tree mallow are of a tender shade of grey-green, setting off the wide, saucer-shaped flowers.

'Veronica Tennant' is especially free with its large, lavender flowers; white-flowered forms are even lovelier in their crystalline purity. They grow rapidly, prefer sun or light shade, and need careful staking in windy sites lest they blow over; but are otherwise tolerant of wind, at least in warm gardens. Elsewhere they do well as bulky wall shrubs, where they might be paired with the scrambling, violet potato-flowered *Solanum crispum* 'Glasnevin', which starts to flower towards the end of the abutilon's season and continues until autumn.

To increase named cultivars of the abutilon, take summer cuttings; or sow seeds, which may give you a range of shades from glacier-pale to an almost intense mauve, as well as white. Specimens grown on a wall should be encouraged to form a single leader and should have their main stem carefully secured, but no other tying-in is needed. It is worth cutting off old flower-heads, as seed is produced so abundantly that the plant may suddenly die of sheer exhaustion; other pruning consists merely in removing dead or frost-damaged wood in late spring, or after flowering if to reduce the shrub's bulk. This must be done with discretion, however, with well-trained specimens, otherwise vigorous lateral growths may develop.

Acer, Japanese maples see overleaf

Acer, snake-bark and paper-bark maples

deciduous trees H 4.5–6m/15–20ft S 15ft/4.5m
autumn and winter Z 5–8

As well as their graceful, slender branched outline and elegant leaf-shape, several maples have striated or peeling bark to add winter interest after the leaves have flared into autumn tint and fallen and the bright-toned winged seeds have spun on the wind to land where they may. *Acer capillipes* has greenish, white-striped bark with coral young shoots, while there are several forms of *A. davidii*, of looser growth with reddish, white-striped bark and purple-red young shoots. The Asiatic *A. rufinerve* has green, white-striped bark, bloomed with white on the young shoots; its American counterpart is *A. pensylvanicum*. The paper-bark maple, *A. griseum*, has shaggy, tan and mahogany bark, and trifoliate leaves, silvery-glaucous beneath, turning to scarlet and crimson in autumn. Like all trees that colour vividly in autumn, they are best set off by dark evergreen foliage – of hollies or mahonias, perhaps.

All these maples will thrive in any fertile garden soil. The smooth-stemmed snake-barks should be encouraged to make a clear leader and, as the tree develops, crossing and crowded branches should be pruned out to display the bark and the graceful outline during winter when the tree is fully dormant. Only small cuts should be made at the end of the growing season, in late summer and early autumn. The paper-bark maple should be pruned similarly, with a clear short trunk and uncluttered main branches.

As the shaggy outer layers of bark, outlined here with hoar frost, peel away, the smooth inner covering on the trunk of the aptly-named paper-bark maple, Acer griseum, *is revealed.*

acer

autumn incandescence

DETAILS FROM TOP:
The incisively drawn outlines of Acer japonicum *leaves are enhanced here by the sunlight.*

The rich maroon-purple of Acer palmatum *f.* atropurpureum *throws into relief the chalk-white trunk of* Betula utilis *var.* jacquemontii.

Acer palmatum *'Sango-kaku' is an individualist; its pale, fresh foliage turns butter yellow in autumn before dropping to reveal coral-red stems in winter.*

Dying, the elegantly symmetrical leaves of Acer palmatum *'Osakazuki' turn to brilliant scarlet-crimson, falling to spread a carpet of ottoman richness on the autumn grass.*

MAIN PICTURE:
Among the most appealing of Japanese maples are those in which the leaves are dissected into lacy delicacy, as in Acer palmatum *var.* dissectum.

ACER, JAPANESE MAPLES

deciduous tree or shrub H 1.5–4.5m/5–15ft
S 1.5–4.5m/5–15ft spring to autumn Z 5–8

The Japanese maples, selections of *Acer palmatum*, are so diverse, and have given rise to so many variants, that their descriptions would fill an entire book. They typically grow into small trees with bright green, five- or seven-lobed leaves, though some of the selections with lacy-fine dissected foliage remain low, hummocky shrubs all their days. Both leaf forms, the sharply-lobed and the finely-cut, come in coppery and purple shades as well as green, and there are variegated and lime-yellow selections as well. All colour brilliantly in autumn. The old 'Osakazuki' remains one of the most vividly incandescent in dying leaf, and is hardly less bright in spring when the young foliage unfurls in shades of scarlet. Similar spring tints belong to 'Shindeshôjô' and 'Shishio', while 'Chitoseyama' is bright coral-pink aging to bronze-green, and 'Katsura' blends buff-orange and coral. Among the finest of purple-leaved Japanese maples are the near-black 'Bloodgood', and finely dissected 'Burgundy Lace' and 'Garnet', and cultivars of *A. palmatum* var. *dissectum:* 'Crimson Queen', 'Inaba shidare' and 'Dissectum Nigrum'. All turn intense scarlet-crimson in autumn. Unusually, the autumn foliage of 'Sango-kaku' ('Senkaki') is yellow; still more unusually, this cultivar has bright coral winter stems. The best of the golden maples is not a form of *A. palmatum*, but the Japanese full moon maple, *A. shirasawanum* 'Aureum' (*A. japonicum* f. *aureum*), with rounded, lobed leaves of tender lime yellow from spring to autumn, when they turn to scarlet.

The golden full moon maple can be tricky to place, as the leaves are apt to scorch in hot sun or drying winds and to turn anaemic green in too much shade. Indeed, a place sheltered from cold winds and fierce sun suits all the Japanese maples best, while their roots prefer cool, leafy soil that does not dry out. They hardly require pruning, unless to remove dead or damaged wood.

The autumn livery of maples so captures the imagination that their value in spring may be overlooked. Acer palmatum *'Osakazuki' is also a flowering tree of merit.*

As the fingered leaves of the shrubby buckeye, Aesculus parviflora, *expand in spring, they fade from copper to pale green, later to ripen to summer's full green. Bluebells grow among the low, spreading branches of this mature specimen.*

RIGHT *A small, many-stemmed tree,* Amelanchier lamarckii *is unrivalled in both the brightness and the dependability of its autumn tints.*

Aesculus parviflora

deciduous shrub H 3m/10ft S 3m/10ft
high summer Z 5–9

The shrubby buckeye, *Aesculus parviflora,* native of the southern United States, is a wide-spreading, mildly suckering shrub with airy panicles of white, red-anthered flowers appearing well after the main horse-chestnut or buckeye season. The palmate foliage is tinted with bronze and pink as it unfurls in spring, and colours again, pleasantly rather than dramatically, in autumn. In growth it is open enough to allow for an underplanting of spring flowers; bluebells assort especially well with its young foliage, or you could echo its apricot tints with pink-trumpeted daffodils and the pinkish young foliage of epimediums.

Any fertile garden soil suits the shrubby buckeye. Layers, pinned into a peaty mixture, root readily, or you can sow the conker-like seeds. The only pruning it may need is to restrict its sideways growth, taking care to keep the outer growths furnished down to ground level. This should be done in winter, while the shrub is dormant and its branch outline can be easily distinguished.

Amelanchier lamarckii

deciduous tree H 4.5m/15ft S 4.5m/15ft
spring and autumn Z 5–8

One of the prettiest of spring-flowering trees for colder regions, the snowy mespilus or June berry bears a mass of starry, white flowers followed by sweet black berries at midsummer (from which little seedlings often grow unaided by the gardener). In autumn it flares into bonfire colours of scarlet, flame and crimson. With its pure

colouring free of any hint of pink, the snowy mespilus is the ideal companion for the sharper tones of spring: the lime and chartreuse of spurges and Bowles' golden grass, the sunshine yellow daisies of doronicums, scarlet- and orange-flowered

Japanese quinces, and small daffodils. If softer tints are more to your taste, set the snowy mespilus among pink azaleas (in acid soils only), or with white or cream half-height daffodils, Solomon's seal or the allied false spikenard (*Smilacina racemosa*), and ferns.

The same moist, acid soil that suits azaleas and false spikenards is ideal for amelanchiers, but they will tolerate any fertile garden soil; they dislike thin, dry chalk. This species, unlike some others, does not sucker, but may form a single-stemmed or multi-stemmed tree; unwanted shoots from the lower stem can be removed as soon as they appear, but the multi-stemmed effect is very appealing.

Arbutus × andrachnoides

evergreen tree H 4.5m/15ft S 4.5m/15ft
year-round Z 7–9 [unless indicated]

The glory of this small tree is not its white, urn-shaped flowers appearing in late autumn and winter, but its flaking, cinnamon and fox-red bark, which invites the passer-by to run an appreciative hand down the stem. The foliage is dark and polished, reflecting every least change in sun, shadow or breeze. A hybrid between the Killarney *Arbutus unedo* and the Grecian *A. andrachne*, this tree inherits the tolerance of lime of the first and is more resistant to frost than the second.

The strawberry trees dislike root disturbance and should be planted from pots, then left to develop with the minimum pruning, consisting only of removal, in spring, of dead inner branchlets as the growth becomes more dense. The main branches tend naturally to grow at a near-horizontal angle, and should be kept as uncluttered as possible to display their bark to fullest advantage. If damaged by storm or frost, strawberry trees can be cut back, hard if necessary, when new growth begins to break out.

Fortunate is the gardener who inherits a mature specimen of Arbutus × andrachnoides *such as this, or who can wait for the sapling he plants to grow strong and tall. For those who have not this privilege, it is a tree to make pilgrimage to, in order to caress its beautiful, richly-coloured bark.*

Berberis

deciduous shrubs H 1.8m/6ft S 1.5m/5ft
year-round, and spring Z 5–8 [unless indicated]

Truly a shrub for all seasons, *Berberis dictyophylla* [Z 6–8] has neat, white-backed, glaucous-blue leaves which turn to rich scarlet and crimson very late in autumn, falling in midwinter to reveal the ➤

Many birches have white bark, but in Betula albo-sinensis septentrionalis *the trunk and limbs are clad in satin-textured apricot, cream and tan.*

whitewashed stems. The flowers are large for a berberis, resembling tiny double, lemon-yellow roses; red fruits, bloomed with white, follow. Older wood loses much of its chalky white bloom, and if unpruned the shrub becomes rather shapeless; to keep both the brilliant whiteness of the winter stems and the fountain-like outline which displays them so well, you need to prune the shrub hard each year or two, removing two- and three-year wood in winter. Wear stout gloves, as protection against the fierce spines. Like most berberis, this one has few fads about soil so long as it is free-draining; it is frost- and wind-hardy. Encourage just-pruned specimens with a mulch and feed. Summer cuttings root reluctantly, in my experience. Mist and bottom heat should help.

Of all the manifestations of *Berberis thunbergii*, 'Golden Ring' is the one I commend to you. Of generous but not over-exuberant proportions, it has oxblood-red foliage lifted out of the ordinary by the wire-fine lime-yellow edge to each leaf. The sparse scarlet berries in autimn are outshone by the brilliant vermilion and crimson of the dying leaves. 'Golden Ring' can be increased by cuttings, and thrives in any fertile, well-drained soil; grow it in full light for the most intense leaf colour.

Betula

deciduous trees H 10m/35ft S 6m/20ft
year-round Z 5–7 [unless indicated]

It is hard to choose just one birch from among so many good species valued for their white, cream, amber, apricot, tan or near-black bark, as well as for their yellow autumn colouring, a contrast to the fiery reds of maples or rowans, with that extra dimension of sound as the dying leaves patter down like golden wafers. They span the northern hemisphere, inhabiting the cooler boreal regions or higher altitudes, ranging from North America's white-stemmed paper-bark or canoe birch, *Betula papyrifera* [Z 3–6], golden-stemmed *B. alleghaniensis* (*B. lutea*) [Z 4–7], and shaggy black river birch, *B. nigra* [Z 4–9], through the graceful silver birch of European and Russian woods and mountain slopes, *B. pendula* [Z 3–7], to the Himalayan, Chinese and Japanese species. Among these are the apricot-barked *B. albo-sinensis septentrionalis* and creamy-peach *B. ermanii*; and my final choice, *B. utilis* var. *jacquemontii*, the brilliantly white-barked birch which hails from the dry western Himalayan ranges and Kashmir (see page 23). It will do well enough in thin, rocky soil, but appreciates the better living of fertile, well-drained garden soil.

If you choose a birch as a shade tree (for deciduous azaleas perhaps, in acid soil, or a carpet of blue *Anemone apennina* if your soil is limy), remember that they have wide-reaching fibrous roots, greedy for surface nutrients. Little pruning is necessary except to encourage a single leader, gradually trimming up the small lower branches when dormant to leave a clear trunk. Most nursery specimens are single-stemmed, but a multi-stemmed birch also has great appeal.

BRACHYGLOTTIS MONROI

evergreen shrub H 60cm/2ft S 90cm/3ft foliage Z 9–10

Brachyglottis (*Senecio*) 'Sunshine' is far more often seen, but *B. monroi* is more appealing, with its low, spreading habit and deckle-edged leaves, grey-felted above and white beneath, the pale reverse visible along the upper margin as though each leaf were touched with hoar frost. It has yellow daisies, which add nothing and can be removed; hard pruning in spring keeps it compact and discourages flowering. Sun and well-drained soil also encourage compact growth, and it stands exposure to sea gales. It can be increased by summer cuttings.

LEFT Brachyglottis monroi *is comely all year, with its grey, crimple-edged leaves outlined in white; the cheery yellow daisies, appearing in summer, can be snipped out if they do not assort with your chosen colour scheme.*

BUDDLEJA

deciduous shrubs H 1.8m/6ft S 1.8m/6ft summer Z 6–9 [unless indicated]

There are just two butterfly bushes I will admit to the company of shrubs endowed with firmness of structure or clarity of outline, both chosen as much for their foliage as their flowers. The hardier of the two is *Buddleja* 'Lochinch', which allies luminously grey foliage and robust growth with stout flower spikes of clear lavender-blue, each tiny floret amber-eyed, and endowed with a sweet, strong honey perfume. The more tender *B. fallowiana* var. *alba* [Z 7–9] is even paler in its white-felted foliage, and its slimmer flower spikes are ivory-white, warmed by the same soft orange centres to the florets. Both are best hard-pruned in spring, without which they may become straggly in growth; both need sun and well-drained, fertile soil; both are easily increased by summer cuttings.

The broad, tapering spires of Buddleja *'Lochinch' are perfectly complemented by its luminous grey foliage.*

Bupleurum fruticosum

evergreen shrub H 1.2m/4ft S 1.2m/4ft summer Z 7–9

A shrubby relative of cow parsley, this has none of the airy grace of Queen Anne's lace, but forms a wide dome of satisfying solidity, with sea-green, oblong leaves and umbellifer heads of small, lime green flowers. It is extremely resistant to sea winds, and thrives in any fertile, well-drained soil, in sun or light shade. Plant it small, to allow it to become wind-firm as it grows. In full exposure it is unlikely to need pruning, but grown in too much shelter it may become leggy. If it is necessary to prune to keep the shrub compact, late spring is the best time. It can be increased by cuttings taken in late summer.

Camellia × williamsii *combines the best qualities of both parents, inheriting especially the elegant shape and tender colouring of the blooms of* C. saluenensis.

Camellia

evergreen shrubs H 3m/10ft S 3m/10ft winter to spring Z 7–9

Given a leafy, acid soil and a modicum of shade and shelter, most camellias are tough and easy-going shrubs, with presentable year-round foliage and flowers that can be as simple and unassuming as a dog-rose, as sumptuous as a peony, or so formal as to seem like carved wax. They do well in tubs and containers (happily for gardeners whose soil is not naturally suitable); try flanking your front door with a matched pair of peony-form or formal double camellias. The singles look best in informal settings. Whether in tubs or in the ground, be sure they are well watered and well fed in summer, when next season's buds are forming; but at all times, beware of overwatering container-grown camellias.

The greatest diversity is encountered in *Camellia japonica*, which has broad, glossy foliage to set off its white, pink, red or striped flowers. In single and semi-double cultivars such as clear red 'Adolphe Audusson' the yellow cluster of stamens add to their allure. The *williamsii* hybrids are among the hardiest (as tough as laurel) and most free-flowering; one parent is *C. japonica*, the other *C. saluenensis*, which has abundant pale pink flowers with deeper veining in spring. The original single pale pink *C.* × *williamsii* 'J. C. Williams' remains one of the best, while the popular 'Donation' is a more showy concoction in come-hither pink. 'Salutation', a cross between *C. reticulata* (a somewhat tender shrub with voluptuous flowers and net-veined leaves) and *C. saluenensis*, has soft pink, semi-double flowers from late winter onwards. 'Cornish Snow' (*C. saluenensis* × *C. cuspidata*) is an adorable single white, flowering in late winter and early spring and weather-resistant, with coppery young growths as a bonus. As a departure from the usual range of colours, 'Jury's Yellow' is over-optimistically named but appealing, in clotted cream with a primrose-yellow anemone centre.

Camellias need very little pruning, unless to remove growths that are spoiling the outline of the shrub, which should be done immediately after flowering. Some varieties are 'self-cleaning', but others hang on disgracefully to their dead flowers, which should be removed.

There is nothing to rival a tree-sized ceanothus in full bloom, each branch a mass of brilliant blue, echoed here by the ranks of paler blue bearded irises leavened with the white of arum lilies.

Ceanothus

evergreen shrubs H 30cm–4.5m/1½–15ft
S 1.8–4.5m/6–15ft early spring to autumn
Z 7–10 [unless indicated]

Most evergreen ceanothus or Californian lilacs are natives of hot, dry Californian slopes, where they form part of the chaparral, or of coastal bluffs, so they need full sun and free-draining soil in the garden. They do not like humidity of any kind.

The taller Californian lilacs make handsome furnishings for a warm, sunny wall in areas too cold to grow them free-standing. In mild climates or urban heat islands *Ceanothus* × *veitchianus* is almost tree-like, spectacular when the neat foliage is almost hidden by the rich blue flowers in spring. Another tallish species, *C. impressus* [Z 8–10], with its tiny, neat foliage and rich blue flowers in late spring, is the perfect accompaniment to the double soft-yellow Banksian rose, or the brighter yellow saucers of *Fremontodendron*.

Coastal species such as the low, wide-spreading *C. thyrsiflorus repens* [Z 8–10], a form of the blue blossom or bluebrush, which has dark foliage to set off its china-blue spring flowers, make fine cover for hot banks, with creamy *Cytisus* × *praecox* perhaps; *Ceanothus griseus* var. *horizontalis* 'Yankee Point' [Z 8–10], a selection of the Carmel ceanothus from the Monterey peninsula, is another spreader with brighter blue flowers in spring. ➤

LEFT *This katsura tree* (Cercidiphyllum japonicum) *is ideally placed, sheltered but with its soft autumn tints lit by the sun.*

BELOW *The reddish-pink pods of* Cercis siliquastrum *are a second and unexpected attraction after the brilliance of the clusters of pea-flowers in spring.*

Though these are among the hardier ceanothus, it is still worth taking a few cuttings each summer as a precaution against losses in hard winters. Seedlings are also apt to pop up here and there, though there is no guarantee that they will resemble their parent. Any pruning must be done little and often; evergreen ceanothus dislike being cut back into old wood.

Cercidiphyllum japonicum

deciduous tree H 6m/20ft S 4.5m/15ft autumn Z 5–8

Pretty in spring, when its heart-shaped leaves, resembling those of the Judas tree but smaller, unfurl in shades of claret and pink, and pleasantly green in summer, this Far Eastern tree is at its finest in autumn, when the leaves turn to shades of yellow or dusky pink. Their dying tints might not, alone, earn the katsura tree a place in our gardens, but as the leaves fall they give off a far-carrying aroma of hot toffee – or, some say, of strawberry jam (if the latter, then definitely jam that has 'caught' over a too-hot flame, burning the sugar). The aroma lasts only while the leaves are falling; in a season when they fall rapidly, this will be a short-lived delight, to be awaited with keen anticipation next season.

Plant the tree in a spot sheltered from scorching sun, searing spring winds or late frosts, in a deep, fertile soil for preference to ensure the foliage is protected from damage in spring. It tends naturally to produce several leaders that will develop into multiple trunks with horizontal branches, and should be allowed to do so without coercive pruning. If you must prune, do so in autumn to late winter, when the tree is dormant.

Cercis

deciduous trees H 4.5m/15ft S 4.5m/15ft spring Z 6–9 [unless indicated]

The Judas tree, *Cercis siliquastrum*, is so-called because it is said to be the tree on which Judas hanged himself – but its spreading slender branches seem hardly strong enough to take the weight of a man. It would be a shame if the legend were to deter anyone from growing the Judas tree, one of the brightest notes of its native Mediterranean regions in late spring, the clusters of bright rosy-purple pea-flowers erupting from the bare branches and even from the trunk (see page 15). Later, the heart-shaped foliage unfurls and the flowers yield to showy purple seedpods, from the contents of which new plants can be raised with ease if indeed they do not spontaneously appear near the parent tree. It has a white-flowered form of great charm, *C. siliquastrum* f. *albida*, with paler green leaves. The Judas tree appreciates a free-draining soil and a place in full sun.

Its North American equivalents are the redbuds, of which *C. canadensis* [Z 4–9], from the eastern regions of the continent, has given rise to a striking purple-leaved form known as 'Forest Pansy' [Z 5–9]; this is best sheltered from scorching sun.

Little or no pruning is needed for the Judas tree and the redbuds, except to remove, in spring, wood damaged by frost, storm or disease (coral spot fungus can be a problem, especially in wet areas). *Cercis* dislike root disturbance and should be planted when still small.

CHAENOMELES

deciduous shrubs H 1–1.5m/3½–5ft S 1.5m/5ft
early spring Z 5–9

The flowering or Japanese quinces are among the brightest of spring shrubs, especially valuable for gardeners whose soil is too limy to grow rhododendrons and azaleas. The typical colour is clear scarlet to orange, with excursions into white, pink, apricot, coral and blood-red. In autumn the branches are decked with large, yellow quinces, almost as aromatic as an orchard quince, and good for making a delicious jelly or simply to leave in a bowl indoors to perfume the room. Among several well-tried varieties are *Chaenomeles speciosa* 'Moerloosei' in apple-blossom pink, *C.* × *superba* (see page 19), and its cultivars: self-explanatory 'Knap Hill Scarlet' and suckering 'Crimson and Gold' The reds make a striking contrast to the white clouds of amelanchier or to the chartreuse bracts of spring-flowering spurges.

Any fertile soil suits the flowering quinces, which will grow in the open or can be wall-trained, flowering with great freedom even on sunless walls.

Grey stone perfectly sets off the pink and white spring freshness of Chaenomeles speciosa *'Moerloosei'*.

In the open they can be left unpruned to develop their naturally informal, tangled growth. Wall-trained plants should be pruned during the growing season, the laterals cut back to five leaves (unless needed to extend the area of wall covered) and sublaterals to two leaves; this promotes flowering and also helps to control aphids.

Amid the bright yellow, polished young leaves of Choisya ternata *'Sundance' play the long-stalked, flared violet lanterns of* Clematis viticella.

Choisya ternata

evergreen shrub H 2.4m/8ft S 2.4m/8ft
spring and autumn Z 7–9

The Mexican orange blossom, *Choisya ternata*, is a handsome evergreen shrub of rounded outline with glossy, dark green, aromatic, trifoliolate leaves; the flowers, borne abundantly in late spring and often again, more sparsely, in autumn, are pure white stars with a sweet orange-blossom fragrance. In colder areas it makes a fine, if bulky, wall shrub, ideal to fill the angle where two walls meet; in warmer gardens it grows free-standing into a big dome of a shrub, substantial enough to host a not too vigorous climber. Its yellow-leaved variant 'Sundance' has quickly become popular for its cheery brightness all year, marred only if planted in too hot and exposed a place (when it may scorch) or in too much shade, which turns it an anaemic green. With the caveats issued for 'Sundance', choisyas thrive in any fertile, well-drained soil, in sun or light shade, and can be increased by cuttings. They should need no regular pruning, but if growing out of bounds can be cut hard back after flowering in late spring; frost-damaged wood should also be removed, in spring, after the risk of severe frost has passsed.

Cistus

evergreen shrubs H 15cm–1.2m/6in–6ft
S 75cm–1.2m/2½–6ft summer Z 7–9

The sun roses, like the Californian lilacs, are evergreen shrubs at their best in sunny, dry places. As natives of the Mediterranean region, they are adapted to the same climatic pattern of hot, dry summers and cool, wet winters. Each flower lasts just a day, but there is a long succession of buds to ensure colour – white, and shades of pink from dog-rose to magenta, sometimes with a maroon blotch at the base of each silk-tissue petal – for a summer season. A few have gummily resinous foliage which wafts the aroma of the *maquis* on warm summer evenings. The gum cistus itself, *Cistus ladanifer*, is upright, with large, pure white, plum-blotched flowers. More frost-resistant is *C. laurifolius*, which has clustered, creamy-white flowers.

Among the medium-sized, mound-forming cistus, *C. salvifolius* and its offspring *C.* × *hybridus* (*C.* × *corbariensis*) have pretty white flowers, the latter from pink buds. Others have pink flowers: *C.* × *skanbergii* in shell-pink over greyish foliage, *C.* 'Peggy Sammons' and *C.* × *pulverulentus* in magenta, the latter at its most potent in 'Sunset'. *C.* × *purpureus* has large rosy-purple flowers with maroon blotches, and *C. albidus* has amethyst-pink flowers over white-woolly leaves. Silvery foliage, and the dusty purple of *Salvia officinalis* Purpurascens Group, make an ideal setting for these pink sun roses.

C. × *dansereaui* (*C.* × *lusitanicus*) 'Decumbens', with white, chocolate-blotched flowers, grows flat to the ground, flowing over rock-faces and banks.

Although cistus are essentially shrubs for summer, the grey and green of their foliage, varied by the cold-weather tones of *C.* × *cyprius* and the russet-purple of *C.* × *hybridus* in winter garb, makes for pleasant year-round cover in mild gardens. All are short-lived, and can be readily increased by cuttings, while species such as *C. laurifolius*, *C. salvifolius* and *C. incanus* (in varying shades of pink) are easy from seed, often sowing themselves freely. Cistus are far better left unpruned, for they resent cuts into the old wood. Any cuts that must be made, say to remove frost-damaged stems, should be done in spring. Best of all is to replace them frequently, for young plants are both hardier and more comely than old, straggly ones.

Cordyline

evergreen shrubs H 3m/10ft S 3m/10ft foliage Z 8–10

In contrast to the domes and mounds of so many shrubs, cordylines add a bold, spiky outline to the border, and are at their most striking in youth, when their rapier or broad-sword leaves still radiate outwards starburst-fashion and before they have formed a distinct trunk and begun to branch. Plumes of fragrant, ivory flowers are borne in spring and may be followed by blue-black fruits. The rapier foliage of *Cordyline australis* is typically dull green, but purple and variegated forms and cultivars add colour as well as contrasting form to the border. Seed-raised purples range from milk-chocolate to oxblood red in colour and are collectively known as Purpurea Group. The older variegated cultivars have been overtaken by the jazzy 'Torbay Dazzler' with its brightly cream and greyish leaves are broader, forming bold rosettes. Named cordylines can be grown from sections of stem. All do best in fertile, well-drained soil, in sun.

Cistus × cyprius *is one of the finest of larger sunroses, with dark, crinkle-edged foliage to set off the pure white flowers with their startling, symmetrical crimson blotches at the base of each silky-papery petal.*

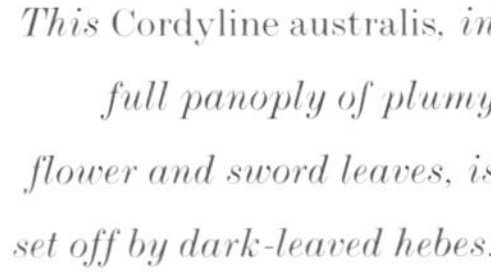

This Cordyline australis, *in full panoply of plumy flower and sword leaves, is set off by dark-leaved hebes.*

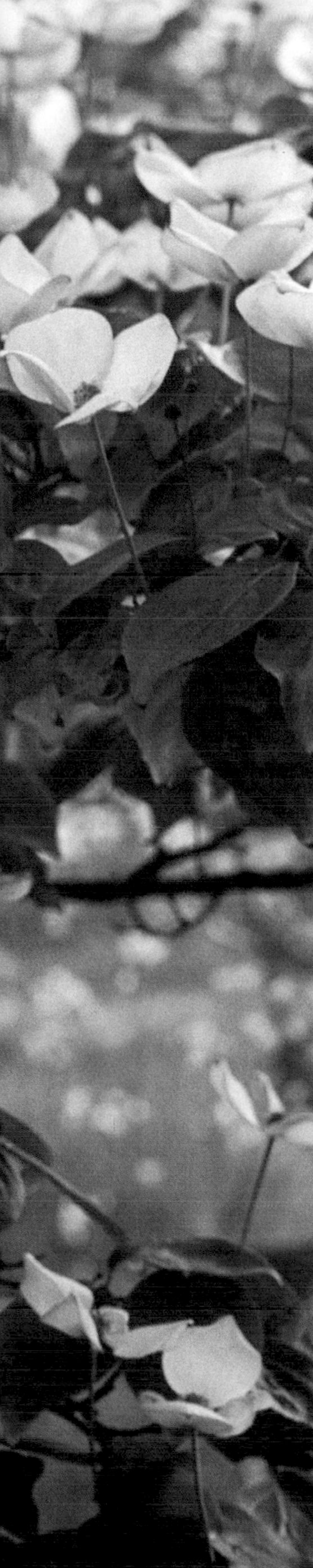

cornus

bracted beauties

DETAILS FROM TOP:
Among the most adaptable of flowering dogwoods is Cornus kousa *var.* chinensis, *with its showy ivory bracts poised above spreading branches.*

The flowers of Cornus kousa *var.* chinensis *are followed, in autumn, by fruits somewhat resembling a strawberry in appearance.*

The dogwood of eastern North America, Cornus florida, *comes not only in white but also in shades of pink to pale ruby known as* C. florida *f.* rubra.

The flowering of dogwoods is followed by a second season of beauty when their dying foliage flushes richly with copper, ruby and tan, as in this Cornus kousa.

MAIN PICTURE:
The horizontally-spreading branches of Cornus kousa *var.* chinensis *display to perfection the hovering, showy white bracts.*

Cornus

deciduous trees H 6m/20ft S 4.5m/15ft
late spring and autumn Z 5–8 [unless indicated]

The flowering dogwoods earn their name from the showy, petal-like bracts that encircle their small flowers. In the Japanese *Cornus kousa* and its more lime-tolerant Chinese form *C. kousa* var. *chinensis*, these bracts are white or cream flushing pink with age, as also in *C. nuttallii* [Z 7–9] from western North America. The flowering dogwood of the eastern United States, *C. florida*, comes in white, pink or rosy red, and is at its best in continental climates (i.e. warm to hot, sunny summers, and cold winters) rather than the cooler, wetter climates that suit the westerner and the Asiatic dogwoods. One of the finest in flower, with broad, white bracts, and combining the climatic tolerance of east and west, is the hybrid between *C. florida* and *C. nuttallii* known as 'Eddie's White Wonder' [Z 7–9]. All colour brightly in autumn.

Cornus nuttallii *is perhaps at its most alluring as the bracts expand in tints of jade, later to fade to cream and ultimately blushing pink.*

The Asiatic *C. controversa* is usually seen in its white-variegated form, nicknamed the wedding cake tree by some on account of its tiered habit. The plain green-leaved form is handsome too, especially in late spring when the near-horizontal branches are covered in the white flowers (no showy bracts here, just an abundance of tiny, foamy inflorescences), and again in autumn when the leaves turn to rich shades of crimson and purple.

Deep, fertile soil, preferably neutral to acid, suits all these tree dogwoods. All should be encouraged to form a single leader; their tiered habit, less marked but still present in the species with showy bracts, will develop naturally.

Corylopsis pauciflora *is one of spring's choicest offerings, with its tassels of fragrant flowers on bare branches, followed by shrimp-pink young leaves.*

Corylopsis

deciduous shrubs H 1.8m/6ft S 1.8m/6ft spring Z 6-8

These shrubs, all with the hazel-like leaves that give them their botanical name, bear their drooping clusters of cowslip-scented blooms on bare branches. All are good, and for small spaces and lime-free soils *Corylopsis pauciflora*, with its fewer but larger flowers and coral-pink young shoots, is a pet. Spread a carpet of soft blue *Anemone apennina* beneath it, or even the more insistent blue of *Chionodoxa sardensis*. And be sure to allow room for the corylopsis to spread, for pruning spoils its natural habit of branching from the base. This also makes it easier to put down layers, by far the best method of increase.

A smoke tree, Cotinus coggygria, *in full hazy bloom silhouetted against a purple filbert* (Corylus maxima *'Purpurea'*), *is accompanied by the handsome, blue-grey lobed leaves of* Macleaya microcarpa, *which will soon lend its tall, airy plumes of palest coral to the picture.*

Cotinus

deciduous shrubs H 2.4m/8ft S 2.4m/8ft summer Z 4–8

The Venetian sumach or smoke tree, *Cotinus coggygria*, earns the latter name from its hazy flower plumes, which open in summer and last long, turning from pinkish-fawn to grey in a smoke-like halo. The rounded leaves turn to brilliant shades of scarlet and flame in autumn, especially in hybrids such as 'Grace', with the blood of the tree-like *C. obovatus*. It is the purple-leaved forms of *C. coggygria*, however, which are deservedly most popular for their rich colouring, superb as the backbone of an all-red planting, or contrasting dramatically with glaucous-blue foliage or pale-coloured flowers. The 'smoke' of the purple-leaved cultivars is a mere wisp compared with the green-leaved cultivars; in any case the best foliage colour comes from hard-pruned specimens, which do not flower much if at all. Cultivars such as 'Royal Purple' (see page 13), or the promising new 'Velvet Cloak', derive from the Rubrifolius Group, which if seed-raised varies from milk-chocolate to deepest blood-red; the former are not to be despised as elements in soft-toned schemes.

The smoke trees need full sun, where the purple cultivars develop their richest tones; poor rather than rich soil helps to ensure the brightest autumn tints. Layering is the easiest method of increase. Specimens growth above all for their foliage should be allowed to form a low, woody framework and then pruned hard each spring, cutting young wood back to the two lowest buds. If they are to be left to grow freely to display the 'smoke' of their inflorescences, no pruning is needed except to remove dead wood.

CUPRESSUS ARIZONICA

evergreen conifer H 9m/30ft S 4.5m/15ft
year-round Z 6–9

The Arizona cypress thrives in hot, dry climates but will do surprisingly well in cooler, wetter areas. Its powdery, grey-blue foliage and neat pyramidal habit give it great allure, whether under a blazing meridional sun with spiky agaves or pink and white oleanders, or as part of a cool planting scheme beneath greyer skies, where it assorts well with glaucous-blue hostas or the blue grasses.

Plant while still small, in well-drained soil, and encourage it to form a single leader if it is to be grown as a specimen. It can also make a good hedge, submitting to regular clipping during the growing season; but is not particularly long-lived. Propagate it by cuttings of side-shoots taken in late summer or autumn, or from seed. Named forms must, of course, be increased by cuttings.

CYTISUS × PRAECOX 'WARMINSTER'

deciduous shrub H 90cm/3ft S 90cm/3ft
late spring Z 7–9

The Warminster broom, a shrub of mounded outline, has arching, almost leafless stems, weighed down in their season by the heavily fragrant, rich cream flowers. It looks well with the blue-flowered *Ceanothus thyrsiflorus repens*, covering a sunny bank. There is a brighter yellow form, 'Allgold', and the cream and cerise 'Hollandia'. All demand full sun and are at their best in fertile, well-drained soil, preferably neutral to acid, even tolerating clay so long as it does not lie wet in winter. They can be increased by summer cuttings. If pruning is necessary to keep them compact, it should be done immediately after flowering. Like all brooms, it does not break from old wood when cut.

DANAE RACEMOSA

evergreen shrub H 90cm/3ft S 90cm/3ft
year-round Z 7–9

The Alexandrian laurel, an elegant relative of the butcher's broom, has arching green stems set with narrow cladodes (leaf-like flattened stems) of gleaming dark green. Enjoying shade and leafy soil, it assorts well with skimmias, green hellebores, ivory-flowered *Ribes laurifolium*, small ferns, epimediums and snowdrops; to display its graceful habit, keep the planting immediately around it low and uncluttered. Cut out older stems in spring as the new shoots emerge at ground-level. Propagation is by division in spring or autumn, or by seed when, after a hot summer, the orange-red fruits ripen.

Whether in its original, creamy-primrose colouring, or the clear lemon yellow of 'Allgold', Cytisus × praecox *lights up the spring garden when its slender green branches are clad from base to tip with flower.*

The high gloss on the cladodes of Danae racemosa *sets off their elegantly tapering form, which makes the plant a favourite not only in the garden but also for cutting.*

DAPHNE PONTICA

evergreen shrub H 30-90cm/1-3ft
S 75cm-1.5m/2½-5ft spring Z 6–9

At first sight *Daphne pontica*, with its discreet chartreuse-green clusters of flowers, seems unexciting. But no other daphne that I know of can rival its airborne, nocturnal perfume, carrying far ➤

In full creamy blossom, Eleagnus angustifolia *makes a pale and fragrant canopy over epimediums, bergenias, ferns, and* Geranium macrorrhizum *'Album'.*

This leaning specimen of Eucalyptus pauciflora *subsp.* niphophila *beautifully displays its ivory, olive-grey and tawny bark.*

on the chill spring air with a poignant sweetness defying description. Furthermore, the shrub makes a satisfying mound, wider than it is high, of glossy, dark green foliage, keeping its good looks all year and needing no pruning. Small dark red fruits follow the flowers; if you save them from the birds and rub off the flesh (taking care, for it is poisonous), you can sow the seeds to make plenty more little daphnes. Plant in cool, leafy soil that does not dry out, in shade.

ELAEAGNUS

deciduous trees and shrubs H 1.8m/6ft S 1.8m/6ft spring Z 2–6 [unless indicated]

The silver berry, *Elaeagnus commutata*, has foliage as platinum-pale as any grey-leaved shrub, with a gleaming metallic finish, each leaf with seductively undulating margins, set off by reddish-brown stems. What is more, it is remarkably frost-hardy. The little flowers are sweetly fragrant, and are followed by small, silvery, egg-shaped fruits. The silver berry grows well in any soil except thin chalk or a bog, spreading slowly by suckers; it is at its brightest in full exposure to sun and wind, and stands even coastal gales with equanimity. The same is true of the Russian wild olive or oleaster, *E. angustifolia* [Z 2–8], a small tree with intensely white foliage on angular, spiny branches, and tiny, fragrant, pale yellow flowers in spring – in cold areas, it makes a splendid visual substitute for the true olive. The only pruning these silvery elaeagnus are likely to need is the removal of dead wood. Pruning to keep them in bounds, or to limb up the oleaster so it develops a trunk, should be carried out after flowering. Propagate by layers or seed or by division of the silver berry.

EUCALYPTUS PAUCIFLORA *SUBSP.* NIPHOPHILA

evergreen tree H 6m/20ft S 4.5m/15ft year-round Z 7–10

As with birches, so with eucalypts, only more so: from a huge number of species that are suitable for Mediterranean, Californian or semi-arid climates, I select just one that is not only beautiful, but also tough enough for cooler, wetter regions: the snow gum. It has quite large, scimitar-shaped, leathery-textured, grey-green leaves on orange stalks, pleasant but hardly able to compete for foliage effect with some of the blue gums: its bark, though, is unmatched, a flaking patchwork of olive-green, cream and grey. The flowers are creamy white.

Slower growing than many gums, and so less likely both to outgrow its station or to blow over at the first gale, the snow gum is unlikely to need pruning, except to encourage the formation of a clean trunk by the gradual removal of lower branches. On no account should it be mutilated by cutting hard back in the manner of the eucalypts grown for their juvenile foliage. Plant in any fertile, drained soil, when still small, avoiding pot-bound specimens, which may never become root-fast. Gums are among the most drought-tolerant of all plants. They can be propagated from seed.

Euphorbia characias

evergreen shrub H 1.2m/4ft S 1.2m/4ft spring Z 7–9

The shrubby spurges of the Mediterranean regions are among the most 'architectural' of hardy plants when in flower, with their tall cylindrical plumes of green to chartreuse-yellow held on thick, latex-filled stems set with narrow, darkly glaucous leaves. *Euphorbia characias* subsp. *characias* has narrow columns of flower with green, chocolate-eyed bracts, while the more easterly *E. characias* subsp. *wulfenii* has broader, more airy inflorescences varying from bright lime-yellow to acid green, without the dark eye.

These shrubby spurges need a sunny place, in well-drained soil. The stems that will flower each year bend, in late winter, like shepherd's crooks, to straighten as the flowers open; later, as they fade, each flowered stem should be cut out at the base to make room for next year's flowering shoots. Seed is the easiest method of increase.

Fatsia japonica

evergreen shrub H 3m/10ft S 3m/10ft autumn Z 7–10

Among the most handsome of hardy evergreen foliage plants, this grand shrub has polished, seven- to nine-fingered leaves, each long narrow lobe with an undulating margin, composing a leaf up to 30cm/1ft wide. The dark green mature foliage contrasts in spring with the tender green baby fingers of the emerging new leaves, and in autumn forms a plinth for the showy panicles of creamy-white flowers in rounded clusters, which emerge from stout pale green buds and are in turn are followed in winter by black berries. There is a variegated form in which the wavy leaf margins are discreetly marked with creamy-white.

The Formosa rice tree or Japanese aralia does well in sun or shade, even deep shade, and stands wind reasonably well; any drained soil suits it, and it does well in tubs. It can be allowed to grow freely to form a sparsely-branched mound with branches arching almost to the ground under their own weight, or pruned up, in mid-spring, onto two or three stems to allow for an underplanting of ferns, hostas and other shade-loving groundlings. Half-ripe to firm cuttings root easily.

Euphorbia characias *subsp.* wulfenii *lasts long in beauty, its tall cylinders of acid green set off by the dark sea-green foliage.*

Fatsia japonica *has some of the largest leaves of hardy evergreen shrubs; in 'Variegata' they are edged with ivory. The blue-grey, lobed leaves alongside belong to* Macleaya.

Brilliant in midsummer flower, the Mount Etna broom (Genista aetnensis) *is a graceful fountain of slender stems for the rest of the year.*

Halimium lasianthum *is one of those precious plants that makes its own colour scheme, the clear yellow, black-blotched flowers set amid grey foliage.*

GENISTA AETNENSIS

deciduous tree H 4.5m/15ft S 4.5m/15ft early summer Z 9–10

The Mount Etna broom makes a small, open-canopied tree with almost leafless branches, casting the lightest of shade, even when arching fountain-like under the weight of its abundant, bright lemon-yellow pea flowers. It thrives in full sun, in well-drained soil, and can be increased by seed or half-ripe cuttings. If stopped low down it forms a big, low-branching shrub; or it can be encouraged to form a single leader by staking a strong shoot for a few years, until it makes mature wood. Thereafter no pruning is needed except to cut out dead wood. It does not regenerate from old wood, like all brooms, but can be lightly trimmed after flowering.

GLEDITSIA TRIACANTHOS

deciduous tree H 9m/30ft S 9m/30ft foliage Z 4–9

The green-leaved honey locust or sweet locust is a large, thorny tree, with elegant foliage composed of many small, bright green leaflets. My choice falls upon two variants selected for their foliage colour: 'Sunburst', and 'Rubylace'. The former has golden-green foliage, brightest in spring, and again in autumn; it is far more appealing, in its neater foliage and subtle colouring, than the unrelentingly bright golden-leaved black locust or false acacia, *Robinia pseudoacacia* 'Frisia'. 'Rubylace' has plum-red young growths maturing to bronze-green, and the same daintiness in mature leaf. Their lightness of foliage and distinctive colouring make them ideal trees for carefully-planned colour schemes: 'Sunburst' over a spread of Bowles' golden grass and spurges, say; or 'Rubylace' with *Euphorbia dulcis* 'Chameleon'.

The honey locusts are tough trees despite their air of foliar fragility, tolerating air pollution, heat, cold and wind, and thriving in any fertile, free-draining soil. Their late-leafing habit makes them very suitable for areas where late spring frosts are a regular hazard. They are unlikely to need pruning, but if any cuts are needed, late summer is the best time, as they bleed profusely in spring.

HALIMIUM and × HALIMIOCISTUS

evergreen shrubs H 30–60cm/1–2ft S 60–75cm/2–2½ft summer Z 8–10

Closely related to cistus, the halimiums introduce another colour, yellow, with grey-felted foliage; like many greys, they thrive in full sun, and do very well in dry places. In *Halimium lasianthum*, a shrub of spreading habit, the clear, bright yellow flowers are enhanced by a blotch of umber-brown at the base of each petal. The foliage of *H. ocymoides* is whiter and neater, and the shrub forms a low mound of rather upright stems rather than the near-horizontal, criss-crossing stems of the bigger species. The flowers are smaller, their clear yellow set off by an almost black spot at the base of each petal; they open from tawny-red buds. Like the true cistus, of which it is a bigeneric hybrid, × *Halimiocistus sahucii* is an ideal cover for hot, dry, sunny slopes, forming a low, wide mound of dark green foliage spangled, over a long season, with squarish, pure white flowers. Like their cousins the cistuses, the petals of halimiocistus fall each day, to be followed by a succession of new buds opening to the sun next morning. This and the halimiums are easily increased by summer cuttings.

Hamamelis

deciduous shrubs H 2.4m/8ft S 3.6m/12ft winter Z 6–8 [unless indicated]

Like many winter flowers, the witch hazels are endearing rather than flashy, their spidery yellow, orange or tawny-red flowers strung along the bare branches as though an army of worshippers had tied tiny prayer-ribbons all over the bush. A mature specimen of *Hamamelis mollis* 'Coombe Wood', the original introduction from China and still one of the best on account of its large, clear yellow, spicy-sweet-scented flowers, is sure to lift the heart on a cold winter's day, especially if it has been foresightfully set against a dark evergreen backdrop. The Japanese *H. japonica* has given us one excellent cultivar, 'Zuccariniana', which bears its lemon-yellow flowers in early spring; and runs to reddish tints, whence some of the richer-coloured hybrids classed under *H.* × *intermedia*. The reddish tints infuse not only the flowers but also the autumn foliage, which is more usually yellow – in witch hazels with yellow flowers, at least. 'Feuerzauber' ('Magic Fire') wins my vote as the only red with a perfume I can detect; but to the eye, if not to the nose, oxblood-red 'Diane' is undeniably finer. 'Jelena' is a striking coppery orange, 'Arnold Promise' a pure yellow with short-petalled but well-filled flowers, and 'Pallida' a great beauty with delectably-scented, pale lemon-primrose flowers. A witch hazel with a difference is *H. vernalis* 'Sandra' [Z 5–8]; hardly showy in yellow late-winter flower, it unfurls its spring foliage in shades of claret and plum-purple, fading to green with a purple flush on the reverse for summer before flaring into brilliant orange, scarlet and flame autumn tints.

Witch hazels are often described as lime-haters, but in my experience they will tolerate some lime so long as the soil is deep, moist and leafy. In drier climates they do best in dappled or passing shade, with shelter from wind; where the air is normally moist and the skies often grey, they flower most freely in a sunny position. Naturally slow-growing, they should be left unpruned to develop their spreading or vase-shaped outline. Resist even the temptation to cut sprigs for the house until you have a bush of good size. Any cuts that must be made are best done in early spring. Crossing growths can then be cut away.

Hamamelis × intermedia *'Pallida' is ideally placed, as here, against a backdrop of dark foliage to set off its pale flowers, lit by the winter sunshine.*

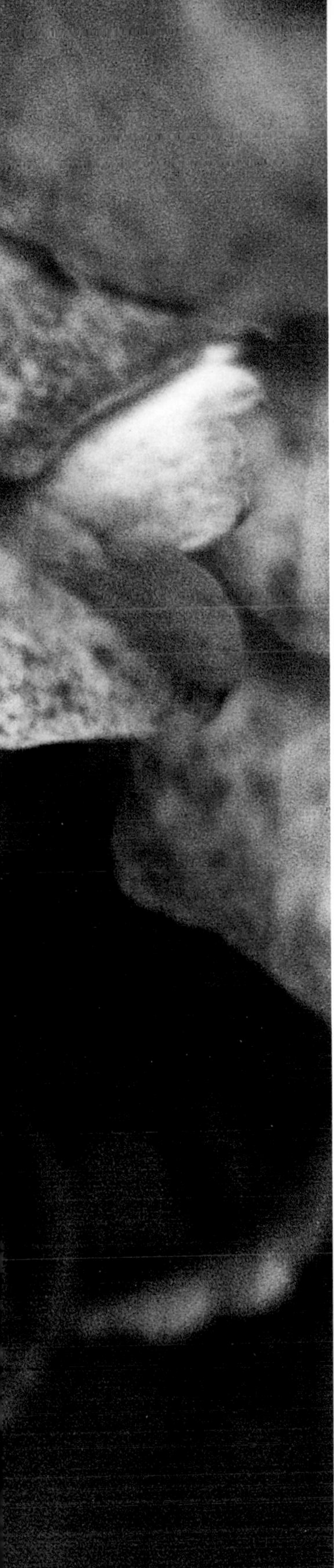

hydrangea

billowing blues

DETAILS FROM TOP:

On hard-pruned bushes, Hydrangea arborescens *'Annabelle' bears huge, flattish domes of florets.*

In flower and leaf alike, Hydrangea serrata *'Preziosa' is of unusually rich colouring, especially where touched by the sun to garnet and ruby depths.*

The rounded outlines of hydrangea bushes, and of their globular heads of flower, are enhanced by the neatly clipped domes and hedges behind.

Bearing flowerheads midway between the solid cones of 'Grandiflora' and the airy lace of 'Kyushu', Hydrangea paniculata *'Floribunda' is a splendid, hardy and handsome shrub.*

MAIN PICTURE:

At their best, the mophead hydrangeas last and last, their flowers aging to intriguing metallic tints of verdigris and steel, flushed with rose.

HYDRANGEA

deciduous shrub H 1–2.4/3½–8ft S 1–1.8m/3½–6ft
summer to autumn Z 7–10 [unless indicated]

Hydrangeas are a diverse lot. The graceful, shade-loving lacecaps are described on page 88. The hortensia of seaside gardens, with its rounded heads of pink, white, lilac or – in acid soils – electric and azure blue, form billows of colour. Among the best are clear pink (or sky blue) 'Générale Vicomtesse de Vibraye'(see page 16), white 'Madame Emile Mouillère', deep red or intense blue, dwarf 'Altona', rich pink 'Europa', as well as 'Ayesha', with incurved florets reminiscent of lilac, in pale pink or blue. All these are cultivars of *Hydrangea macrophylla*; 'Preziosa', a dwarf with mophead flowers opening blush and turning to deep crimson among coppery-red foliage, belongs to *H. serrata*.

The mopheads are thirsty and greedy, needing rich, deep soil that does not dry out. Those that would naturally come blue in suitable soils can be encouraged, when growing in neutral soils, to turn from mauve to blue by with the use of a proprietary 'blueing powder'. Leaving the flowerheads unpruned until spring helps protect against winter frosts; as the new buds break, the flowerheads are cut back to strong buds and old, weak, much-branched wood can be cut right out. Unpruned bushes flower well enough but bear smaller flowerheads. From time to time they can be cut right back to the ground, in spring, to make entirely new growth; this means sacrificing a season's flower. Cuttings root with ease at almost any time of year.

Hydrangea macrophylla *'Altona' is decked with the sultry blue, nodding lanterns of* Clematis integrifolia *which dies down each winter to leave the hydrangea uncluttered.*

Different treatment suits the hardy, white-flowered hydrangeas that flower on the current season's wood. *H. arborescens* 'Annabelle' [Z 4–9] bears wide, flattish domes of many small florets, opening from green buds to ivory-white and fading again towards cream. The variants of *H. paniculata* [Z 4–8] form cone-shaped panicles, at their most appealing when fertile and sterile florets mix to give a frothy effect, as in 'Floribunda', 'Kyushu' and the later-flowering 'Tardiva'. 'Grandiflora' makes heavy, all-sterile flowerheads, at their most massive on bushes hard-pruned in spring. All will grow in any fertile soil. Cuttings root easily and are best taken at midsummer.

The slender, catkin-like tassels of Itea ilicifolia *are displayed at their best when, as here, they hang clear of the main stems trained to a wall.*

The Chinese privet, Ligustrum lucidum, *is transformed, in late summer, from a handsome foliage tree to a foamy mass of ivory-white blossom.*

Itea ilicifolia

evergreen shrub H 3m/10ft S 3m/10ft late summer Z 8–10

This Chinese shrub has leaves as dark and gleaming as holly, though its toothed margins have no sharp spines; they are handsome all year, the new spring growths bronze-tinted, and in late summer they form the setting for long, catkin-like tassels of alabaster-green, fragrant flowers. Of rather lax growth, it makes a handsome wall shrub, as happy in light shade as in sun. If good evergreen foliage and understated flowers appeal to you, and you have a sizeable wall to cover, it could accompany the winter-flowering, vanilla custard-scented *Azara microphylla*, the evergreen climbing hydrangea-relative *Pileostegia viburnoides* which bears its cones of creamy froth in late summer, and the hummocky, green-flowered *Bupleurum fruticosum*.

In mild areas, and where space allows, *Itea ilicifolia* can be allowed to grow as a free-standing shrub or, if against a wall, billowing forward unrestrained except for tying in the main branches. Where wall shelter is needed to protect it against winter cold, it should be pruned and tied-in more rigorously; the best flowers come on the previous year's strong young growths, so older, twiggy stems can be pruned right out in spring and the new stems tied in each year. Late summer cuttings root easily.

Ligustrum lucidum

evergreen tree H 9m/30ft S 9m/30ft late summer Z 8–10

A mature specimen of this Chinese privet is a compelling sight, forming a shapely, high-domed tree, its branches densely set with dark, glittering, pointed leaves almost like those of *Camellia japonica*. In late summer this mass of foliage is obscured by innumerable, bold panicles of many small, ivory-white flowers opening from creamy-green buds.

If you have not room for a tree-sized privet, you can keep it in bounds by careful pruning in spring. But this is not a tree to treat as though it were the common hedging privet; its elegance, and the beauty of its leaf and flower, should be respected. Its variegated forms are naturally more restrained in growth. Any fertile, well-drained soil suits this privet, in sun or shade. Cuttings root easily, taken in summer or autumn.

Much of the colour in this mixed planting comes from shrubs and conifers. The steely blue cone of Chamaecyparis pisifera *'Boulevard' contrasts sharply with the bright yellow foliage of a young* Choisya ternata *'Sundance', and the wide sprawl of burgundy-red belonging to* Cotinus coggygria *is cooled, and kept from quarrelling with the vivid choisya, by the grey-green of* Elaeagnus × ebbingei. *The green swords of crocosmia foliage, between the cotinus and another purple-leaved shrub,* Berberis × thunbergii *'Atropurpurea Nana', bring a change of outline to the mainly rounded or dome-shaped plants.*

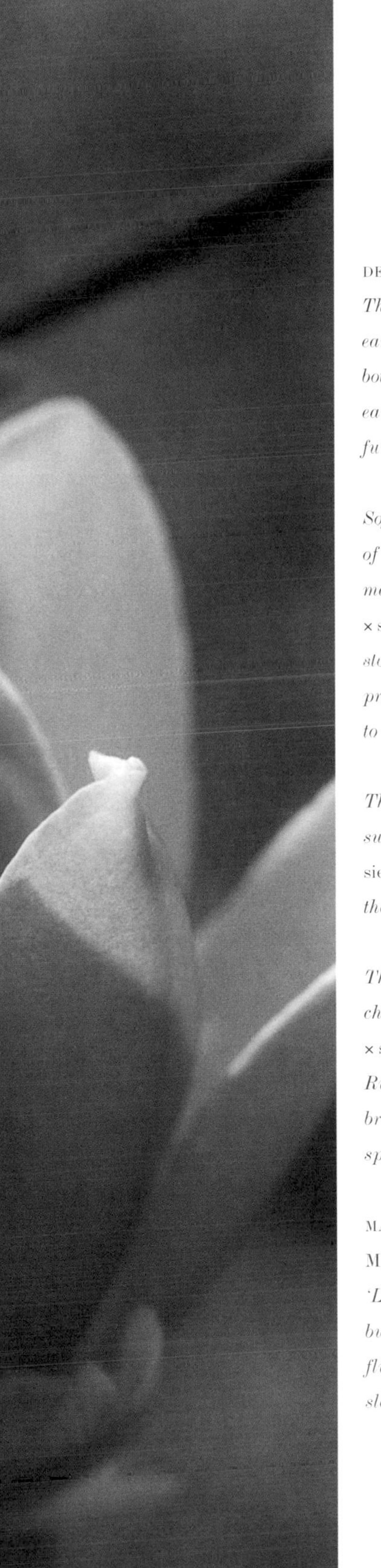

magnolia

waxen chalices

DETAILS FROM TOP:
The starry flowers that earn Magnolia stellata *its botanical name open in early spring from grey-furred winter buds.*

Soft-furred buds are typical of the spring-flowering magnolias: in Magnolia × soulangeana *they tip the stout branchlets, a winter promise of spring glory to come.*

The waxen petals of summer-flowering Magnolia sieboldii *are cupped around the central boss of stamens.*

The ample, ruby-pink chalices of Magnolia × soulangeana *'Rustica Rubra' are borne on bare branches before the pale spring foliage unfurls.*

MAIN PICTURE:
Magnolia × loebneri *'Leonard Messel' has small but abundant flowers flushed with pink, borne on slender branches.*

MAGNOLIA

deciduous trees H 3–9m/10–30ft S 3–9m/10–30ft
spring and summer Z 5–9 [unless indicated]

The familiar *Magnolia* × *soulangeana* is as tough as a flowering cherry. In spring the fat, furry buds open into white or pink or wine-red globes or chalices before the foliage unfurls. Two fine cultivars are 'Brozzonii', a late-flowering white with just a hint of pink at the base of the petals, and the still-later 'Lennei', with flowers like vast purple tulips. There are other, still more desirable magnolias to choose from if you have the right soil. This need not be lime-free; even on chalk, so long as it does not dry out, *M.* × *loebneri* should thrive. A small-leafed tree, it has several cultivars, including 'Leonard Messel', its many-petalled, creamy-white flowers suffused with mauve-pink, and 'Merrill', with starry, semi-double, white flowers. *M. salicifolia* [Z 6–9] is a slender, twiggy tree for lime-free soil, with countless small, pure white flowers scented like orange-blossom. For a slow-growing, mound-shaped shrub, there is *M. stellata*, with pure white flowers of many narrow petals (there are pink-flushed forms too, and 'Water Lily', with larger, fuller flowers).

The deciduous *M. sinensis*, or *M. wilsonii* are lime-tolerant, the shrubbier *M. sieboldii*, which has broad, glaucous-backed leaves, decidedly lime-hating. They have in common their early- to late-summer season (longest in *M. sieboldii*) of fragrant, nodding, bowl-shaped flowers with waxy white petals around a boss of crimson stamens with a lemon or green club at their heart, followed by showy fruits, composed of a ruby-red, fleshy receptacle splitting to show scarlet seeds. Whether lime-tolerant or not, all magnolias are at their best in a leafy, moist yet drained soil. Their fleshy roots are easily damaged and they are therefore best planted when still small, and thereafter left undisturbed. If pruning is needed to maintain the desired branching structure or repair wind damage (for the branches of magnolias tend to be brittle) it should be done shortly after midsummer to reduce bleeding and allow time for healing before winter. Some magnolias can be propagated by cuttings, but for non-professionals layering is much easier. Species can also be raised from seed.

A big, flopping bush rather than a tree, similar in habit to Magnolia x soulangeana *'Lennei',* M. liliiflora *'Nigra' is one of the last to flower.*

Mahonia × media *'Arthur Menzies' is typical of this group of winter-flowering shrubs, with its bold, holly-like foliage in ordered ranks, and its tall candles of yellow flower.*

The fragrant, pincushion flowers of Myrtus communis *are one of the delights of summer, and the glossy foliage is comely all year.*

MAHONIA

evergreen shrubs H 23cm–3m/9in–10ft S 45cm–3m/18in–10ft winter Z 7–10 [unless indicated]

Two fine shrubs have united to produce *Mahonia* × *media*, among the best of winter-flowering evergreens: *M. japonica*, a great mound of a shrub with bold leaves of several holly-like leaflets and drooping sprays of clear yellow flowers reminiscent both in outline and fragrance of lily-of-the-valley; and *M. lomariifolia* [Z 8–10], a tall, gangly thing with bare stems topped by ruffs of leaves of many narrow leaflets, and upright yellow candles. The hybrids have inherited the upright clusters of close-packed, scarcely-scented flowers of the second together with the frost-resistance and good temper of the first. 'Charity' is perhaps the most famous of the hybrids. Another is 'Arthur Menzies'. 'Winter Sun', which is noticeably endowed with the lily-of-the-valley fragrance, is among the best. In full sun the foliage of these mahonias becomes bronzed or even reddish-apricot in winter. A simple companion planting to set off the bold foliage is best: the paddles of bergenias, the spears of *Iris foetidissima*. Any fertile garden soil suits these mahonias, in sun or shade. They can be increased by one-node cuttings, taken in early spring. They can be cut back quite severely, if need be, after flowering, and will soon to refurnish themselves with fresh foliage.

The simplest of settings – a carpet of moss, or merely a mulch of crumbly leafmould – in dappled shade, is also what will most flatter *M. nervosa* [Z 6–9], a low, spreading shrub with an appeal out of all proportion to its size. A slow-growing, modestly suckering carpeter, it has hard-textured leaflets of clear-cut outline, dark green in summer and often flushed with maroon in winter. The yellow flowers appear in spring. It can be increased by cuttings or division, and is unlikely to need any pruning. If you must, prune it after flowering.

MYRTUS COMMUNIS

evergreen shrub H 3m/10ft S 3m/10ft summer Z 8–10

The common myrtle of Mediterranean regions, *Myrtus communis*, has dark, aromatic foliage glittering in the sun, and fragrant flowers that are hardly more than a brush of creamy stamens emerging from rounded buds, borne in great abundance. There is a double-flowered form, 'Flore Pleno' and another, 'Variegata', with cream-margined leaves. Myrtles make fine hedges; the tiny-leaved *M. communis* subsp. *tarentina* ('Jenny Reitenbach') is one of the best for this purpose.

The Mediterranean myrtle needs a place in the sun, in well-drained soil, and can be increased by summer cuttings. It stands clipping well, and if frost-damaged, can be cut hard back; so long as there is sound basal wood, it will regenerate. Similarly, a myrtle that has outgrown its space (perhaps in a sheltered, sunny corner against a wall) can be cut back severely. This is best done in spring.

NANDINA DOMESTICA

evergreen shrub H 75cm–2.4m/2½–8ft S 75cm–2.4m/2½–8ft summer Z 7–9

The sacred bamboo is so-named, we are told, because the Japanese like to plant it by their house doors and confide their fears and secrets to it. It is not a bamboo, but a berberis-relative; but its frond-like foliage on unbranched canes does – rather remotely – call to mind some elegant bamboo. In spring, and again in autumn, the foliage may be flushed with coppery-red, and cultivars such as 'Firepower' have been chosen for this quality. For small spaces there is the knee-high 'Pygmaea'. In hot, sunny climates nandinas flower freely, their creamy plumes giving way to red fruits.

Any fertile, well-drained soil suits nandinas. Cuttings are not that easy to root; the best time is summer. Provided there are strong new growths coming from the base, older, tatty stems can be cut right out at ground level in spring; no other pruning should be needed.

OLEARIA

evergreen shrub H 1.8m/6ft S 1.8m/6ft
spring summer Z 8–9

With its pewter-grey, holly-like leaves and sprays of white daisies, *Olearia macrodonta* is one of the finest shrubs for mild gardens, tolerating full exposure to sea winds; in such places it forms a dome-shaped shrub clad to the ground with foliage. If sheltered from the wind it will grow leggy, revealing stems with peeling, pale beige bark. It is one of the few 'greys' to retain its colouring in shady places.

Pruning depends on whether you want to encourage compact leafy growth or to display the papery bark; in the former case, straggly stems should be cut back, while in the latter, cluttering lower branches should be cut right out. These operations, or any radical surgery on specimens that have grown out of bounds should be carried out in late spring, or after flowering.Cuttings root easily if taken in summer or early autumn.

PAEONIA DELAVAYI

deciduous shrub H 2.4m/8ft
S 2.4m/8ft late spring to summer
Z 6–9 [hybrids Z 5–8]

The tree peonies are, for the most part, big, muscular shrubs with boldly jagged leaves and an abundance of cupped, waxy-petalled flowers. They range from the alluring colours of *Paeonia delavayi*, at their best deep blood crimson set off by glaucous-blue foliage, to the yellow-flowered, green-leaved *P. delavayi* var. *ludlowii* (*P. lutea* var. *ludlowii*).

The tree peonies thrive in any well-drained soil, preferring full sun and shelter from late spring frosts, to which their early-leafing habit makes them susceptible. They can be increased by seed, or by careful removal of rooted suckers. They need almost no pruning; removing old flower stalks is worth doing for cosmetic reasons after the leaves fall, and old, worn wood can be removed at ground level at the same time.

Seedlings of red-flowered parents such as this Paeonia delavayi *hybrid are apt to vary, though always appealing in their range of copper, terracotta and blood-red tints.*

PHILADELPHUS

deciduous shrubs H 1.2–2.4m/4–8ft S 1.2–2.4m/4–8ft summer Z 5–8

Philadelphus *'Belle Etoile' remains one of the best of the hybrid mock oranges, despite its age: it was raised around a century ago. Its crimson heart enhances the whiteness of the petals.*

Although it has not the most showy flowers, if I were restricted to only one mock orange it would have to be *Philadelphus coronarius* 'Aureus', on account of its lime-yellow foliage and the potent orange-blossom perfume of its creamy-white flowers. Not that others, with finer flowers though commonplace green foliage, lack perfume. 'Belle Etoile' has squarish, maroon-hearted flowers with a distinct pineapple fragrance, and some of the double-flowered cultivars, such as the tall, bulky 'Virginal', are also perfumed. There is no point in a scentless mock orange, when there are fragrant ones of equal beauty.

Any well-drained soil, in sun, suits the mock oranges, except that *P. coronarius* 'Aureus' is apt to scorch in dry soils in too hot a place, while overcompensating with too much shade turns it green. They are easily increased by summer cuttings. Flowered wood should be pruned after flowering, cutting back to strong new growth; if there are new stems coming from ground level, one or two of the oldest stems can be cut out entirely so the bush gradually renews itself.

The translucent garnet and ruby tints of the young foliage of Photinia × fraseri *'Red Robin' are given full value when, as here, they are back-lit by the spring sun.*

PHOTINIA × FRASERI

evergreen shrub H 4.5m/15ft S 4.5m/15ft spring Z 8–9

The splendour of these hawthorn-relatives is their vivid scarlet or cinnabar spring foliage, rivalling the pierises. These pyrotechnics are staged against a background of the mature, dark green, glossy foliage. The unglamorously named 'Birmingham' has coppery-red spring foliage, and is outshone in both name and brilliance by 'Red Robin' in scarlet young leaf. 'Redstart' is allied, and just as bright.

Any good, well-drained soil, from acid to alkaline, suits the photinias. A modicum of shelter from late spring frosts helps to preserve the display, though they are less susceptible to burn than the pierises. They need little or no pruning, but if any cuts must be made, the best time is late spring, as the bright foliage fades to green. Propagation is by cuttings, taken in summer or autumn – the later in the season they are struck, the longer they will take to root.

PICEA BREWERIANA

evergreen conifer H 9m/30ft S 6m/20ft year-round Z 6–8

Brewer's weeping spruce is rare in the wild, growing in only a few places in the Siskiyou Mountains of northern California; but, unlike some plants that have such a restricted distribution, it has readily adapted itself to captivity. It is one of the most beautiful conifers for cool climates, its spreading, dipping branches decked with hanging curtains of slender branchlets clad with glossy, dark blue-green needles (see page 15).

It deserves a well-nourished soil kept clear of competing plants to allow its natural branching habit to develop, and should be encouraged to form a clear leader from babyhood. It is increased from seed, and grows very slowly at first.

PINUS

evergreen conifers H 9m/30ft S 6m/20ft
year-round Z 5–9 [unless indicated]

Of the many pines suitable for gardens, I have chosen just two, one for milder regions and one adapted to cooler climates. *Pinus patula* [Z 8–9] is a graceful Mexican species, with long, drooping, bright green needles, more elegant if less imposing than the massive Montezuma pine. The Japanese white pine, *P. parviflora*, naturally develops, with age, a picturesque outline, which can be heightened by judicious pruning; it has short tufts of deep blue-green needles.

Most pines are easy from seed; as with the spruces, a clear leader should be encouraged as the seedlings develop. They are at their best in an open position, in deep, fertile, well-drained soil.

PITTOSPORUM TOBIRA

evergreen shrub H 2.4m/8ft S 2.4m/8ft
late spring Z 8–10

The tobira or Japanese mock orange is handsome all year, with its blunt-ended, polished, bright green leaves in whorls. The showy ivory-cream flowers are endowed with a potent orange-blossom fragrance, and are followed by blue-green berries with orange seeds. It is slow-growing but ultimately quite bulky; there is a naturally dwarf form 'Nanum', growing to waist height with time, while 'Variegatum' has cream-edged leaves.

Pinus patula *adds a special quality to the garden, with its hanging curtains of long, slender needles.*

The tobira is amazingly tolerant of dry conditions and general neglect, as dusty hedges of it in Mediterranean towns testify. It deserves better, however. It can be increased by summer cuttings or seed, and is unlikely to need any pruning unless damaged by frost. This is best done in mid-spring when the plant is already in growth.

PRUNUS

deciduous trees H 6–15m/20–50ft
S 6–15m/20–50ft spring, autumn, winter
Z 5–7 [unless indicated]

With so many flowering cherries to choose from, it is not hard to insist on one that offers more than just a frou-frou of blossom in spring followed by months of boring leaf. No doubt those who adore sugar-pink and don't mind the clash with the sharper colours of spring – to say nothing of the coppery young foliage – will not approve of my choice among Japanese cherries. However, to the discerning eye, there are finer pink cherries than the Japanese, and among the Japanese cherries themselves, two white-flowered cultivars are outstanding in beauty: 'Shirotae' and 'Taihaku' (see next page). The first, also known as 'Mount ➤

Whorls of gleaming leaves frame the posies of waxen flowers of Pittosporum tobira, *known as the Japanese mock orange because of its heady fragrance.*

Fuji', needs plenty of lateral space to allow full expression to its wide-spreading, horizontal or gracefully drooping branches, which are covered in very large, semi-double, pure white flowers hanging in long bunches; for added value, they are fragrant. The great white cherry, 'Taihaku', has huge, single, pure white flowers amid bronzed young foliage.

If ever a tree deserved the poet A. E. Housman's line "Loveliest of trees, the cherry now/Is hung with bloom along the bough", it is 'Taihaku', the most beautiful of all Japanese cherries.

The Yoshino cherry, *Prunus × yedoensis* [Z 6–8], is a pretty tree with arching branches abundantly set, early in the cherry season, with almond-scented, palest pink to white flowers (see page 183). In flower, Sargent's cherry, *P. sargentii*, cannot compare with the more obvious charms of these selected Japanese cherries, but it has the elegance of a wildling, with its single, pink flowers amid bright tawny-red spring foliage, and its incandescent autumn tints. Even in winter it is attractive, on account of its rich brown bark. However, in this it is outdone by *P. serrula*, the mahogany-barked cherry, a willow-leaved tree with small white flowers and a trunk and branches as polished as its common name implies. The appeal of *P. subhirtella* [Z 4–8] is its winter-flowering cultivars 'Autumnalis', in white, and 'Autumnalis Rosea' in pink. Their tiny flowers might not turn many heads in spring, but on the bare winter branches they enchant.

Given plenty of space, there are few cherries to compare with the double gean or mazzard, a selection of the wild cherry of Europe that, in other manifestations, has developed into the fruiting sweet cherries. *P. avium* 'Plena' [Z 4–8], in maturity, is an imposing tree, a mass of white in spring and a bonfire of orange and crimson as the leaves die away in autumn.

The flowering cherries are, on the whole, greedy trees, needing a fertile, well-drained soil. Except for *P. serrula*, which should be trained to form a distinct trunk to show off its beautiful bark by removing low branches when still small, they should need no pruning, but if large branches must be removed the work should be done after flowering but before high summer to minimise the risk of disease and gumming. As with many other ornamental trees, they are probably more often bought in than propagated by amateurs, but it is worth trying summer cuttings, especially of *P. × yedoensis* and 'Taihaku'.

QUERCUS

deciduous tree H 18m/60ft S 12m/40ft autumn Z 5–8

Many oaks are forest rather than garden trees; but the deciduous oaks are such fine shade-trees for rhododendrons (which follow them in this chapter, courtesy of the alphabet) that I include the scarlet oak, *Quercus coccinea* 'Splendens', and the pin oak, *Q. palustris*, for your consideration. They are fairly similar, with deeply and sharply lobed leaves turning in autumn to fiery scarlet. The pin oak is the more elegant of the two, graceful in habit and with smaller, more deeply cut leaves. Even in youth they are handsome, and as they mature and the texture of the soil beneath them becomes moist and crumbly from their decaying leaves, they come into their own as shade trees *par excellence*.

To achieve their full glory they need a deep, moist, lime-free soil. They can be grown from seed, which will germinate so long as the acorns are not allowed to dry out; seedlings grow reasonably fast and should be encouraged to form a clear leader.

RHODODENDRON, AZALEAS

evergreen and deciduous shrubs
H 60cm–1.8m/2–6ft S 60cm–1.8m/2–6ft
early to late spring Z 5–8

Azaleas, whether evergreen or deciduous, are sufficiently distinct to have been at one time classed in their own genus, and though they have long been considered members of the genus *Rhododendron*, they have their own series for botanical purposes and their own character for the gardener's purposes. The change in classification led to a name change for the honeysuckle azalea, no longer *Azalea pontica* but *Rhododendron luteum*. A large shrub, it remains popular for its warm yellow flowers with a far-carrying, powerful fragrance, and for its bright autumn colour.

There are many other wild deciduous azaleas, and dozens or even hundreds of named cultivars; restricted to a handful, I would choose late-flowering, mostly fragrant Ghent hybrids such as 'Daviesii', with dainty white, yellow-flared trumpets, or the soft yellow, hose-in-hose 'Narcissiflorum'.

Evergreen azaleas give double value, once when smothered in flower in spring, and again in winter when, if grown in exposed positions, the foliage burnishes to mahogany and bronze. The colours are mainly in the pink-crimson-magenta range, with white of course, of which one of the finest is stark white 'Palestrina'. *R. kaempferi* is semi-evergreen and has flowers in coral and apricot shades.

Azaleas need the same leafy, acid soil as rhododendrons. The species can be grown from seed; all can be layered; and the evergreen azaleas can be propagated by summer cuttings. They seldom or never need pruning, though if they become leggy or too large for their space, they can be pruned after flowering.

Even a young sapling of the scarlet oak, Quercus coccinea, *will draw the eye in its brilliant autumn garb, giving yearly pleasure as it matures alongside its owner.*

The breeder's art, though it has brought us named azaleas by the dozen, has produced not one that can compete with Rhododendron luteum, *the honeysuckle azalea, for fragrance; the opulent perfume of its yellow flowers wafts far on the spring air.*

rhododendron

opulent refinement

DETAILS FROM TOP:

Rhododendron *'Loderi King George' combines opulence and refinement in bloom, with the added charm of spring foliage like slender candles set in pink bracts that echo the pink of the unopened flower buds.*

With its soft coral bells in late spring, the Fabia Group is one of the loveliest of medium-sized hybrids.

The white flowers of Rhododendron *'Loderi Mintern' seem all the purer for their setting of clear green foliage.*

Among rhododendron hardy hybrids, with their full heads of bloom, 'Sappho' is in a class of her own with white, black-blotched flowers.

MAIN PICTURE:

Rhododendron *Cilpinense Group flowers early, and so needs some protection from untimely frosts, if its pale pink blooms with their brown anthers are not to be singed by the cold.*

RHODODENDRON, HYBRIDS

evergreen shrubs H 30cm–4.5m/1–15ft
S 30cm–4.5m/1–15ft early to late spring Z 6–8 [unless indicated]

The pure scarlet bells of Rhododendron *Elizabeth Group, her compact growth, and easy, undemanding ways ensure her enduring popularity.*

If there are hundreds of rhododendron species, there are thousands of hybrids; rhododendronitis is a contagious disease that has infected many growers, especially wealthy amateurs with large estates. They have bred many fine things for smaller spaces, however. Some of the most appealing among them are the dwarf 'blue' rhododendrons, with their amethyst, slate or violet-blue flowers and neat foliage: the Blue Diamond, Blue Tit and Bluebird Groups, and others like 'Sapphire'. They derive from the tall *Rhododendron augustinii* [Z 6–7], the dwarf *R. russatum*, tiny-leaved *R. impeditum* [Z 4–7] and others, the first essentially a woodland shrub, the others happier in open spaces. They look well with the dwarf yellow-flowered rhododendrons such as 'Princess Anne' and 'Chikor' [both Z 6–8], or the taller, slender Yellow Hammer Group [Z 6–8], with its tubular lemon flowers that often give a repeat show in autumn. If the pink shades are more to your taste, there are the Bow Bells Group [Z 6–8], *williamsianum* hybrids with bright coppery-bronze new growths and carmine buds opening to soft pink bells, and the Temple Belle Group [Z 7–8], which rather takes after its other parent, *R. orbiculare* [Z 7–8], with rounded, white-backed leaves and clear pink bells. Or you could choose the early-flowering Cilpinense Group, which has pink-flushed white bells opening from pink buds. The Seta Group is of upright rather than mounded habit, with narrow bells white at the base and vivid pink at the tips. The dwarf scarlet Elizabeth Group [Z 7–9] is very popular, but I prefer 'Carmen' [Z 7–9], on account of its waxy, deepest blood-crimson bells.

Among more substantial hybrids, the Fabia Group [Z 6–8] has flowers of coral to tangerine, lovely with the sharp greens of unfurling oak leaves and ferns. 'Naomi' [Z 6–8] is a *R. fortunei* hybrid with some of that species' fragrance, and wide, pale lilac trumpets flushed with lime-green in the throat. If you have space for rhododendrons that will ultimately become large, you must grow a Loderi rhododendron [Z 7–9]. These hybrids of *R. fortunei* and ➤

Rhododendron leucaspis *is a gem for early spring, with its fringed leaves and brown-stamened white flowers .*

Rhododendron bureaui *is among the best of small species, with tawny-felted leaves and stems.*

R. griffithianum are at their most beautiful as teenagers. A mature Loderi does, it is true, display its beautiful peeling, pink and grey bark; but the lovely,powerfully fragrant lily-like flowers, white, pink or blush, are then held way above your head.

Most of the foregoing are still close in character to the species, with the grace and poise of wildlings combined with hybrid vigour. If the conditions you can offer are less than ideal – too exposed, too cold – for these lovely things, there are some very tough rhododendrons you could attempt. 'Cunningham's White' [z 5–7] has the blood of the thuggish *R. ponticum* in it, and is corressondingly easy-going; it has white funnels opening from mauve buds. 'Fastuosum Flore Pleno' [z 5–7] is in effect a double-flowered ponticum, but of cleaner colouring, rich lilac-mauve. The white-flowered, purple-black-blotched 'Sappho' [z 5–7] is one of the most showy of hardy hybrids, unless all those magenta-reds are to your taste. Slightly less hardy are the fragrant, lily-flowered species and cultivars such as *R. johnstoneanum*, 'Lady Alice Fitzwilliam' and 'Fragrantissimum'[all z 7–8]. Their flowers are white or ivory-cream, sometimes with a pinkish flush along the ribs on the outside, and often waxen in texture. Where they will thrive, few shrubs are lovelier. Warm, moist woodland conditions, or the nearest equivalent that can be contrived by growing them in containers and shifting them to frost-free winter shelter, are what they require.

The dwarf rhododendrons, and the tender lily-flowered species, can be increased by cuttings. Layering is an easy method of increase of the larger rhododendrons. Little or no pruning is needed, but both for cosmetic reasons and to direct the plant's energies into growth rather than seed production, dead flowers should be removed, at least until the shrubs become too large for you to reach them.

Rhododendron – species

evergreen shrubs H 30cm–6m/1–20ft
S 30cm–6m/1–20ft spring/year round
z 4–8 [unless indicated]

Even if you set aside the azaleas and the hybrids, the genus rhododendron is very large and diverse; from over five hundred species I offer the following, all-too-limited, selection to tempt you. First, a handful of small- and medium-sized species to fit into almost any garden with the right soil. The genus offers several carpeting or mounded shrublets for cool, leafy, lime-free soil, in dappled shade or open-skied but not baking hot positions. They make good cover in high-rainfall areas, but you need patience; meanwhile, they are a delight in themselves. The blood of *Rhododendron impeditum* [z 4–7] runs in many of the blue-flowered hybrids, but none has inherited such appealing, glaucous-blue foliage, to emphasize the blue-lilac flowers. In *R. calostrotum* [z 6–8] grey-green foliage sets off bright magenta or cherry-crimson saucers, large for such a little shrub. 'Gigha' is a fine selection with rich wine-red flowers. The taxonomists have decreed that this species should absorb *R. keleticum* (now *R. calostrotum* subsp. *keleticum*), which has plum-red saucer-flowers, and *R. radicans* (now *R. calostrotum* subsp. *keleticum* Radicans Group), with similar flowers but with shining green foliage. In *R. campylogynum* Myrtilloides Group [z 7–8] tiny, glossy green leaves set off waxy, plum-purple bells. Rather larger than these is *R. leucaspis* [z 7–8], which needs a sheltered place; its creamy-white flowers, enhanced by dark anthers, open very early in the year. All these little rhododendrons, and many others which there is no space to mention here, can be increased by cuttings or layers.

Up a size or so, and a particular favourite of mine, pretty in leaf and flower, is *R. williamsianum* [Z 5–7], a compact, flattened dome of a shrub with small, circular leaves, coppery-chocolate in colour when young, and shell-pink bells; it needs some shelter, but too much shade may mean too few flowers. Taller again is *R. oreotrephes* [Z 6–7], which has glaucous-blue foliage and clear lilac-mauve flowers, which hint at the funnel shape of the lapageria-flowered rhododendrons.

Some rhododendrons are desired above all for their foliage. The compact, slow-growing *R. bureaui* [Z 6–7] is modest in pink flower, but splendid in tan-felted leaf; as the leaves mature, they turn deep green above, retaining the fox-red coating beneath.

One of the first rhododendrons to be introduced to western gardens from its native Himalayas was *R. arboreum* [Z 7–8]. As its name implies, it may reach tree stature; its flowers are held in tight, spherical trusses, and range in colour from white through pink to blood red, opening early in the year. The foliage is often white-backed. 'Sir Charles Lemon' is a noble selection with a thick, rich brown felting on the undersides of the leaves, and mahogany stems, to set off pure white flowers.

Rhododendron species can be grown from their dust-fine seed, though they may not come true if cross-pollination has taken place. They need little or no pruning, but must be given the right soil conditions, leafy, moisture-retaining and acid. They form a fibrous root-ball which means they can easily be moved even when quite large; the roots should be covered only with a layer of leaf litter, not with soil. They need shelter from scorching or drying winds, and the larger the leaf, the more shade and shelter they require: small-leaved species will grow fully in the open so long as they are not baked dry at any time.

ROBINIA

deciduous trees and shrubs H/S 3-4.5m/10–15ft early summer Z 4–8 [unless indicated]

The false acacia or black locust, *Robinia pseudoacacia*, is a big suckering tree, beautiful in leaf and in fragrant creamy flower, but rather unmanageable in the average-sized garden. However, it has some fine selected cultivars, such as 'Umbraculifera', the mop-headed acacia (see page 17), which forms a rounded head set with the same piles of elegant foliage; and 'Frisia', its lemon-green foliage among the brightest incidents of leaf from spring to autumn, when it turns to gold.

Robinias all tend to have brittle wood, liable to suffer damage in high winds. For this reason the rose acacia, *R. hispida* [Z 6–8], is best grown with its long, bristly branches trained against a wall or onto a firm frame, where its short racemes of flower look rather like a deep rose-pink wisteria in early summer. It needs a sunny position and, like the false acacia, it tolerates any soil as long as it is well-drained. Again like its kin, it suckers freely. It is commercially propagated by grafting onto *R. pseudoacacia* rootstocks.

Robinia hispida *has been given the treatment classically accorded to laburnum, trained on hoops into a tunnel of foliage hung with tassels of pink flowers in early summer.*

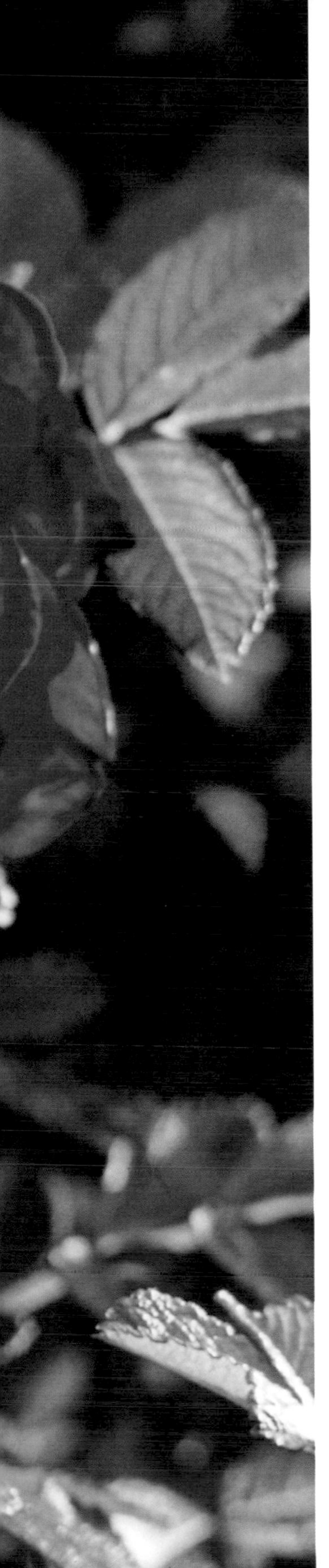

rosa

perfumed panoply

DETAILS FROM TOP:
Rosa *'Tuscany Superb', a gallica rose, is a superior version of the old velvet rose 'Tuscany', with petals as velvety-rich as the common name implies.*

The rugosa rose 'Fru Dagmar Hastrup' makes a compact shrub, with big tomato-red hips to follow the clear pink flowers.

'Belle de Crécy' is a nineteenth-century gallica rose, while dawn-pink 'Fritz Nobis' is a so-called modern shrub rose.

Most hybrid musk roses waft a fruity fragrance, but in 'Cornelia' the musk perfume is dominant.

MAIN PICTURE:
Try floating a few richly-perfumed petals of Rosa rugosa *'Roseraie de l'Haÿ' in a cup of Earl Grey tea for a rare taste experience.*

Rosa

deciduous shrubs H 90cm/2.4m/3–8ft
S 90cm–2.4m/3–8ft summer Z 4–9 [unless indicated]

From the tiny-leaved, simple white-flowered burnet rose of northern Europe and Asia to the muscular *Rosa rugosa* [Z 3–9] of Japan's shores there is a great variety of shrub rose species. And from the wild China rose to the scrolled perfection of a modern large-flowered hybrid tea there is not only a great visual, aesthetic leap, but also genetic mutations and the breeding of centuries. What follows is a tiny selection of species, 'old' roses, modern shrub roses.

The burnet rose, *R. pimpinellifolia* (*R. spinosissima*) [Z 4–8], has running roots and thin stems set with many straight prickles and bristles; it varies from barely knee-height to head-height. It was at one time immensely popular, and some of the most enchanting selections of its heyday survive, still valued for their cupped, white or pink flowers appearing early in the rose season, and above all for their sweet, fresh perfume. Near-black hips follow, enhanced by autumn tints of muted plum, crimson and orange. *R.* × *harisonii* 'Harison's Yellow' [Z 4–8] is effectively a yellow burnet rose. Of several wild yellow-flowered species, all desirable, *R. primula* [Z 5–8] not only has pretty, primrose-yellow flowers, but also strongly aromatic young foliage, whence its name incense rose. From North America come two smaller species that are as valuable as the burnets in informal settings and thin soils: *R. nitida* and *R. virginiana* [both Z 3–7], both with single pink flowers at high summer, neat, glossy foliage turning to brilliant scarlet and orange in autumn, long-lasting bright red hips, and russet-red winter stems.

R. willmottiae [Z 6–8] is a tall Chinese species with tiny, grey-glaucous leaflets on pinkish stems, and small but very abundant lilac-pink flowers followed by vermilion hips. In *R. soulieana* [Z 7–8] the effect is creamy-grey, for the glaucous foliage on grey stems is the setting for rather larger, fragrant white flowers opening from primrose buds. It is a lax shrub compared with the gracefully-arching, mounded stems of *R. willmottiae*. The most intensely glaucous in leaf of all roses is *R. glauca* [Z 4–9], of ➤

The tea fragrance of the Bourbon rose 'Souvenir de la Malmaison' is as subtle as its tender colouring.

which the former name, *R. rubrifolia*, speaks of the overlay of plum-purple that colours the foliage where kissed by the sun. The flowers are bright pink and are followed by showy bunches of milk-chocolate to scarlet hips.

The rugosa roses [all Z 3–9] are more robust in appearance, with strong, prickly stems, glossy, corrugated, rich green leaves turning corn-gold in autumn, and pointed buds opening to silky-petalled flowers, followed by big, shining, red hips. Typically magenta-pink, the rugosas also come in white ('Alba'), clear pink ('Fru Dagmar Hastrup'), bright magenta ('Scabrosa'), and doubles: white 'Blanche Double de Coubert', and the glorious magenta-purple 'Roseraie de l'Haÿ'. All have a voluptuous, free-floating fragrance, and all flower both early and late.

The hybrid musks also bear their flowers in summer and again in autumn, and waft their fruity perfume far on the air. 'Buff Beauty' [Z 6–9] has bronzed young foliage and coral buds opening to apricot; 'Moonlight' [Z 5–9] is creamy-pale, with rich mahogany young growths; 'Cornelia' [Z 5–9] has musk-scented, apricot-pink flowers; 'Ballerina' has small, pink flowers, and 'Penelope' [Z 5–9] has salmon-pink buds opening to pale pink flowers that quickly fade to ivory-white and are followed by coral-pink hips.

If the gentle tints of 'Buff Beauty' appeal to you, then so will those of *R.* × *odorata* 'Mutabilis' [Z 6–9], a China rose with mahogany young growths and slender, bright orange buds opening to single flowers. At first buff-yellow touched with flame, they change to tawny pink after pollination and, a day later, to crimson before the petals fall.

Such roses, though bred in the early years of this century or earlier, are not what are conventionally called 'old roses'. This title belongs to the moss roses, the centifolias or Provence roses, the damasks, gallicas and albas, and the Bourbons, the group that are the bridge between the old roses and the moderns, being repeat-flowering ancestors of the hybrid perpetuals that in turn gave rise to the hybrid teas. One of the oldest is *R. gallica* var. *officinalis* [Z 4–9], the apothecary's rose or red rose of Lancaster, a low-growing shrub with semi-double, pinkish-crimson, fragrant flowers with yellow stamens. The white roses or albas (to which belongs the white rose of York) are not all white; 'Céleste' [Z 3–9] is of the purest shade of shell-pink, its semi-double blooms opening from scrolled buds and set off by greyish foliage. My preferred damask is pure white 'Madame Hardy' [Z 4–9], with perfectly-formed, flat blooms revealing a little green eye.

A fully open bloom of the gallica rose 'Charles de Mills' [Z 4–9] (see page 15) reminds me of the underside of a mushroom, so full of petals, so flat and regular is it; the colour is rich, deep crimson-maroon to burgundy. 'Tuscany Superb' [Z 4–9] is another gallica, with flowers of deep, velvety crimson-maroon, beautiful when highlighted by primrose or citron companion blooms. The colour of the moss rose 'Nuits de Young' [Z 4–9] is similar, intensified by the rather dark, burnished foliage and moss. It is another moss rose, however, 'William Lobb' [Z 4–9], which has earned the nickname 'old velvet moss'. This big shrub has flowers of the extraordinary colouring, muted crimson-purple fading to grey-purple, lilac-mauve, and lavender, making it the ideal companion for *Clematis viticella* 'Purpurea Plena Elegans', which bears pompon-double blooms of soft grey-purple among grey and silver leaves, and *Salvia officinalis* Purpurascens Group, which has foliage of similar understated grey-purple. The same gentle colouring belongs to the hybrid perpetual rose 'Reine des Violettes' [Z 4–9], which looks closer in style to the Bourbons.

It is to the Bourbons that the famous thornless rose 'Zéphyrine Drouhin' [Z 5–9] belongs. She has a rich perfume, almost endless season of flower, and good temper. But her colouring is a somewhat crude sugar pink (best at dusk, when it seems to glow with inner fire); I prefer her sport 'Kathleen Harrop' [Z 5–9], with flowers of pure, clear pink. 'Souvenir de la Malmaison' [Z 5–9] is not thornless, but unsurpassed in its palest peach-pink to ivory tones.

That leaves me just a handful of shrub roses I would not wish to be without. The season begins in late spring with

'Frühlingsgold'. A big shrub with arching branches, it bears an abundance of single, clear yellow flowers with amber stamens, endowed with a rich, fruity-spicy perfume. At midsummer it is the turn of 'Geranium' [Z 4–9], a manageably-sized derivative of the leggy *R. moyesii* [Z 4–9], with thick textured, bright cinnabar-scarlet, Tudor-rose flowers followed by vermilion, flask-shaped hips.

I have never grown, but have long been tempted by, David Austin's English Roses [Z 5–8], a growing band of compact, repeat-flowering, mainly fragrant cultivars with flowers of 'old-fashioned' style in many different colours.

On the commercial scale, roses are almost always budded, but summer cuttings generally root quite easily, and 'own root' roses do not sucker – or at least, if they do, you get more of the same. How you prune depends on the rose's character and what you expect from it. It is possible not to prune these shrub roses at all, but they can become very large with time. You can remove whole branches – the oldest stems with many twiggy growths – at the base from repeat-flowering roses and the ones with showy hips, doing the job in late winter; new, strong stems should replace them from ground level, especially if the bush is generously fed. Similar treatment suits the once-flowering roses that do not produce hips, except that you can do it after the flowers fade. The rugosas can be clipped over in late winter to make dense bushes covered with flower by summer. If you want *R. glauca* to produce the finest foliage, you can cut it hard back in late winter each year and sacrifice the flowers and hips. Unpruned, it is less handsome in leaf, and taller; and may well provide you with self-sown seedlings. Other species can be grown from seed, too, though they will not necessarily come true.

On the whole, shrub roses are more free of diseases than the highly-bred modern kinds. If they do get a touch of black spot or mildew, they are generally vigorous enough to overcome it without your intervention. Give them a well-nourished soil rich in organic matter, and they will more or less take care of themselves.

OPPOSITE FROM TOP:
White forms of the rugosa rose such as the double 'Blanche Double de Coubert' have petals of stark paper white, lacking the hint of cream that is almost inevitably present in white roses.

Rosa xanthina *'Canary Bird' is one of the brightest in flower of the early, yellow-flowered species.*

The flat-faced, petal-packed flowers of the ivory-white damask rose 'Madame Hardy' are enhanced by the tiny green 'eye' at their hearts.

David Austin's English roses have flowers of 'old-fashioned' style, subtly coloured and fragrant, on stocky bushes ideally suited today's smaller gardens; this is 'Charles Austin'.

RIGHT:
Roses vary greatly in fragrance; in Constance Spry, a climbing shrub rose, the perfume is distinctly musky.

Rosmarinus officinalis

evergreen shrub H 30cm–1.2m/1–4ft S 1.5m/5ft
late spring Z 6–10

The Mediterranean, sun-loving rosemaries vary greatly in habit, from the fully prostrate forms with pale blue flowers known as the Prostratus Group, to the fastigiate, which have no place in this chapter. In between are those of sprawling, spreading habit, of which some have particular appeal for the rich blue-mauve colouring of their flowers as well as for the warmly pungent aroma of the foliage (try a few fresh leaves chopped onto potatoes roasted in olive oil ...). One of the best is 'Severn Sea'; another is 'Tuscan Blue'. They need a well-drained soil, and are easily increased by summer cuttings. They can be pruned in spring if it is necessary to cut them back hard; or lightly trimmed in early summer after the flowers fade.

Beautiful against these warm tones of weathered brick, Rosmarinus officinalis *also assorts well with other aromatic, sun-loving plants – sage, lavender and the like. Ideally, grow it where you can tweak an aromatic sprig as you pass.*

Salix

deciduous shrubs H 75cm–2.4m/2½–8ft
S 75cm–2.4m/2½–8ft foliage Z 3–8 [unless indicated]

Handsome though a full-grown weeping willow can be, it has no place in small gardens. At the other end of the scale are willows so tiny that they are best grown in a rock garden or even a trough. Among those of shrub stature, the tall *Salix exigua* [Z 3–7] has long, needle-fine, intensely silvered leaves on a fountain of upright, slender stems; uniquely (so far as I am aware) for a willow, it suckers. The rosemary-leaved willow, *S. elaeagnos* [Z 4–8], grows into a graceful dome, its slender, dark maroon stems densely set with long, grey-green needles backed with white felt, at its best when a breeze ruffles its feathers into a play of grey and silver.

Willows are often believed to require moist or even wet soil, but these will grow in any good garden soil, and *S. exigua* will tolerate quite dry conditions. *S. elaeagnos*, in my experience, is adept at sopping up excess soil moisture; I have used it successfully as a lazy alternative to laying drains where water lay ankle-deep after every heavy rainfall. They are easily increased by cuttings, or division of the suckering roots of *S. exigua*. If they need pruning to restrict size, they can be cut hard back with no ill effects. This is best done in winter.

Sambucus

deciduous shrubs H 1.8–2.4m/6–8ft
S 1.8–2.4m/6–8ft foliage Z 4–8 [unless indicated]

The froth of creamy, muscat-scented heads of elderflower is a fine sight in late spring hedgerows, and the black fruits of *Sambucus nigra* [Z 5–7] hold the promise of wine and throat-soothing syrups, while the coral berries of *S. racemosa* [z 4–8] are vivid in the subalpine landscape of Europe. But it is as foliage shrubs that I recommend *S. nigra* f. *laciniata* and *S. racemosa* 'Sutherland Gold' or the foliage forms of *S. nigra*. The first has lacy-fine green foliage (others, only a little less appealing, have the normal elder foliage in a range of variants, gold, purple and variegated). The golden elder has more sharply-cut foliage, which emerges tinted with copper and coral before unfurling to bright chartreuse faintly touched with bronze.

Any fertile garden soil suits the elders. They can be cut back if they grow too large; to get the best foliage from 'Sutherland Gold', cut back severely each winter to a low framework of branches. Good feeding is essential for hard-pruned specimens. The combination of full, baking sun and dry soil may scorch its foliage, but too much shade turns it a sickly green. Summer cuttings root easily.

Sarcococca hookeriana *var.* digyna

evergreen shrub H 60cm/2ft S 60cm/2ft winter Z 7–9

The Christmas box is an understated little thicketing shrub, with narrow, dark green leaves on erect, plum-purple stems, and tiny, creamy-pink flowers which fill the cold winter air with honeyed fragrance. It will spread a carpet of foliage beneath deciduous shrubs, as it might below *Viburnum* × *bodnantense*, whose pink flowers will echo its own tiny tassels. It grows well in shady places, in any fertile, well-drained soil. The only pruning needed is to remove dead stems in spring. The suckering stems can be divided to make more plants.

Skimmia

evergreen shrubs H 90cm/3ft S 90cm-1.8m/3-6ft winter to spring Z 7–9

If you grow your skimmias for their shiny red fruits in winter, you will need a female plant, and a male to pollinate her (one male can take care of several females). My choice, however, falls on a male plant: *Skimmia japonica* 'Rubella', which displays crimson-red buds all winter, making it a favourite component of smart town window-boxes. In spring the flowers open to whitish, lily-of-the-valley scented flowers. Skimmias look well with other shade-lovers – *Geranium macrorrhizum* 'Album' to prolong the season of pale flower, ferns and Lenten roses. If suited in neutral to acid soil, moist and well-nourished and away from scorching sun and searing winds, it has lustrous, dark green foliage. Cuttings root well if taken in summer or autumn. No pruning is necessary, but if it needs cutting back to keep it in bounds, this is best done after the flowers fade, in late spring.

Sophora tetraptera

evergreen tree H 4.5m/15ft S 3m/10ft late spring Z 9-10

This little, open-branched New Zealand tree has foliage composed of up to forty-one tiny leaflets on each pinnate leaf. The decorative patterns they form are the setting for hanging, claw-shaped, rich yellow flowers. The flowers are followed by pods that look like strings of winged beads; new plants are easily raised from the seeds within. No pruning is needed; indeed, sophoras rather resent it. They grow in any fertile, well-drained soil, in sun.

There is no more graceful willow than Salix exigua, *especially when its slender, platinum-pale needle leaves are ruffled by the breeze.*

The fragrant domes of Skimmia japonica *'Rubella' that appear in the spring are accompanied here by scarlet young leaves and creamy sprays of a pieris.*

Sorbus cashmiriana *is perhaps the perfect small, deciduous tree for today's gardens, with its four seasons of beauty. Here it is decked in its pure white fruits, set off by the last of autumn's crimson foliage.*

Sorbus

deciduous trees H 6m/20ft S 4.5m/15ft year-round Z 6–7 [unless indicated]

The finest rowans come from Asia. One of the brightest in autumn is *Sorbus commixta*, for its glossy leaves, coppery in spring, turn to fiery tints amid the large clusters of small, vermilion berries. Other rowans bear white or pink fruits. For the smallest gardens, *S. vilmorinii* is a pet, with extremely fine foliage of many tiny leaflets, and berries that are at first crimson-rose amid the red and plum-purple autumn leaves, hanging on through winter as they gradually fade through pink to white. The larger, more rounded leaflets of *S. hupehensis* are glaucous-tinted, turning to madder and plum in autumn, and its small fruits are white, or pink. Perhaps the finest of all, though, is *S. cashmiriana* [Z 5–7], for it has many seasons of charm. In spring the young leaves unfurl in rich shades of pinkish-crimson; by the time they have fully expanded, the soft pink flowers have opened; and in autumn the leaves again turn to rich purple, crimson and maroon, amid which the marble-sized, opaque white fruits gleam, remaining long after the leaves have fallen.

Any fertile, well-drained soil except thin chalk, suits the rowans . The pink- and white-fruited rowans have the obliging habit of coming true from seed; you can, of course, sow seed of red-fruited rowans too, but anything may come up. The seedlings should be encouraged to form a strong leader. Any necessary pruning for this purpose, or to remove crossing branches, should be done from autumn to early spring.

Stewartia

deciduous trees H 4.5m/15ft S 4.5m/15ft summer Z 5–7

These camellia relatives are among a handful of summer-flowering trees which form the ideal supporting cast for a collection of choice rhododendrons. They make small trees, their white or cream flowers borne over a long season, barely over before autumn's chill turns the leaves to flame, scarlet and crimson. On older trees the bark is beautiful too, flaking away in patches of tan, fawn and cream. *Stewartia pseudocamellia* makes a tree of somewhat open habit, its white, cupped flowers enhanced by a central boss of yellow stamens. Of more upright habit, *S. pseudocamellia* Koreana Group has flowers that open wider to a saucer shape; and it has the brightest autumn tints of the species.

Stewartias thrive in woodland conditions, in a leafy soil that does not dry out, and benefit from a good annual mulch of leafmould. They need no pruning, except for cosmetic reasons, to enhance the lovely, marbled bark by carefully removing selected branches to leave an uncluttered trunk and lower limbs.

Styrax japonicus

deciduous tree H 4.5m/15ft S 4.5m/15ft summer Z 6–8

Another pretty tree to associate with rhododendrons, the snowbell tree earns its name from the countless little white bells that hang from beneath gracefully-spreading branches in summer. They are followed by fruits like small, suede-coated, jade green marbles. The pattern of the branches and the dainty, fresh green foliage adds lightness to the heavier foliage of rhododendrons, for which the snowbell tree provides a light and grateful shade. It flowers with such abandon that an annual mulch of nutritious leafmould is almost essential. It needs no pruning except to remove dead wood. Layering is a possible means of increase.

Few trees flower quite so profusely as the snowbell tree, Styrax japonicus; *and its near-horizontal branching structure might have been designed to display the little bells to their best advantage.*

SYRINGA MICROPHYLLA *'SUPERBA'*

deciduous shrub H 1.8m/6ft S 1.5m/5ft
late spring to autumn Z 5–8

Small and neat of leaf, this little lilac makes a stocky, rounded bush liberally sprinkled in late spring with short panicles of lilac-pink, deliciously fragrant flowers. After the main burst of flower, more are produced off and on until autumn. It assorts prettily with *Rosa glauca*, purple sage (*Salvia officinalis* Purpurascens Group) and silvery foliage such as that of artemisia or elaeagnus.

An open position in fertile, well-drained soil is ideal. Little or no pruning is needed, for the shrub is naturally compact in growth. Propagate by summer cuttings.

TAMARIX RAMOSISSIMA

deciduous shrub H 4.5m/15ft S 3m/10ft summer
Z 3–8

Tamarisks have slender branches set with tiny, scale-like leaves, often sea-green or palely glaucous in colour, making a cloudy mass which, at flowering time, is transformed into a haze of feathery pink plumes. *Tamarix ramosissima* (*T. pentandra*), left unpruned, will develop into a large shrub or even a small tree; but since it flowers in summer, on the current season's growths, it can be hard-pruned each spring to remain compact without loss of flower. For brighter pink flowers choose 'Pink Cascade'.

A place in the sun, in a well-drained soil except shallow chalk, suits tamarisks, which are very wind-tolerant and make first-rate seaside shrubs. They root easily from hardwood cuttings.

VIBURNUM

deciduous and evergreen shrubs H 1.5–2.4m/5–8ft S 1.5–2.4m/5–8ft winter, spring, summer, autumn Z 5–9 [unless indicated]

By planting a selection of viburnums, you could have flowers at every season, handsome evergreen foliage, bright autumn colour and vivid fruits. The winter-flowering viburnums, *Viburnum farreri* [Z 7–8] and its hybrid offspring *V.* × *bodnantense* [Z 6–8], are widely grown for the potent, free-floating almond fragrance of their little clusters of white, blush or pink flowers. The cultivars of the hybrid all lean to blush or pink and all are good: 'Charles Lamont', 'Dawn', and 'Deben' [all Z 6–8]. All flower over a long, late-autumn to late-winter season and make large, many-stemmed shrubs from which, if they grow out of bounds, entire, older stems can be removed to leave a vase-shaped outline. Minor cuts are best made in early spring, immediately after flowering; major overhauls later in spring. The other winter-flowering species is the laurustinus, a sombre cloud of matt evergreenery spangled with scentless white flowers opening from pink buds throughout mild, maritime winters, or holding back until spring to make more of a show in regions with more clearly defined seasons. My choice would be *V. tinus* 'Gwenllian' [Z 8–10], which is compact in growth, with pretty flowers and small indigo-black fruits to follow.

The daphne-scented Viburnum carlesii *is one of a choice group of spring-flowering viburnums with white, snowball flowers that open from pink buds.*

The season between the winter- and spring-flowering viburnums is bridged by *V.* × *burkwoodii* [Z 4–9], a glossy-leaved semi-evergreen with pink buds opening to white domes. In flower it is outdone by the more properly spring-flowering *V. carlesii* [Z 4–9], its rounded clusters of pure white flowers opening from pink buds endowed with the same strong, sweet carnation fragrance. 'Aurora' retains its pink colouring even when fully open.

Late spring to early summer is the season of the lacecap viburnums, *V. plicatum* and its cultivars. One of the most popular of these, in fact, is the Japanese snowball, often called simply *V. plicatum*, sometimes labelled with the qualifying 'Sterile', on account of its ivory-white globes, their weight arching the branches over their long season. It is greatly superior to the later-flowering snowball form of the guelder rose, *V. opulus* [Z 3–8], appealing though this is at all stages from jade-green bud to white maturity (see page 17). The lacecap forms of *V. plicatum* are grand shrubs, especially at home in informal or even woodland settings, making ample sideways growth and increasing in height by piling layer upon layer of horizontal branches, set with fresh green, pleated leaves, which in flower are concealed under a froth of white lace. 'Mariesii' shows the tiered habit most markedly (see page 17); 'Rowallane' and 'Lanarth' are more upright in growth, and the first is most free with its showy clusters of small, cinnabar-red fruits in autumn. 'Pink Beauty' departs from the usual white flower-colouring to blush deeper with age. All display sombre crimson and plum autumn tints, especially when grown in full exposure to light. The guelder rose is naturally also of lacecap type, and the flowers are followed by vivid, translucent fruits like redcurrants, or, in *V. opulus* 'Xanthocarpum', amber yellow. Of similar character to the European guelder rose is the Asian *V. sargentii* [Z 4–7]; the cultivar 'Onondaga' [Z 4–7] is outstanding, with young foliage of mahogany-plum and crimson, and deep, rich autumn tints.

I am left, in this all too brief selection of viburnums, with three first-rate foliage plants. *V. cinnamomifolium* [Z 7–10] somewhat calls to mind the dumpy *V. davidii* [Z 7–10], but is a much larger shrub, with bolder leaves of thinner texture with a more polished sheen, and the same three deep, longitudinal veins which give them such character. Neither the off-white flowers nor the little blue-black fruits are up to much. If *V. japonicum* [Z 8–9] never flowered it would still be worth growing – though the fragrant, white, rounded clusters at midsummer are welcome when they do appear, in the shrub's maturity – for here is a generous shrub with large, leathery, highly-polished, rich green leaves. Lastly, the entirely desirable *V. henryi* [Z 7–9], an open-branched, more or less upright shrub with narrow, pointed, very dark shining green leaves to set off, at midsummer, its nubbly cones of white flower that turn to sprays of red fruits aging to black, both colours in the cluster at once. If I could grow only one viburnum, desipite its lack of fragrance, it would be this.

Viburnums of the *carlesii* [Z 4–9] type are tricky to raise from cuttings, but semi-ripe late summer cuttings of the winter-flowering kinds, the lacecaps and the choice evergreens are not too difficult. Cuttings of the laurustinus root almost whenever they are taken. Except as noted for the winter-flowering kinds, little or no pruning is needed. If necessary, prune *V. tinus* in early summer after it has flowered, *V. plicatum* in summer as the flowers fade, and the fragrant *carlesii* types at midsummer if absolutely essential.

On still, cold winter days, the air will be filled with the far-carrying almond fragrance of Viburnum farreri, *announcing its pink clusters of flower even before they come into sight.*

verticals

plants to clothe & climb

A rambling rose tumbling down from the topmost branches of an old orchard tree; the azure, ultramarine and lapis trumpets of morning glory decking the dark pines of the Mediterranean coasts and rivalling the colour of the sea itself; a white-barked silver birch hung with a vine such as Vitis coignetiae, *the autumn sun shining through its huge, scarlet and orange leaves; a grey-leaved sea buckthorn large enough to embrace in its thorny branches the little curved bugles of the Chilean glory vine in burnt orange, cinnabar-scarlet or amber, to prefigure the sea buckthorn's own amber-yellow winter berries: these imply a garden already mature. And it takes time, too, for a vine or a wisteria to clothe a pergola with the full glory of leaf or flower. While waiting for the ripe maturity of the noblest woody climbers, there are annuals and perennials ready with a season's growth generous enough to deck trellis, pillars and walls.*

Wisteria is almost the perfect flowering climber for a pergola, with its elegant hanging tassels of sweet-scented flower. Wisteria floribunda *'Alba' is here beautifully set off here by the strong, dark horizontals of the pergola and the warmly-coloured wall.*

verticals

Clematis and roses are a classic combination. By the time the smoky 'old man's beards' of this early-flowering Clematis macropetala *have formed, the candy-pink* Rosa *'Débutante' has opened to complete a soft-toned colour scheme.*

The flowers of Clematis macropetala *resemble a flared skirt with a frou-frou of petticoats beneath. Later the flowers are succeeded by silky, wig-like seedheads.*

Climbers are the opportunists of the plant world. Growing among shrubs or in the shelter of trees, they use their neighbours' sturdier branches to hoist themselves towards the light.

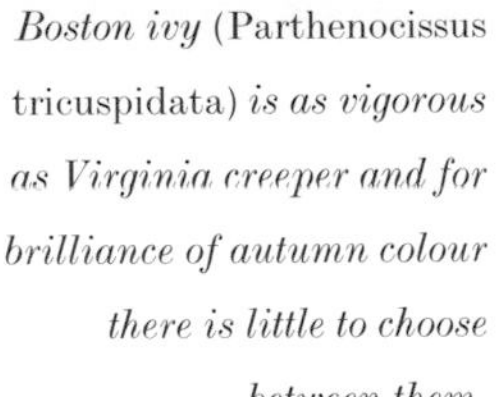

Boston ivy (Parthenocissus tricuspidata) *is as vigorous as Virginia creeper and for brilliance of autumn colour there is little to choose between them.*

An old apple tree, even if barren, is too valuable to fell, making the ideal host for a climbing rose, such as 'Félicité Perpetué' that will cascade from the branches.

Though plant catalogues often bracket in one section 'climbers and wall plants', a garden need not be blessed with walls or graced by a pergola for climbers to enhance its vertical dimension. In the wild, climbers use their neighbouring shrubs and trees as supports by which to reach light and air; they have evolved twining stems, coiling leafstalks or tendrils (sometimes with adhesive tips), aerial roots or even hooked prickles the better to haul themselves upwards.

In the garden, this natural association of climber and host can be exploited for aesthetic ends. Combinations of shrubs and climbers allow for striking associations of colour, form and texture, to say nothing of extending the season as flower succeeds flower and is, in turn, overtaken by fruit and autumn tints. The best companions for shrubs are the viticella and other clematis hybrids of not too vigorous growth, that are cut down each winter to free the host from the clematis' old stems. A single climber, the double, dusty-purple *Clematis viticella* 'Purpurea Plena Elegans', for example, may link two hosts such as the grey-leaved *Buddleja* 'Lochinch' and the old purple moss rose 'William Lobb'. The popular *Cornus alba* 'Elegantissima' can be given a new look by hosting a richly-coloured clematis, the purple or velvety crimson or violet-blue flowers set off by the dogwood's white-variegated leaves.

The great synstylae roses, that is those with the blood of the wild musk rose and its allies, are never so lovely as when they have drawn themselves up through a tree – an old apple tree, perhaps, or a dark conifer – to cascade down in a waterfall of ivory-white, fragrant blossom. Honeysuckle, too, is most at home when twining through the branches of a host tree; this, after all, is how honeysuckles grow in the wild, at woodland margins.

Hedges may also be decked with climbers. A clipped yew hedge, even within a few years of planting, will be substantial enough to glow with the small, fiercely scarlet nasturtiums and pale, frail foliage of *Tropaeolum speciosum*. Woodbine or honeysuckle, *Lonicera periclymenum*, will embrace a rough hawthorn hedge as readily as it will scale a tree, to fill the air, at dawn and dusk, with its sweet, insinuating fragrance.

Not that walls are not welcome as both shelter and support for many a climber. A vigorous climber such as Virginia creeper (*Parthenocissus quinquefolia*), or Boston ivy (*P. tricuspidata*) with its coarser foliage, can easily on its own cover a wide expanse of wall, making a fiery sheet of colour in the autumn before the leaves fall. Even on walls and on free-standing artificial supports, such as trellis, pergolas, poles and pyramids, climbers are almost always at their best when grown with other plants, as they are in the wild. Combining climbers with other climbers, or with wall or pillar shrubs, gives scope for yet more striking or subtle combinations of flower and foliage.

Thus the incandescent scarlet of Virginia creeper will be heightened if mingled with an ivy such as *Hedera colchica* 'Dentata Variegata', its large, leathery leaves green margined with cream and butter-yellow all year round. Or imagine a pergola covered with *Vitis vinifera* 'Purpurea', the teinturier vine, its muted purple foliage dusted with white on first emerging. Then add in your mind's eye a pink rambling rose, or an amethyst-mauve clematis or – more unusually – a passion flower of similar colouring, such as *Passiflora* × *caeruleo-racemosa*. The opulent, full blooms of climbing and pillar roses are flattered by the blue-violet, purple, lavender and mauve tones of clematis, or may be subtly matched with white or mauve-pink cultivars.

This is not to say that you can simply plant a climber and forget about pruning or grooming it. Even ivy is the better for a comb-through in spring, to remove tired old foliage, and on a wall it may be trimmed back to make a dense, close cover. Large-flowered roses and clematis soon become cluttered with old, dead growths if not pruned yearly. Honeysuckles have a strangler mentality and may choke a supporting tree unless watched and, if necessary, disciplined.

Since climbers in the wild grow in company with other plants, they face competition for nutrients from their hosts, but also enjoy the cool, leafy soil and shade from burning sun that the canopy provides. Cool roots and head in the sun is a good rule of thumb for climbers. When planting, it is worth preparing the site thoroughly, adding organic matter and perhaps a slow-acting fertilizer as well, to ensure an ample supply of nutrients. The host shrub or tree will immediately appropriate much of these nutrients, of course, and to give the climber a good start – especially if the host is a greedy, rooty tree – it is worth taking a little extra trouble. One way is to plant the climber outside the reach of the roots and lead its stems into the host by means of a cane or stout string. Another is to try and find a space free of feeding roots close up against the trunk, among the

Two fragrant flowers mingle: double mock orange, Philadelphus *'Manteau d'Hermine' hosts woodbine or honeysuckle,* Lonicera periclymenum.

Irish ivy (Hedera hibernica), *mingling with* Clematis *'Marie Boisselot' forms the backdrop for this autumnal scene, with the tawny dying leaves of* Hosta sieboldiana *var.* elegans *and the great lobed blades of* Macleaya. *Clipped box globes* (Buxus sempervirens) *will remain to frame the stone* putti *after the hostas die away entirely.*

Flowering in late summer and autumn, Clematis flammula *is more often seen in relaxed mood, scrambling through a host tree or falling over a wall. Here it has been captured into a globe of starry, hawthorn-scented flower, with the fuzzy spikes of* Sanguisorba *around it.*

'New Dawn' is one of the great climbing roses of all time, perpetual-flowering, glossy-leaved, and with delectably-scented blooms of softest shell pink. It is equally at ease on a wall or trellis, or gracefully falling over a hedge or fence.

anchoring roots, and to incorporate as much organic matter as possible to help the climber establish. An annual mulch of nutrient-rich organic matter, and plenty of moisture during the growing season, should ensure that your climber not only grows but thrives and flowers.

Planting climbers against a wall also calls for care. The soil near a wall can be extremely dry, and overhanging eaves may keep much of the rain away. Then again, the soil at the foot of a wall may be more rubble than loam, and perhaps contaminated with cement or lime mortar. Wall climbers will benefit from being started in a generous planting hole, filled with enriched soil, and may need extra watering, and feeding, not only at the time of planting, but all through the growing season, year after year. The risk of drying out at the root is especially great with climbers that need protection against frost, so that you are tempted to tuck them as close as possible into the shelter of the wall. Extra dryness in winter, however, is often beneficial to tender plants.

However you grow your climbers, and be they gaudy or elegant, untamed wildling or highly-bred and stylized, chosen for flower or fruit or foliage, their great gift is to add romantic profusion to the garden in a minimum of lateral space. A starveling is is in no state to achieve this; climbers need and deserve generous treatment, and will repay it in kind.

clematis

gem-tinted diversity

DETAILS FROM TOP:

The flowers of 'Perle d'Azur' are of the tender colour often called Wedgwood blue.

The dusky mauve-pink of 'Hagley Hybrid' is echoed by the buds of the lilac-mauve rambling rose 'Veilchenblau'.

Magenta-red can be a difficult colour; the answer is to flaunt it assertively, as does 'Ville de Lyon'.

Both white and pink forms of Clematis montana *are found in the wild; the pinks, known as var.* rubens, *develop their best colour in full light.*

MAIN PICTURE:

Texture and colour combine to give 'Gipsy Queen' its velvety richness.

Clematis

deciduous leaf-tendril climbers H/S 1.8–6m/6–20ft
spring, summer, autumn z 4–9 [unless indicated]

The flowers of 'Duchess of Albany' seem as though a tulip had absent-mindedly grown skywards. But no tulip ever burst into silken wigs in seed.

The clematis season opens with the alpines and macropetalas, their nodding, blue, white or dusky pink bells very different from the wide-open flowers that characterize the large-flowered clematis. *Clematis alpina*, in the wild, scrambles over rocks and shrubs in open woodland, and in the garden looks more at home in informal settings than trained on a wall. Combine any of the blue-flowered cultivars – broad-petalled 'Pamela Jackman' in deep blue, or paler 'Columbine' – or the whites such as 'White Columbine' or subsp. *sibirica* 'White Moth' with scarlet Japanese quince (*Chaenomeles*) or orange *Berberis darwinii*, or contrast the blues with the lime-yellow foliage of *Choisya ternata* 'Sundance' (see page 32). There are several dusty pinks: deep pink 'Rosie O'Grady', paler *C. alpina* 'Willy', rosy-purple *C. alpina* 'Ruby', *C. alpina* 'Rosy Pagoda', or *C. macropetala* 'Markham's Pink' [z 5–9]. *C. macropetala* [z 5–9] (see page 70) also comes in blue ('Maidwell Hall') or white ('Snowbird', 'White Swan'). Its flowers are fuller of petals than those of *C. alpina*, giving an almost double effect. In both, the flowers are followed by silky, grey-white, wig-like seed heads. The only time these spring-flowering clematis need pruning is if they outgrow their space, when flowered shoots are cut back immediately after flowering.

The flowers of *C. montana* [z 6–9] open flat in the more conventional clematis style. Typically, they are white, and for visual impact the one to go for is snowy white f. *grandiflora*. 'Alexander', in ivory-white, is vanilla-scented, like the pale pink 'Elizabeth', which fades to white if grown in shade. 'Pink Perfection' is slightly deeper pink; the deepest pink of all, var. *rubens*, has bronzed foliage but little or no scent. Most montanas are very vigorous, quite able to reach the top of a sizeable tree – indeed, there are few finer sights in spring than a tall conifer with dark green foliage wearing the bridal white of *C. montana* f. *grandiflora*. They are pruned in the same way as the atragenes, but if space is limited it may be necessary to cut them back frequently. ➤

From high summer to autumn the yellow lantern-flowered and cowslip-flowered clematis come into flower. Several species have thick, lemon-peel petals with their incurving tips forming a Chinese lantern outline: *C. tangutica* [z 3–8] and *C. tibetana* subsp. *vernayi* [z 5–9], which used to be known as *C. orientalis*. Like most clematis, the flowers are followed by grey 'wigs', at first silky and then fluffy. *C. tangutica* is a rumbustious species, its long season ensuring a mix of flowers and 'wigs' as the weeks pass. 'Bill Mackenzie' has large, long, well-shaped, rich yellow lanterns and silky seed heads and is the one to go for unless you especially prefer the paler, lemon shades of yellow – in which case you will fall for *C. serratifolia* [z 6–9], which has purple stamens and a lemony fragrance. Given plenty of space, you can leave your lantern-flowered clematis unpruned, but they make a considerable tangle before long; alternatively, cut them hard back each late winter, when they will be more manageable but will start to flower later in the season. The cowslip-scented *C. rehderiana* [z 6–9] is another vigorous, late-flowering species, with hairy leaves and an abundance of soft primrose flowers in sprays. The hawthorn-scented *C. flammula* (see page 72) adorns autumn with a cloud of starry, white flowers.

The summer-flowering clematis which are hybrids of *C. texensis* [z 5–9] are semi-herbaceous, and have inherited something of its pure red colouring. 'Duchess of Albany' has long, erect flowers of almost pure pink, like lily-flowered tulips. The nodding, open bells of 'Etoile Rose' are cherry-red margined with pink and open over a three-month long summer season. 'Gravetye Beauty' has rich ruby-crimson flowers that open to wide stars. All can be cut hard back in late winter.

And so to clematis that bear their large, wide-open flowers in summer. They are the most spectacular, and come in a wide range of colours from pure white through shades of lilac-pink to deepest velvety crimson, magenta, and wine-red, silvery-mauve to rich purple, and palest lavender to periwinkle- and violet-blue. Some, such as the famous 'Nelly Moser', have pinky-mauve flowers with a bold carmine stripe along each tepal; and a very few are described as yellow – about as yellow as clotted cream. Those that flower on wood of the previous season are the first to bloom, and should be pruned only lightly (removing dead stems and cutting healthy ones back to the topmost plump bud, in winter); those that flower on new growths can be cut hard back in late winter, down to 90cm/3ft or less from the ground. All clematis, but especially these highly-bred creatures, are at their best in enriched soil, and a good mulch to keep their roots cool.

The finest of the whites is 'Marie Boisselot', which bears its huge, rounded flowers on both old and new wood. 'Comtesse de Bouchaud' is a fine mauve-pink, flowering on new wood and combining to perfection with the glaucous and plum-purple foliage of *Rosa glauca*, or with pink Japanese anemones and purple sage. In these shades of dusty mauve-pink, 'Hagley Hybrid' is one of the best, with dark eyelashes and a three-month season. Of the reds, 'Ville de Lyon' is bright carmine-crimson, 'Ernest Markham' an eye-wiping magenta; both flower on old and new wood. But neither can compare with 'Niobe', which bears the deepest, most velvety maroon-crimson blooms of all.

For an almost indestructible violet-purple clematis, there is only one choice: 'Jackmanii Superba', which should be pruned hard in late winter, like 'Niobe', to flower after midsummer. For a long season from late spring, 'The President' is unsurpassed for its blue-purple flowers, slightly cupped to show off their silvery reverse. With more red in its purple is 'Gipsy Queen', flowering from late summer to autumn.

Among blues, 'Lasurstern' is a stunner in rich, deep blue, best when lightly pruned. The outright winner among blue clematis – to my taste, indeed, among all large-flowered clematis, whatever their colour – is 'Perle d'Azur', which bears quantities of porcelain-blue flowers all summer.

There are double-flowered clematis too, all bearing double flowers in their first flush on the previous year's growths, and single flowers thereafter on the new season's stems. 'Beauty of Worcester' is a superb blue, 'Daniel Deronda' deep violet, 'Belle of Woking' a glacial silvery mauve, 'Proteus' a splendid, very full mauve-pink, and 'Duchess of Edinburgh' a many-petalled white with alabaster-green tints.

The one drawback to large-flowered clematis, apart from the fiddle of tying in new growths, is that they may suddenly succumb to wilt, one or more stems, or even the whole plant, collapsing almost overnight. Cut out the diseased wood and treat the plant with a fungicide, and guard the new shoots carefuly lest they get damaged. If the idea of losing a treasured clematis is too much to contemplate, the answer is to grow the *C. viticella* hybrids [z 3–8]. Their flowers are not so large, but they are tough and easy to grow, are best pruned hard each winter, and come in much the same range of colours. 'Alba Luxurians' is white, tinged with green; 'Huldine' is mother-of-pearl white with pale mauve reverse; 'Abundance' is light claret and 'Kermesina' deep wine-crimson; 'Etoile Violette' describes itself; and the bicolors ('Little Nell', 'Minuet' and 'Venosa Violacea') are all white margined with mauve to purple. There is a wholly enchanting double form of *C. viticella* called 'Purpurea Plena Elegans', with neat little petal-packed rosettes of soft, grey-washed purple-lilac.

Clematis used almost invariably to be propagated by grafting, but they are not too difficult to root as cuttings. Take internodal, rather than nodal cuttings from midsummer onwards, reducing the leaf area by removing one of the pair of leaflets entirely and the terminal leaflet of the other if it is very large, so that there is no overlap of leaves when the cuttings are stuck in gritty compost – they readily succumb to grey mould without this precaution. Watering them in with a fungicide solution is another helpful preventive. Leave them undisturbed until spring, when they can be individually potted and staked. The easiest to root in this way are the montanas and atragenes. Clematis species can also be grown from seed.

OPPOSITE FROM TOP:
The dark stamens of 'Henryi' intensify the whiteness of the tepals.

The thick, pointed tepals of Clematis tibetana *curve around a central boss of stamens.*

'Snow Queen' is another fine white clematis, its charms heightened by the ribbed tepals that guide the eye to the dark stamens.

The white tepals of 'Alba Luxurians' are sometimes almost wholly green.

RIGHT:
'Bill Mackenzie', a tangutica clematis, displays its lemon-peel lanterns on gracefully curving stems.

The curved trumpets of Eccremocarpus scaber *are borne in profusion over a long summer season, producing an abundance of seed that often germinates as freely as mustard and cress. Grow it through another climber, or drape it over host shrubs. The amber-yellow form is best set off by dark green foliage, while a strong colour scheme can be made with the coppery-crimson form hosted by a golden-leaved shrub such as* Cornus alba *'Aurea'.*

Eccremocarpus scaber

annual/tender tendril climber H/S 4m/13ft summer to autumn Z 7–10

The Chilean glory vine, which climbs by leaf tendrils, is easily raised from seed to flower in its first year, often sowing itself for next year's display, and, even if its stems are frosted, will regenerate from the roots if these are protected from frost by surrounding vegetation or a deep mulch. Though vigorous, it is not a heavyweight, and can be paired with another climber to extend the season or add contrasting colour. The flowers are little, narrow, lopsided trumpets, typically orange with the tiny flared lips paling to yolk yellow, but seedlings with coppery-red or amber-yellow flowers sometimes crop up. Any fertile, well-drained garden soil, in sun or light shade, suits it.

Cobaea scandens

annual/tender perennial tendril climber H/S 2.4m/8ft summer to autumn Z 9–10

A frost-tender perennial that can be treated as an annual, raised from seed to flower in its first year, *Cobaea scandens* has tubby, cup and saucer bells opening from greenish-white buds. Typically, the flowers soon age to deep purple, making a subtle play of colours over the plant. There is also an exquisite form which remains alabaster-white, *C. scandens alba*. Its subtle colouring is best set off by a sombre background: phillyrea, perhaps, or yew, as host. Any fertile, well-drained garden soil suits cobaea, in sun or light shade. It climbs by means of tendrils at the end of the pinnate leaves. To encourage a bushy habit, pinch out the growing tips regularly.

The exquisite white form of Cobaea scandens alba *deserves to be planted where it can be seen at close quarters, for it is fascinating at every stage, from plump bud framed in the green saucer of the calyx, to open, flared bell with protruding anthers.*

Hedera

evergreen self-clinging climbers H/S 1.8–9m/6–30ft year-round Z 5–9 [unless indicated]

In the wild, ivies grow on trees, often scaling a tall host to the very topmost branches; and they have been quick to cover and romanticize ruined buildings. In the garden the many fancy ivies with unusually-shaped leaves, often variegated with white, cream or yellow, take precedence, and fortunately most are more restrained in growth than the wildling. Among the larger garden ivies are two handsome variegated forms of the Persian ivy, *Hedera colchica* [Z 5–9]. They have bold, heart-shaped, leathery leaves, in 'Dentata Variegata' irregularly margined with primrose yellow which

The bold-leaved Irish ivy, Hedera hibernica, *embowers this leafy grouping in which the ribbed, bloomy plates of* Hosta sieboldiana *var.* elegans *and the boldly lobed, celadon-green foliage of* Macleaya microcarpa *'Kelway's Coral Plume' contrast with the small leaves of clipped box domes.*

partly overlays the dark green of the centre to make a greyish zone between yellow and green; and in 'Sulphur Heart' displaying a bright splash of yellow at the centre of the leaf. The cultivars of *H. helix*, the common ivy of Europe and Asia, are legion, offering many combinations of vigour, leaf form and colour. Among the quieter variegations is that of 'Glacier', a vigorous ivy with silvery-grey and cream leaves on reddish stems. Brighter than these is 'Goldheart', with a central yellow splash, as its name implies, on neatly triangular leaves. The Irish ivy, *H. hibernica*, is a big, strong grower, with bold, shining dark green leaves that several times larger than those of 'Goldheart' or 'Glacier'.

Most ivies will grow anywhere, including dark places, in any well-drained soil, and if given a little encouragement at first will quickly develop the aerial roots which make them such efficient self-stickers to walls, fences or tree-trunks. They can be increased by cuttings. Ivies on walls can be clipped back in spring to keep them close and neat, and at the same time dead leaves can be combed out. Ivies are unlikely to damage a sound wall; indeed, they help to keep it dry.

The lacy froth of Hydrangea anomala *subsp.* petiolaris *seems all the whiter when spangled with the intense blood-red nasturtium flowers of* Tropaeolum speciosum, *a frail-stemmed climber that dies back to its fleshy roots each winter.*

The continent of South America is rich in beautiful plants, but few surpass Lapageria rosea. *Its narrow, high-shouldered bells, looking as though they were carved from wax, are the epitome of elegance.*

HYDRANGEA ANOMALA *SUBSP.* PETIOLARIS

deciduous self-clinging climber H/S 9m/30ft summer Z5–8

This climbing hydrangea will cover a wall or tree-trunk or make mounded, spreading ground-cover, in sun or light shade. It needs ample light to flower freely, however, and when it does, the fresh green foliage is almost concealed beneath a foaming mass of white lace-cap heads. It is happy in any fertile, well-drained soil and needs no pruning unless it grows out of bounds. The best time to prune is after flowering, for it flowers on the previous season's growths. If grown in a tree, it will cover the trunk with foliage and bear flowers only on the growths that reach the light. It may be slow-growing at first, and if the adhesive stem-roots have dried out they may be reluctant to take hold; try cutting one or more stems back to encourage strong new growth, held against the intended support by a cane or tie. Layers root easily, and summer cuttings are another means of increase.

LAPAGERIA ROSEA

evergreen twining climber H/S 4.5m/15ft summer Z9-10

Named for an empress – Joséphine de la Pagerie, Napoleon's wife – this is a queen among climbers, with hanging, waxy, narrowly flared bells in shades of pink from pale crimson to the ivory-white of *Lapageria rosea albiflora*. These exquisite confections hang on slender stems set with heart-shaped, pointed, leathery evergreen leaves. So beautiful a plant deserves the very best: a deep, moist, lime-free soil in a sheltered, shady place. However, I have seen it growing, apparently happy, in full sun facing the cold easterly winds. The type can be raised from fresh seeds.

LATHYRUS

annual or perennial tendril climbers H/S 1.8–3.5m/6–13ft summer Z5–8

Turn to any seed catalogue, and you will find sweet peas in an extraordinary range of colours, many with frilled flowers, and even a few fragrant enough to remind you why they are called 'sweet peas'. But for the true, intense fragrance of the old-fashioned sweet pea, I commend to you *Lathyrus odoratus* 'Painted Lady', with rose-pink and white flowers. Specialist seedsmen sometimes offer it, or you may find seedlings for sale, and save seed to grow your own in future. Though it has no scent, the annual *L. sativus* is admired for its gentian-blue to azure pea flowers. Most perennial peas are scentless too, but the exuberance, long flowering season and easy temper of the everlasting pea, *L. latifolius*, earns it a place – especially as the annual stems will climb, scramble, flop down a bank, or cover up a bare space in the border where some early-flowering perennial has gone to ground. Typically, it is bright magenta-pink; there is a paler pink, too, and a handsome pure white, 'White Pearl'. They come near enough true from seed, or you can take basal cuttings for absolute certainty. Any fertile garden soil suits them, in a sunny place.

Lonicera

deciduous twining climbers H/S 6m/20ft
summer Z 5–9

Though not the most showy of honeysuckles, the woodbine of European copses and hedgerows, *Lonicera periclymenum*, is one of the most fragrant, its sweet, evocative perfume free on the air, especially at dawn and dusk. Its most colourful cultivar is 'Serotina', the late Dutch honeysuckle, in which the creamy yellow flowers are overlaid with madder-purple, at its most intense where touched by the sun and fading to pink and cream in shade, and flowering into autumn. 'Graham Thomas' is an excellent newer cultivar with large, cream, very fragrant flowers. All honeysuckles do best with their roots in the shade, in fertile soil, and many flower most abundantly with their heads in the sun or dappled shade. Their twining stems can choke a host plant, but they are ideal for giving body to a thinning hedge. They are increased by summer or autumn cuttings. Pruning, if needed, is best done after flowering, when the flowered shoots can be cut back by one-third.

The common woodbine or honeysuckle, Lonicera periclymenum, *is endowed with a delicious, free-floating perfume. The flowers vary in colour, from creamy white aging to Naples yellow to forms, like this one, that are flushed with rose-red, at its most intense where touched by the sun.*

Whether in shades of magenta to pale pink or, exquisitely, in white, the everlasting pea, Lathyrus latifolius, *is an easy-going, long-flowering perennial climber which will sprawl sideways or scramble up peasticks or a host shrub with equal enthusiasm.*

The five-fingered leaves of Parthenocissus henryana *are velvety green with the veins picked out in white and pink, dying away in autumn in rich shades of crimson and flame. If you have room for only one ornamental vine, this is the one to choose in preference to the more familiar Virginia creeper.*

MAURANDYA and LOPHOSPERMUM

herbaceous climbers H/S 90cm–1.8m/3–6ft
summer Z 9–10

The climbing snapdragons are still often listed under *Asarina*, while some species now considered to belong to *Lophospermum* may also be found under *Maurandya* – which is why they are grouped together here. Their flowers are perhaps more like foxgloves than snapdragons; certainly that is true of *M. barclayana*, which has purple, pink or white flowers over many weeks, amid softly downy, heart-shaped leaves. *L. erubescens* is known as the creeping gloxinia; it has large, rose pink flowers and sticky, grey-green leaves over a very long season. Easily raised from seed or cuttings to flower in their first year, they are ideal fillers in the border, dying back to the ground in winter. If the roots are protected from frost they will grow again from the base the following spring. They appreciate a sheltered, sunny place in fertile, well-drained soil and can be provided with pea-sticks as support, or allowed to scramble through a host shrub.

PARTHENOCISSUS

deciduous self-clinging climbers H/S 7.5m/25ft
summer and autumn Z 4–9

Rivalling the Virginia creeper (*Parthenocissus quinquefolia*) and the coarser Boston ivy (*P. tricuspidata*) [Z 5–8] in the beauty of its crimson autumn tints (see page 71), *Parthenocissus henryana* [Z 7–8] is far more handsome than they in its summer livery, for the leaves of three to five leaflets are dark velvety green with a maroon-bronze flush, picked out in white and rose-pink along the veins. The best colour comes from plants grown in shade. The other species are happy in sun or shade. Like its cousins, it adheres to its support by means of the little adhesive pads at the ends of the leaf tendrils, and like them, it is best pruned in late winter.

Any fertile, well-drained garden soil suits it. It can be increased by late summer cuttings.

PASSIFLORA

evergreen tendril climbers H/S 9m/30ft summer Z 7–10 [unless indicated]

When Spanish priests in South America first encountered the flowers of these striking climbers, they saw in them the symbols of Christ's passion: the tepals representing the apostles, the corona or ring of filaments within the tepals the crown of thorns, the five stamens the five wounds, and the three stigmas the three nails. Thus the genus gained both its popular name – passion flower – and its botanical one. One of the most frost resistant is the blue *Passiflora caerulea*, a vigorous species with divided, dark green leaves and white tepals around a blue, white and purple corona. Its hybrid offspring *P.* × *caeruleoracemosa* [Z 9–10] is no less vigorous; its flowers are constructed in the same intricate way, but the tepals are lilac and the corona purple. The ideal companion is the claret vine, *Vitis vinifera* 'Purpurea', and you could add *Rhodochiton atrosanguineum* for a subfusc blend of colours.

The passion flowers need a sheltered place, in full sun to encourage plenty of flowers (and their orange, egg-shaped fruit, where the summers are long). They thrive in any fertile, well-drained soil; so long as the soil remains unfrozen in winter, they will normally regenerate from the base even if the topgrowth is killed by frost. By the same token, if they outgrow their space, they can be hard-pruned in spring, easily making 4.5m/15ft of new growth in a season. They are increased by cuttings in summer.

The intricate structure that inspired the name 'passion flower' is clearly visible in this fully open bloom of Passiflora caerulea, *one of a group of species with similarly constructed flowers in colours ranging from ivory white through to violet and dusky purple.*

RHODOCHITON ATROSANGUINEUM

herbaceous or annual twining climber H/S 3m/10ft summer Z 9–11

The flowers of this slender climber resemble little, muted magenta umbrellas, from which hang narrow trumpets with flared lips, of so dark a maroon-purple as to be almost black. In the balloon-like, papery seedpods which follow, many tiny winged seeds form, which can be sown to make new plants that will flower in their first year (the plant is, in fact, a herbaceous perennial). The leaves are heart-shaped, and tinted with maroon, especially where touched by the sun; their leaf-stalks twine around any suitable support.

When touched with dew or raindrops, as here, the papery rose-maroon calyces of Rhodochiton atrosanguineum *remind one irresistibly of* les parapluies de Cherbourg, *except that no umbrella ever had so bold a handle of velvety black as these long trumpets.*

Rosa

deciduous scramblers H/S 2.4/9m/8–30ft
spring, summer, autumn Z 5–9 [unless indicated]

The synstylae roses are a group of vigorous species and their nearly-allied hybrid descendants with many small flowers in each wide cluster, often followed by small, orange or red hips. Though everyone thinks of them as climbers or ramblers, these roses have no tendrils, twining stems, or aerial roots to hoist themselves skywards; at best, their long stems hook themselves onto any suitable support by means of more or less curved prickles. For all that, a full-grown synstylae rose is well able to hold itself secure in a host tree, to tumble out in a cascade of ivory or white or pastel-toned blossom, which gives out a sweet, free-floating perfume. Among species, my choice falls not on the famous *Rosa filipes* 'Kiftsgate' [Z 7–10], but upon *R. longicuspis* [Z 9–10], flowering rather later than most, at or after midsummer, endowed with good, glossy foliage, mahogany-red young growths, and huge heads of creamy flowers, as many as 150 in each cluster; and on *R. gentiliana*, which used to be known as 'Polyantha Grandiflora', a name which describes both its many-flowered clusters and the ample size of each individual flower, ivory with a yolk-yellow cluster of stamens at their hearts and a rich, fruity perfume. They are followed by colourful orange-red hips in autumn. There are several close allies, in both white and soft colours. 'Rambling Rector' is a splendid, vigorous and generous cultivar with ivory-white, semi-double flowers, and 'Bobbie James' is only a little more restrained, with polished foliage and white flowers. In lilac-pink, there is the tall 'Paul's Himalayan Musk', which has small, rosette flowers in hanging clusters on slender stems, while the newer 'Treasure Trove' has creamy apricot flowers and coppery-mahogany young growths.

The easy grace of this rambler, 'Adélaïde d'Orléans', with her nodding blooms, is far removed from the stiff, scrolled perfection of modern hybrid roses. The green 'eye' at the heart of each frail-textured flower only adds to their charm, while the dainty buds add a discreet touch of colour.

The Banksian rose, *R. banksiae* [Z 6–9], also has clusters of many small flowers, but there the resemblance ends, for it has thornless green stems and fresh green foliage; and it flowers right at the start of the rose season, in late spring. The flowers may be single or double, white or soft yellow; for fragrance, the singles are superior, though the double white *R. banksiae banksiae* has a sweet violet perfume. The double yellow, *R. banksiae* 'Lutea', has almost none, but is undeniably the prettiest, charming combined with lilac wisteria or with the pure ultramarine blue of a spring-flowering ceanothus. All the Banksian roses are best on a wall unless in climates mild enough for them to be spared frost-damage in winter, when they can be encouraged to grow into a host tree or left to sprawl as a huge, lax bush in the open ground. On a wall, once they have filled their space the Banksian roses need a modicum of annual pruning to keep them in bounds. After flowering, some of the oldest sideshoots – though not main framework stems, unless very old and debilitated and there are strong new basal shoots to replace an old stem – can be cut out and young growths tied in as replacements. In autumn, young growths that have strayed away from the wall should be tied in for extra winter protection.

If the lilac and mauve tints of wisteria are to your taste, you can have more of them as the season advances, from a quartet of 'blue' rambling roses. Of course they are no more true blue than the blue hybrid teas that breeders seek and occasionally promise, but are none the worse for that. The first to open, at midsummer, is 'Veilchenblau', its small, clustered flowers magenta and purple streaked with white, fading to violet and mauve; uniquely in the set, they are scented. Next it is the turn of 'Violette', which has more crimson in its newly-opened flowers and fades towards maroon and lilac-mauve. 'Rose Marie Viaud' quickly follows, at first purple and crimson, fading to lilac and violet-mauve. These two both have almost thornless stems and noticeably pale, fresh-looking foliage. Finally comes 'Bleu Magenta', with the largest flowers of the four, in deep purple fading to violet and grey-mauve (see page 74). All make delightful companions for the dusty miller vine, *Vitis vinifera* 'Incana', with its powdered, greyish foliage. They are pruned in the conventional rambler fashion, with the old, flowered stems cut out each year after flowering and the new shoots growing from the base tied in as replacements. They need to be grown where the air can blow freely through their stems, to minimize the risk of disfiguring mildew.

There are many repeat-flowering climbing roses, and faced with such diversity I offer you most particularly the old glory rose, 'Gloire de Dijon'. Unlike other noisette roses, she will grow on a sunny or lightly shaded wall, giving a long season of fully double, richly scented flowers, in that unique blend of buff and warm yellow and peach which inspired D. H. Lawrence to liken the glory rose to the ripe beauty of his beloved. Of viginal delicacy compared with the ripe maturity of the glory rose, 'New Dawn'(see page 73) is an exquisite creature in shell pink, her looks opening from scrolled buds over a long season.

Almost any rose can be grown from cuttings, taken in summer or early autumn; the resulting plants have the great advantage that they will not sucker, or at least if they do, it will be more of the same that you get, not an interloper. They all enjoy good living, in enriched soil, to produce the abundance of flower we demand of roses.

'Gloire de Dijon' is still unbeatable for its robust constitution and good temper. The perfumed flowers, in tender tints of amber, peach and cream, are voluptuous in their full-petalled amplitude.

Senecio scandens

semi-herbaceous scrambler H/S 4.5m/15ft
autumn Z 9–10

The abundant, small, citron-yellow daisies and fresh green, heart-shaped leaves of *Senecio scandens* bring a spring-like touch to autumn, whether contrasting with ripening scarlet and orange hips and berries or set amid the dark, glossy foliage of a host tree such as a holly or phillyrea. The slender stems may be cut back by frost, but so long as the roots are not frozen the plant will shoot again from the base; as this obliging characteristic suggests, it can be hard-pruned in spring to remove damaged wood or to keep it within bounds. It is easily increased by cuttings, and thrives in any fertile, well-drained soil, in a sunny place.

Solanum crispum *'Glasnevin'*

semi-evergreen scrambler H/S 4.5m/15ft
summer to autumn Z 7–10 [unless indicated]

This fast-growing, semi-shrubby, semi-scrambling potato-relative bears its flowers in clusters over a very long summer to autumn season. They are rich violet enlivened by a central cone of bright yellow stamens. Where not cut back by frost *Solanum crispum* 'Glasnevin' forms a big sprawl of stems that can be allowed to cover a fence or shed, or ramble through a host shrub. This might be *Abutilon vitifolium*, the first of the potato flowers coinciding with the last of the mallow's glacier-mauve saucers. The solanum can also be trained against a wall to display its showy flowers to best advantage. It is hardier than *S. jasminoides* 'Album' [Z 8–10], a true climber with starry white flowers over a long summer-to-autumn season. Whether in the open or on a wall, it is the better for having any weak or damaged shoots pruned away in spring; wall-trained plants will have been tied in in autumn, so the spring pruning is also an occasion for a general tidy-up of stray shoots. It is happy in any fertile, well-drained soil, in full sun, and can be increased by late summer cuttings.

Solanum crispum *'Glasnevin', the climbing potato, is here paired with another vigorous climber, the golden hop* (Humulus lupulus *'Aureus'), its green-gold foliage echoing the golden pointel at the heart of each violet potato flower.*

Sollya heterophylla

evergreen twining climber H/S 1.8m/6ft
summer to autumn Z 9–10

The bluebell creeper from Australia is ideal for small spaces, with its slender, twining stems, exiguous foliage and azure blue bells over a long season. It grows in sun or light shade, in any fertile, well-drained soil, and is easily raised from seed or summer cuttings.

Trachelospermum

evergreen twining/self-clinging climber
H/S 6m/20ft summer Z 7–10 [unless indicated]

The trachelospermums are among the most valuable of all-seasons wall coverings, with half-twining, half self-clinging stems and glossy, evergreen foliage, smaller, denser and neater in *Trachelospermum asiaticum*, which is the more efficient self-sticker and has sweetly perfumed, creamy-white flowers aging to buff yellow. The bolder foliage of *T. jasminoides*, the star jasmine, tends to burnish to coppery, mahogany and crimson in winter, especially in the form known by its collector's number, 'Wilsonii' W 776; in the US the cultivar 'Madison' is the one to choose for winter colour and hardiness The flowers of the star jasmine are larger, the better to display their propellor outline, and at first white, aging to cream; they are no less fragrant. It has a variegated cultivar, imaginatively known as 'Variegatum' [Z 8–10], which is handsome all year, margined and splashed with cream on dark green in summer and turning to crimson and pink in winter, especially if grown in full light. Any fertile, well-drained soil, and a sheltered wall in sun or part shade suits the trachelospermums. They can be increased by layers or summer cuttings. Pruning is a simple matter of cutting out dead and spindly shoots in spring; stray growths, if strong and healthy, are best tied back or tucked in rather than removed, unless the available space is really limited.

TROPAEOLUM

herbaceous climbers H/S 1.2–3m/4–10ft
late winter to spring, summer, autumn Z 7–9

Not all forms of the climbing nasturtium *Tropaeoleum tuberosum* can be relied on to flower from summer onwards; look for one described as early-flowering, or choose the cultivar *T. tuberosum* var. *lineamaculatum* 'Ken Aslet'. The roots are tuberous; indeed, they are part of the staple diet in their native South America, but never caught on here as did the (also South American) potato. The leaves are broadly five-lobed, and the flowers are narrow, open-mouthed, long-spurred confections of soft orange-scarlet with rich yolk-yellow lobes. If you grow the plant horizontally, twining over pea-sticks half-snapped and bent over at right angles, the flowers will hover above the mass of foliage. The tubers increase freely, and those that have piled up near or above the soil surface can be lifted and stored in just-moist peat or other sterile medium, frost-free, for the winter, while those that remain in the ground should survive if well mulched with grit to exclude frost. This species needs a sunny position, in any fertile, free-draining soil. The Scottish flame flower, *T. speciosum*, is a plant for a cool place, in soil that is preferably lime-free. Its dainty, fresh green foliage makes decorative patterns against a dark background, as it might be twining its way through a yew hedge, but its real allure lies in the vivid scarlet nasturtium flowers which open in late summer and autumn (see page 80). These may be followed by bright blue fruits from which new plants can be raised; another, rather tricky method of increase is to chop up the fleshy roots into sections each bearing a growing point, and lay them horizontally in pots of peaty compost.

OPPOSITE *The propellor-shaped white flowers of* Trachelospermum asiaticum *are delectably fragrant, and the polished foliage makes a comely wall-covering all year round.*

RIGHT Tropaeolum tuberosum, *grown horizontally over half-snapped, bent-over pea-sticks, displays its countless long-tubed nasturtiums on slender red stems, so that the flowers seem to dance over the pretty, lobed foliage.*

The cool tones of a classic stone ball and pillar heighten the brilliance of Vitis coignetiae *in its autumn livery of scarlet, flame and claret.*

Tweedia caerulea

perennial twining climber H/S 1.2m/4ft
summer Z 10

Some plants create their own, self-contained colour schemes, as does *Tweedia caerulea* (formerly *Oxypetalum coeruleum*), a delightful, modest creature with softly velvety, grey-furred, heart-shaped leaves and fleshy, sky-blue flowers tinged with opaline pink as they fade. It can be increased by soft summer cuttings or seed, which will produce flowering plants in the first year.

Vitis

deciduous tendril climbers H/S 6–9m/20–30ft
autumn Z 5–9

The true vines are among the best of climbers for autumn colour, and their foliage is handsome all summer. The claret or teinturier vine, *Vitis vinifera* 'Purpurea', indeed, is essentially a foliage plant, the young shoots powdered white, turning to dusty wine-purple, the perfect accompaniment to grey foliage or to mauve, pink or lilac flowers. It often bears bunches of black grapes, which – unlike ordinary black grapes – are coloured even when unripe. Boldest of all in leaf is *V. coignetiae*, its great, rounded leaves as big as dinner plates on thriving plants, turning to scarlet and burnished coppery-crimson in autumn. It is handsome against a grey stone wall, and breathtaking if you can contrive to hang its stems in the branches of a silver birch so as to see the foliage with the sun behind it, lighting it up like a stained glass winter.

The vines all grow in any fertile, well-drained soil, in sun, and can be increased by eye cuttings in winter or layers. If space is limited they can be pruned back to a framework each winter (they bleed copiously if this is done during the growing season); young wood is cut back to one or two buds. In summer some of the excess leafy growth can be nipped back to just above a node at five to six leaves. Anyone who has lived in a wine-producing area will recognize this rhythm of 'la taille' in winter and 'l'effeuillage' (de-leafing) in summer. Vines grown in a tree can be left alone.

Wisteria

deciduous twining climbers H/S 9m/30ft
late spring Z 5–9 [unless indicated]

At their best, wisterias are spectacular. The Chinese *Wisteria sinensis* can fill a 30m/100ft tree if allowed to, but lends itself very well to wall training, to display its tassels of lilac-mauve, purple-blue or white pea-flowers with their characteristic bean-field scent, especially noticeable in the white 'Alba' and blue-purple 'Caroline'. The Japanese *W. floribunda* [Z 4–9], which twines in the opposite direction, clockwise, has a fainter fragrance and longer tassels, especially in lilac-blue 'Multijuga' ('Macrobotrys'), where they can be as long as your arm. A pergola, or a stone balustrade, makes the ideal support, so that the tassels can hang free (see page 69).

Plenty of sun is the recipe for plenty of flowers. Too rich a soil or too little sun, and they run to masses of leafage. Careful pruning can also help to encourage flowering. In the early years, tie in the shoots to the wall or structure they are to decorate, and thin them out to encourage the formation of stouter, stronger growths. Twice a year, prune the side shoots – in summer to about 15cm/6in, and in winter right back to two or three buds. Wisterias can be increased by late summer cuttings. It is better to resist the temptation to grow them from seed: seedlings may take years to reach flowering size, and be worthless when they do.

Wisteria in relaxed mood, its long tassels of bean-scented flowers cascading over the formal stone balustrade and mottled steps in a symphony of cool spring colours.

broadbrush effects

long-lasting shrubs and perennials

In early autumn the border is illumined by a quality of light that high summer can never deliver. Here the plumes of Miscanthus *catch the lowering sun, with* Persicaria amplexicaulis *glowing crimson and backed by the old-rose fuzz of* Eupatorium.

Drifts and billows of colour fill the summer borders of our dreams: a haze of meadow rue, the flat plates of yarrow and warmly aromatic duvets of phlox, yielding, as the days decline lazily towards autumn, to butterfly-clad ice plant and clouds of starry asters, and punctuated by the heraldic fleur-de-lis of irises, steepling red hot pokers, spiky ruffs of sea holly, and blue globes of agapanthus; the sharp tints of spurges add zest. Hostas expand their calm, broad leaves from spring snouts like shellcases, and the bold swords of crocosmias stand guard, while blades of blue or brightly-striped grasses ripple and sway with every breeze. On hot summer afternoons, what could be more agreeable than to sit in the garden, the eye entranced by the play of colour and shape, the ear distracted by the hum of bees and the rustle of grasses; for a moment the world retreats and intimations of the gracious living of years gone by, in the heyday of the classic flower border, assail us with a delicious nostalgia.

Small-flowered daylilies (Hemerocallis) *such as 'Corky' have a grace often lacking from the modern hybrids with larger blooms. Here the warm yellow trumpets are poised amid the ruby-red and metallic purple leaves of annual* Atriplex hortensis *var.* rubra.

Orchestrating all these lovely things is as pleasurable as observing them. From a single association one may build harmonies or contrasts of colour, of form, of texture, until the border nears perfection.

Few gardeners today are content with a traditional border, with a single concentrated season of flower, and little to offer at other times. Today's borders have to look good for as long as possible, even if that means they never approach the impact of a Gertrude Jekyll-style border at peak season. To achieve this means using not only the classic elements of the herbaceous border, but also shrubs, bulbs, annuals, bedding plants, or whatever else seems good to achieve your aesthetic objective. This chapter concentrates on the first two elements – perennials and shrubs. Many of the shrubs from Chapter 1 could also find a place in a mixed border; here I include chiefly those that are best grouped for impact rather than standing alone as specimens.

I find it helpful to think of plants that make a more or less permanent framework and those that provide the broadbrushes of colour or texture. Borders, like the gardens they adorn, are the better for a firm structure to frame sweeps of colour or set off fleeting incidents of flower. Comfortable mounds and domes of santolina and lavender, rue and artemisia, contrast with the spiky rosettes of yuccas and soaring fans of phormiums and with fountains of graceful grasses, or set off *Melianthus major* with its leaves like the plumage of some huge bird. Textures and outlines such as those plants offer, often overlooked in the pursuit of colour, are just as important in creating a satisfying border.

Though some of the classic border flowers have indifferent foliage – such as Michaelmas and Shasta daisies or phlox – many of those I have selected for their ability to provide those great drifts of colour have attractive foliage. Some are primarily chosen for their flowers, and the leaves are a bonus; others are above all foliage plants. Their outlines, colours and textures are wonderfully diverse: the spears of iris and daylily and crocosmia; the arching blades of grasses; the silver filigree of achilleas; the scalloped, dew-catching, softly felted foliage of *Alchemilla mollis* and the broad, pleated leaves of *Veratrum*; the dissected, glossy foliage of monkshood and the figured velvet of *Geranium renardii*. Texture is, of course, both a visual and a tactile concept. To indulge the sense of touch there are leaves felted or silken, high-polished or nubbly, stickily resinous

Form, as much as colour, creates the ambience of the border. The arching blades and cloudy golden inflorescences of grasses contrast with pink mallow, crimson pokers of Persicaria amplexicaulis, *and the solid, tapering maroon heads of* Allium sphaerocephalum.

The common yarrow (Achillea) *of meadows and pastures is transformed, in the Summer Pastels group, into a tapestry of gentle pink, lilac and crimson, apricot and cream tints, the flattish flower-heads held over feathery-fine foliage.*

or pale with a bloom as delicate as that of grape. For the eye there is the impression of wind-ruffled young corn created by some grasses; or the contrast between similar shades of green with different surfaces, shiny or matt, or leaf size – the minute leaves of box or the big blades of hostas.

The varied shapes of border plants are as much part of their allure as colour. The vertical lines of foxgloves or epilobiums in massed ranks contrast with the domes and mounds of phlox, the horizontals of sedum or achillea, or the globes of agapanthus, while in other plants – iris, eryngium, hemerocallis – each individual flower has its characteristic outline that is not lost even in the mass.

The ribbed leaves of hostas form an elegantly sculptured receptacle to catch candy-pink azalea blooms as they fall. From spring to autumn these broad blades are an emollient accompaniment to the va-et-vient of flower-colour in the border.

An ideal front-of-border plant, Dicentra *'Stuart Boothman' is unusual, even in a genus known for its charm, in the grace and poise of its soft ruby-pink lockets, set off by the steely blue-grey tints of the finely dissected foliage.*

Even before their flowers have opened or their foliage expanded to its full growth, many border plants have another, more understated season of appeal. In spring, the new growths that push through the soil clothe the border in shades of fresh green, amid which the pale lemon-green spears of daylilies and the mahogany-crimson new growths of peonies stand out. These leafy clumps are the ideal setting for the spring bulbs which feature in the next chapter, or can simply be allowed to make their own statement (see page 122). Far from being a monochrome, green is astonishingly varied: there are celadon and jade and almond, chartreuse and lime, deep-sea green, and the greens of peridot and emerald and malachite, to say nothing of foliage that is other than green, embracing oxblood red and tender grey-purple, and the metallic tones of silver, pewter and platinum, copper and bronze and steely blue.

At the other end of the growing season, there is something nostalgically endearing about the flowers of autumn. Some of them have all the freshness of spring: Japanese anemones, notably. In others, the mellowness of autumn is the dominant note: late kniphofias in glowing colours, sulky-blue monkshoods, *Aster lateriflorus* 'Horizontalis' with its burnished foliage to set off tiny lilac stars, *Sedum* 'Herbstfreude' as it turns from dusty pink to russet. To accompany them in their embered cadences, the foliage of some border plants dies gracefully: hostas turn to corn-gold, grasses to parchment. In the pale light of autumn, too, silver and grey-leaved plants, pearled with the night's dew and morning's mist, take on a luminosity that is softer in quality than their platinum brilliance in summer, and thereby the more perfectly complements the fiery tints of red hot pokers or of autumn-flaring shrubs.

In winter the border sleeps; but even during the cold months – unless in climates so severe that snow covers everything and plants have to be wrapped in burlap for protection – there can be incidents to draw the eye. Some grasses and sedums retain their outlines unless dashed to the ground by winter's storms, and evergreen perennials, such as bergenias and iris, brave the cold and rough weather. Only the greys and silvers are apt to look disconsolate.

Borders composed of the plants described in this chapter, chosen for attributes that go far beyond the impact of their flowers, may never reach the acme of perfection for a single short season; but nor will they be dull or derelict for months on end. If you opt for the full palette of colours, they may be displayed

The formality of clipped santolina hedges, with lavender (Lavandula × intermedia) *at the corners, frames flowery, leafy incidents – here, a tree peony,* Paeonia suffruticosa, *soon to open its opulent blooms, captures the foreground, and standard* Rhaphiolepis × delacourii *presides over* Scilla peruviana.

à la Jekyll in graduated harmonies or grouped in a series of associations. Working within a restricted palette is often more aesthetically satisfying, especially in a small space, as well as easier to manage, but even then, the choice lies between harmonies and contrasts; or even one colour only. In nature, wide expanses of terrain with only a single dominant flower, are common; stands of foxgloves or rosebay, grassy banks white with ox-eye daisies, verges blue with lupin or cornfields scarlet with poppies. Borders are not the place for such expansive gestures, but the lesson of massing a single colour is one that can be well taken. Miss Jekyll, again, demonstrated how effective can be a border of a single colour or a narrow range of related tones; the opalescense of blue, lilac, mauve and pink, for example, or all the yellows from acid to amber. And she taught us that a touch of a complementary colour may be essential to lift a single-colour planting: soft yellow amid blue, or pure scarlet to add vibrancy to mauves and purples. The best borders are those planned with a painter's eye, with colours associated so that each enhances the others. In some people it is innate: but it is also a skill that can be learned.

Unlike a painting, a border is a living, changing creation. With the rhythm of the seasons and the march of time, it glows with summer colours or withdraws into the secret slumber of winter; its plants grow from youth to maturity and lapse into senescence, inviting the gardener to devise new groupings of flower and leaf for our enduring delectation.

Achillea millefolium *'Cerise Queen' is a fine old cultivar, still unsurpassed for the brightness and clarity of its deep pink flowers, set off by the feathery-soft foliage typical of yarrows.*

Achillea

evergreen perennials H 60cm/2ft S 60cm/2ft
summer Z 3–8

The yarrows have flat heads of many tiny, usually rayless daisy flowers over feathery foliage. In the common yarrow, *Achillea millefolium*, they are typically off-white, varying to shades of pink; named cultivars include 'Cerise Queen' and 'Lilac Beauty'. The lovely hybrid 'Taygetea' has grey-green foliage and primrose-yellow flowers, while 'Moonshine' has pewter-grey foliage and brighter daffodil-yellow flowers, without the tendency to fade towards mustard of the taller *A. filipendulina*. It makes a striking companion to the velvety blood-red gallica rose 'Tuscany Superb', and the slender canary-yellow pokers of *Kniphofia* 'Goldelse'. A range of hybrids has been introduced which adds blush white 'Apfelblüte' ('Appleblossom'), 'Lachsschönheit' ('Salmon Beauty') and soft peachy pastels to the colour range.

They all thrive in full sun, in well-drained but not too dry soils, and can be increased by division. For the grey-leaved, yellow-flowered kinds this is best done in spring.

Aconitum

herbaceous perennials H 60cm–1.8m/2–6ft
S 30–60cm/1–2ft summer, early autumn
Z 3–8 [unless indicated]

Most monkshoods or wolf's banes bear their sultry indigo or slate-blue, helmeted flowers in late summer or early autumn on tall stems over handsome, finely-cut foliage; among the finest are 'Bressingham Spire' [Z 5–8] in violet-blue, midnight-blue 'Spark's Variety' [Z 5–8], blue and white *Aconitum* × *cammarum* 'Bicolor' and paler blue *A. carmichaelii* Wilsonii Group 'Barker's Variety', reaching head-height or more. They thrive in moist soils, in sun or shade, and assort well with other plants enjoying similar conditions, such as bugbanes (*Cimicifuga* species), with the creamy plumes of *Artemisia lactiflora* and the slender crimson pokers of *Persicaria amplexicaulis*. 'Ivorine' (see page 117) is a low-growing monkshood of different stamp, bearing its abundant, ivory-cream flowers in summer ; it derives perhaps from the pale yellow-flowered *Aconitum lycoctonum* subsp. *vulparia* [Z 4–8], but is less floppy in habit. Unlike the blue-flowered species, which have tuberous roots, these are fibrous-rooted; all may be increased by division, and the species by seed, as may 'Barker's Variety', an exception to the general rule that cultivars do not come true from seed.

The curious helmeted flowers of Aconitum carmichaelii *are typical of the genus; no wonder one of the common names is 'monkshood'. Another is 'wolf's bane' – these are highly poisonous plants.*

AGAPANTHUS

evergreen or herbaceous perennials
H 60cm–1.2m/2–4ft S 45–60cm/1½–2ft
late summer Z 8–10 [unless indicated]

The first African lily to be introduced to European gardens was a comparatively short-growing species with broad, evergreen leaves and spherical heads of deep blue or white flowers, *Agapanthus africanus*. Another of this type, rather taller in growth, is *A. praecox* subsp. *orientalis* [Z 9–11], which is often grown in tubs in regions where the winters are too cold for it to survive in the open ground. A little hardier than these two species is *A. campanulatus*, which has flattish heads of pale to dark blue or white flowers; it is also distinguished by its narrower, greyish, deciduous leaves. This extra frost-resistance has been bequeathed to the Headbourne Hybrids; there is also a wide selection of named cultivars, short and tall, in every shade of blue as well as pure white or white from purple-flushed buds. All are good, so the main criterion for selection will be, simply, the colour and size that best suit your planting scheme.

Agapanthus need a fertile soil which is well drained but not too dry, and plenty of sun. They are increased by division – for the cultivars – or seed. The striking seed heads can be left standing until winter's weather finally defeats them.

ALCHEMILLA MOLLIS

herbaceous perennial H 45cm/18in S 45cm/18in
summer Z 3–7

The lady's mantle earns a place in the garden for its appeal in both foliage and flower. The rounded, pleated leaves are softly downy and of a gentle shade of green; after dew or rain, they are beaded with pearls of moisture, with a large drop nestling at the base of the leaf. They form a dense, weed-excluding mound topped, in summer, by the foamy sprays of many tiny, lime-yellow flowers. Its free-seeding ways allow a quick build-up of young plants to make drifts and patches in the border or among shrubs; it has a talent for placing itself with companions you might never have thought of (I recall a group of alchemilla, *Eryngium giganteum* and sword-leaved *Sisyrinchium striatum*, all self-sown in a paving crack in a harmony of differing greens and greys contrasting in outline), and for ➤

The buds of white agapanthus – this is 'Cherry Hall' – are often touched with a warming hint of lilac. This calls for care in choosing their companions; flowers or foliage in the lilac to purple range, or grey and purple foliage, best enhance the subtle colouring of the agapanthus.

broadbrush effects

Lady's mantle, Alchemilla mollis, *is made-to-measure for broadbrush effects, with its appealing foliage and generous lime-yellow froth of flower. In this planting it sets off the spires of yellow foxgloves* (Digitalis grandiflora, *and the smaller-flowered* D. lutea) *and white* Hydrangea arborescens *'Grandiflora', with mauve* Geranium sylvaticum *'Mayflower' beyond.*

landing in the midst of a choice plant from which it must be extracted while still small. After flowering it may look a little tatty; this is the time to cut it down, leaves and all, to the crown, water generously, and watch fresh new leaves unfurl to remain fresh until the frosts of autumn. Any fertile, well-drained soil suits it, in sun or shade. As well as waiting for self-sown seedlings, you can divide the crowns to make more plants.

ANEMONE, JAPANESE ANEMONES

herbaceous perennials H 60cm–1.5m/2–5ft
S 45–60cm/1½–2ft late summer, early autumn
Z 5–8

The season of the Japanese anemones opens with *Anemone hupehensis*, a short-growing species with pink flowers; its cultivars include rich pink 'Hadspen Abundance', while cultivars of the closely related *A. hupehensis* var. *japonica* include deep pink semi-double 'Bressingham Glow'and 'Prinz Heinrich' and lilac-pink 'September Charm'. The tall *A. tomentosa* (*A. vitifolia* of gardens) also bears its soft pink flowers in late summer. The autumn-flowering pink Japanese anemone is *A.* × *hybrida* (*A. japonica*). It is even more beautiful in white: especially the lovely, long-flowering 'Honorine Jobert', in which the simple purity of the flower, lit by the golden stamens at its heart, far surpasses the semi-double white 'Whirlwind'. If you like the effect of the extra petals, there is rich pink 'Margarete' ('Lady Gilmour'). The pinks make fine companions for *Fuchsia magellanica* 'Versicolor', which has narrow, crimson and violet flowers and foliage that is dove-grey in shade and flushed with crimson-pink in the sun, or for the glaucous and plum foliage of *Rosa glauca*. White Japanese anemones are never lovelier than when set against a simple background of dark green, such as a yew hedge.

Happy in sun or shade, the Japanese anemones do best in a well-nourished soil, coping well with sticky clay but apt to run too freely at the root in light soils. They are increased by division, and can be slow to settle down after this disturbance; but the corollary is that they can be left alone for years without the need for replanting.

ANTHEMIS PUNCTATA *SUBSP.* CUPANIANA

evergreen perennial H 30cm/1ft S 75cm/2½ft
late spring Z 5–8

The combination of finely-divided, silvery-white foliage and bold, pure white, yellow-eyed daisies in late spring is unusual and irresistible. After flowering the flowered stems should be cut right back to new growth to keep the desired low, dense spread of silver which is such as asset in the summer border amid bright or pastel shades. Full sun and well-drained soil are a must; soils that lie heavy and wet in winter are not to its taste. It can be increased by soft tip cuttings taken in summer.

ARTEMISIA

evergreen shrubs and perennials H 90cm/3ft
S 1.2m/4ft foliage Z 5–8

Artemisia 'Powis Castle' makes a wide dome of platinum filigree foliage seldom marred by the urge, common in too many grey-leaved plants, to rush into flower to the detriment of their looks. It is a remarkably hardy shrub, though unhappy in cold, wet winters; a free-draining soil is recommended, and it will even cope with dry, rooty soil, though it must be grown in full light. It can be increased by summer cuttings. To keep it compact, cut it back in spring.

Of different style, though no less silvery, is *A. ludoviciana*, a free-ranging perennial with willow-like leaves, more or less dissected in certain forms. As other silvers, they are the perfect emollient for strong colours, or give full value to pastel tints, and can be increased by division.

The brilliantly white daisies of Anthemis punctata *subsp.* cupaniana *are set off by the chartreuse of a spring-flowering spurge, and its finely divided grey foliage is echoed by the fern.*

The crystalline petals of white Japanese anemones, such as the fine old Anemone × hybrida *'Honorine Jobert', bring the freshness and purity of spring to the mellowness of autumn.*

Simplicity and generosity of planting – broadbrush effects at their best. The clean lines of clipped topiary yews are set off by the stiffly branching stems and countless tiny pink flowers of Aster lateriflorus *'Horizontalis', glowing in the low rays of autumn sun.*

The arching sword leaves of Astelia chathamica *'Silver Spear' are touched to platinum by their coating of fine white hairs. Here they are set off by the bronzed blades of a phormium.*

Astelia chathamica

evergreen perennial H 90cm/3ft S 1.5m/5ft
foliage Z 8–10

Although the silvery-silky sheen on its arching, broadsword leaves might suggest that it needs sun and dry soil, this New Zealand lily-relative prefers a rich soil that does not dry out, and is happier in dappled shade than in full sun. The flowers are unexciting brownish or greenish spikes, followed by orange berries, from which new plants can be raised. Choose, however, if you can, *Astelia chathamica* 'Silver Spear', selected for its notably fine, silver-grey, white-backed leaves in bold rosettes. This must be increased by division.

Aster

herbaceous perennials H 45–90cm/1½–3ft
S 30–60cm/1–2ft summer to autumn
Z 4–8 [unless indicated]

The mildew-beset Michaelmas daisies (cultivars of *Aster novi-belgii*) are not for me, however appealing the great plumes of starry, soft lilac-blue daisies of the wild type may be in autumn amid the bonfire tints of dying leaves. But the genus has much else to offer, among which I single out just two. From summer through to autumn the wide, lavender-blue daisies of *A.* × *frikartii* 'Mönch' [Z 5–8], borne on branching stems, grace the border. The autumn-flowering *A. lateriflorus* 'Horizontalis' is of upright habit – the cultivar name refers to the densely horizontal branching habit, the slender twigs set with tiny leaves turning to coppery bronze in autumn, in contrast to the massed, little pale mauve daisies with deep rose-madder eyes.

These asters thrive in well-drained, fertile soils, in sun or light shade, and are increased by division.

Astrantia

herbaceous perennials H 60cm/2ft S 30cm/1ft
summer Z 5–7

I have never had much affection for the common masterwort, *Astrantia major*, though many rave about its alabaster-white, pin-cushiony flowers with their jade collars (see page 132). However, the garnet-red *A. carniolica* var. *rubra*, a smaller plant, does appeal. It needs companions of equal charm and discretion: *Dicentra* 'Stuart Boothman', blue-leaved hostas. Deep ruby *A. major* 'Hadspen Blood' is another astrantia that well deserves garden space. The astrantias thrive in well-drained, fertile soil, in shade or sun, and are increased by division, or seed (for the species).

BERGENIA

evergreen perennials H 30cm/1ft S 75cm/2½ft
foliage/spring Z 4–8 [unless indicated]

Big-leaved bergenias such as *Bergenia cordifolia*, with (in the grand old cultivar 'Purpurea') its shocking-pink flowers on rhubarb-red stems, make the better weed-excluders, but of more modest dimensions is *B. purpurascens* [Z 5–8]. For a bergenia it has narrow leaves, spoon-shaped and leathery, turning to rich shades of mahogany, liver and oxblood red in winter. 'Sunningdale' has the same intense winter colouring. Though bergenias will grow willingly enough in shade, for winter colour they must be grown in full light. They assort well with sword-leaved plants, set off any plant with airy sprays of flower, and look especially appropriate against stone paving or topping a low, retaining stone wall. A combination I particularly like for winter is one of these coloured bergenias with the ivory-striped *Iris foetidissima* 'Variegata', and the old-gold whipcord stems of *Hebe* 'James Stirling'. Any fertile, well-drained soil suits them. They are increased by division of the thick roots.

CAMPANULA

evergreen and herbaceous perennials
H 60–90cm/2–3ft S 30cm/1ft summer Z 4–8

There is no more appealing bellflower than the tiny alpine harebell; but since we are making borders here, not alpine meadows, I offer you *Campanula persicifolia*, the peach-leaved bellflower, which needs a bit of management, for it tends to run at the root too slowly to find the fresh nutrients it needs; so you may need to lift it regularly, dividing the evergreen rosettes of narrow leaves, and replant it in fresh soil. It comes in conventional campanula colours, pale to deep lavender-blue or white, its wide-open saucers barely nodding on wiry stems. 'Telham Beauty' is a fine, tall blue, good with pink or soft yellow roses, though it is the pure white single, *C. persicifolia alba*, that has my vote, beautiful in a green and white planting where it will accompany the lime-yellow froth of *Alchemilla mollis* amid white-variegated hostas, following on from white foxgloves and white columbines and sweet Cicely. A number of named cultivars and forms are on offer in both colours: not just singles, ➤

The leathery paddles of bergenias and the lacy elegance of ferns make enduring foliage contrasts that can be set off by more fleeting incidents – here, the magenta spikes of Dactylorhiza foliosa (Orchis maderensis).

broadbrush effects

Whether in white, glacier blue or the deepest shades of lilac-tinted blue, the peach-leaved bellflower, Campanula persicifolia, *is one of early summer's delights. Here it is accompanied by white foxgloves,* Digitalis purpurea *f.* albiflora.

but hose-in-hose and cup-and-saucer, loose raggedy doubles and formal rosetted doubles, often simply described by colour and shape. Named doubles include white 'Boule de Neige', as well as several that collectors exchange among themselves.

These campanulas are equally happy in sun or part-shade, in any well-drained, fertile soil.

'Kew Blue' is a richly coloured selection of Caryopteris × clandonensis, *its violet-blue flowers seeming the more intense against the neat grey foliage.*

Caryopteris × clandonensis

deciduous shrub H 75cm/2½ft S 75cm/2½ft
late summer Z 5–9

Certain shrubs – some of them chosen for thier flowers, some for foliage, a few for both – lend themselves exceptionally well to border plantings not because they provide a firm structure but precisely because they do not: because they are soft-wooded and rather flimsy, but can be cut hard back in spring to grow into mounds of colour by high to late summer. Just so *Caryopteris × clandonensis*, which if pruned to stumps after the risk of hard frosts is over will rapidly reclothe itself with grey, turpentiney-aromatic foliage almost completely hidden, later in the season, by the fuzzy, lavender-blue flowers that, in turn, yield to verdigris-green seed heads. Named cultivars with deeper blue flowers are, in the main, even less decidedly woody than the original hybrid; among the finest are 'Heavenly Blue' and 'Kew Blue'. With the same rich blue flowers over soft lime-yellow foliage, 'Worcester Gold' has become rapidly popular. All are easily increased by cuttings, and thrive in full sun, in well-drained soil.

Convolvulus

herbaceous perennial and shrub H 30–90cm/1–3ft
S 30–90cm/1–3ft summer Z 8–9

Convolvulus sabatius (*C. mauritanicus*) has satiny flowers of soft lilac-blue on trailing stems with small oval green leaves; there is also a form of more intense colouring. So far they have not been given separate names. The paler form is enchanting with silver-leaved, chalky pink-flowered *Geranium traversii* 'Elegans'. It can be helped through cold winters if planted where its roots can retire beneath a sheltering rock.

The northern Mediterranean *C. cneorum* is one of the most silvery shrubs I know, its pointed leaves seeming to be coated with sheeny platinum; in flower it is paler still, as scrolled shell-pink buds open to ivory, fluted funnels touched with butter-yellow at their hearts.

Both species enjoy full sun and well-drained soil, and are increased by soft summer cuttings.

Coreopsis verticillata

herbaceous perennial H 60cm/2ft S 45cm/1½ft
summer to autumn Z 3–9

Among the bright flowers that decorate the rather sombre corridors of my family house is always, in summer, a vase of coreopsis, usually *Coreopsis auriculata*, its yellow daisies set off by the maroon blotch at their hearts. They are grown from seed each year, but *C. verticillata* is a true perennial, and one with more quality than most yellow daisies. Its tiny, thread-like leaves of fresh green, on wiry stems that need no staking, are the setting for lazy daisies of vivid, glistening yellow. 'Grandiflora' has large flowers of warm tone, but, fine though it is, it is outclassed by the lovely 'Moonbeam', in which the soft primrose to citron daisies, with the same luminous sheen, fade gracefully to cream. Give them a sunny place in well-drained, fertile soil, and increase them by division.

The fluted saucers of Convolvulus sabatius *open from tightly scrolled buds over a long summer season. Both colour-forms, the pale and the richer lilac-blue, are have the same satin finish.*

Crocosmia

cormous perennials h 60cm–1.2m/2–4ft
s 23–30cm/9in–1ft late summer, early autumn
z 5–9

From time to time purists complain that there are too many cultivars to choose from these days; but there were far more, of certain genera at least, a hundred years ago than now. Certainly that was true of crocosmias, of which Lemoine, the great French nurserymen, raised and named dozens – to say nothing of the English breeders who took them up. Small-flowered or large, brightly-coloured or soft-toned, all the cultivars that survive are desirable, a far cry from the old montbretia (*Crocosmia* × *crocosmiiflora*) with its small, vermilion and orange flowers and fresh green blades. True, this is not to be scorned if you have a difficult corner to clothe – it will grow almost anywhere and keeps weeds at bay, though apt to turn into one itself. Let me just tempt you, however, with a few cultivars. First, those with smallish flowers, which are almost as tough and free-growing as the old montbretia: the clear yellow cultivar invariably, though it seems wrongly, known as 'Golden Fleece' ('Citronella'), and the similar 'Canary Bird' and 'Norwich Canary'; and, most irresistible of all, 'Solfaterre', with milk-chocolate to bronze sword leaves and flowers the ➤

Flowers of pure vermilion are not that common, among hardy perennials at least; in Crocosmia *'Lucifer' the pure colouring is allied to striking form and good, rich green sword leaves, making it one of summer's boldest highlights.*

colour of freshly squeezed tangerine juice. The most enduring of large-flowered crocosmias is 'Emily McKenzie', its wide, nodding flowers in burnt orange and cinnabar red.

The vermilion flowers of *Crocosmia masoniorum* are differently disposed on arching stems, curving upwards rather than nodding downwards; and the foliage is more ample, though not so broad as the pleated blades of *C. paniculata*. 'Lucifer' is a splendid hybrid between the two, bold and handsome in leaf, with brilliant scarlet flowers on tall stems; wonderful with big red hot pokers (scarlet and yellow 'Royal Standard', perhaps), *Fuchsia* 'Genii' and *Hypericum* 'Hidcote', or cooled with lemon daylilies and white phlox. Crocosmias thrive in any good, well-drained soil, in sun or light shade; most increase rapidly, to form dense clumps which can be lifted and divided for increase.

Dianthus

evergreen perennials H 23cm/9in S 23cm/9in
summer Z 4–8

Pinks and clove carnations have been grown in gardens for centuries – Chaucer wrote about the 'clove gilofre', and the clove-like fragrance is recognized in the Arabic name, qaranful – meaning both carnation and the spice – as well as in Chaucer's English. It is mildly heretical, therefore, not to love dianthus unreservedly; yet despite their manifold qualities, I have never felt the urge to collect them as I have many other plants. But I do have great affection for 'Mrs Sinkins', a double white (perhaps because of her reputedly humble origins in a workhouse garden). She has the narrow, glaucous foliage that is one of the pinks' good qualities, making them ideal front-of-the-border plants, with the glaucous-purple *Sedum* 'Vera Jameson' perhaps. They need well-drained soil, sun, and regular propagation by summer cuttings pulled off with a heel and stuck in sandy soil; without this attention they soon become tatty and dwindle away.

Diascia

herbaceous or subshrubby perennials
H 30–45cm/1–1½ft S 45–60cm/1½–2ft
summer to autumn Z 7–9 [unless indicated]

When I first began to garden, the only diascias to be had were *Diascia barberae* and its hybrid 'Ruby Field', which are hardly big enough except for the most midget of borders. Then, suddenly, *D. rigescens* [Z 8–9] was everywhere, and no wonder, for cuttings root in days, and grow fast into a sprawling heap of stems with long, densely-packed spires of warm pink, nemesia-like flowers that go on for weeks if you are scrupulous about dead-heading. It was not long before other species arrived, many of them more graceful in growth and with fewer, larger flowers airily disposed on less flopsome stems. *D. fetcaniensis* [Z 8–9] is of much the same rich colouring as *D. rigescens*; *D. vigilis* is the prettiest of all, with more exiguous foliage, and flowers of tender, satiny shell pink enhanced by a dab of purple at the centre. Lately a gaggle of peach, apricot and dawn-pink cultivars have been introduced, every one of them desirable. All do best in full sun, in fertile, well-drained but not dry soils.

Dicentra

herbaceous perennials H 30–60cm/1–2ft
S 45–60cm/1½–2ft late spring
Z 3–8 [unless indicated]

The bleeding heart – or, more poetically, lyre flower – is one of the loveliest flowers of spring, its rose-pink flowers, lyre-shaped in bud and tipped with white when open, dangling from slender, arching stems over pretty, divided foliage. Its pure white form is prosaically known as *Dicentra spectabilis* 'Alba'; and indeed, so exquisite a flower needs no fancy name to sell it. The lyre flower thrives in any fertile soil, in part shade or sun, and is increased by division or seed. *D. macrantha* [Z 5–8] is very distinct in its more sharply dissected leaves, and above all in its large, honey-yellow lockets appearing in spring; it dislikes wind and burns in the sun, but in cool, sheltered shade is not difficult.

The smaller species, *D. eximia*, *D. formosa* and their garden derivatives, challenge the hapless garden writer to fit them into the arbitrariness of chapters, for they are equally at home, and equally appealing, in the cooler, shaded parts of the border, or spreading their carpets of filigree foliage beneath shrubs or trees. Typically, *D. formosa* has soft plum-pink lockets (see page 197), *D. formosa alba* is a pretty white with very pale green foliage, and 'Stuart Boothman' is a gem with rich pink flowers and steel-blue foliage (see page 94). There are several cultivars of mixed blood: rosy mauve 'Bountiful', deep plum 'Bacchanal', garnet-crimson 'Adrian Bloom', ruby 'Luxuriant', grey-leaved, blush-white 'Langtrees', pure white 'Snowflakes'. All spread rapidly at the root in loose, leafy soil, and 'Bountiful' seeds itself around with abandon too; they can be increased by division, almost any scrap of the fleshy roots willing to make a new plant.

The white lyre flowers of Dicentra spectabilis 'Alba', *hanging beneath arching stems through the spring, are of the same heart-shaped outline as the typical deep pink form, for which another familiar name is bleeding heart; or, in French,* coeur de Marie.

Digitalis grandiflora

evergreen perennial H 60cm/2ft S 30cm/1ft
summer Z 3–8

Though a good perennial, *Digitalis grandiflora* (*D. ambigua*) (see page 98) seeds itself as freely as the biennial purple foxglove, which means you can quickly create a drift in your border, concentrated at the front where you can admire its nodding bells of soft buff-yellow, freckled with tan and lightly whiskered within, borne over narrow leaves. It is happy in sun or shade (ideal, therefore, for straying back among larger border shrubs) in any fertile, well-drained soil, and can be divided if you need more and have absent-mindedly hoed away all its seedlings. In any case, the seedlings are apt to need thinning so those you leave have space to develop.

The spiky-soft blue ruffs of the sea holly Eryngium alpinum *are surrounded by pink* Salvia sclarea *var.* turkestanica *(left), pale lilac* Campanula lactiflora, *the shell pink spires of* Linaria purpurea *'Canon Went', blue* Borago officinalis, *and the brilliant magenta dusty miller* (Lychnis coronaria) *and* Geranium psilostemon *(right). The glaucous-purple foliage to the left belongs to* Rosa glauca.

Elymus

deciduous grasses H 45cm–1.2m/1½–4ft S 30cm/1ft foliage Z 4–9

First, a warning: the lyme grass, often labelled *Elymus glaucus* or *E. arenarius* (properly *Leymus arenarius*), is beautiful with its arching, grey-blue blades and tall wheat-spikes of the same colour in summer, but if you admit it to your garden you will need forever to conduct a containment campaign against its aggressively territorial ambitions. There is no such problem, happily, with *E. hispidus*, except that it too may be labelled *E. glaucus* (or *Agropyron glaucus*); it is equally blue-bladed. The best advice I can give is to see what you are getting, and get it from a nurseryman you can trust not to sell you the runner for the stay-at-home. All these grasses are at their best in full sun, in well-drained soils, and can be increased by division or seed.

Epilobium

herbaceous perennials H 75cm/2½ft S 60cm/2ft summer Z 2–7

The white form of the rose bay willow herb, *Epilobium angustifolium album*, is a lovely thing and much less invasive than the rosy pink type, but the species I love best is *E. dodonaei*. One of those precious plants with its own self-contained colour scheme, it has narrow, grey leaves (hence the other name it sometimes bears, *E. rosmarinifolium*) and long steeples of lilac-pink flowers held in madder calyces. Give it a sunny place in well-drained soil, and increase it by division or seed.

Eryngium

herbaceous perennials H 75cm/2½ft S 60cm/2ft summer Z 5–8

Striking though the evergreen South American eryngiums are, they are accent plants above all, unsuited to broadbrush effect. I propose, therefore, to confine myself here to the European sea hollies. They have in common heads of thistle-like flowers, mostly in shades of steel, lapis or sea blue, long-lasting both on the plant and as 'drieds' in vases. One of the most distinct is *Eryngium alpinum*, which – unlike other species – is not sharply prickly but wears, instead, a wide, softly bristly ruff of rich blue around its blue thimbles. In *E.* × *tripartitum* the individual flowers are much smaller – thimbles for a child's little finger, each with a collar of little blue spikes – and borne several to a branching head. Give them full sun and a well-drained soil; they thrive even in sandy or gravelly soils. They can be increased by division or by root cuttings, and *E. alpinum* can also be seed-raised.

EUPHORBIA

herbaceous perennials H 45–90cm/1½–3ft
s 45–60cm/1½–2ft spring, summer
z 4–9 [unless indicated]

Almost without exception, the hardy spurges bring sharp tones of lime or chartreuse to the border; but this near-uniformity of colour must not be taken to imply monotony. One of the first to flower in spring is *Euphorbia polychroma*, a low, wide mound with flat heads of bright acid yellow, lasting several weeks. It is equally happy in sun or light shade, but *E. seguierana* subsp. *niciciana* [z 5–8] is a sun-lover with glaucous foliage and chartreuse-yellow flowerheads, on a plant of less substance, with needle leaves and thin stems. The late summer-flowering *E. schillingii* [z 5–8], taller than the others I commend to you, has ample, lime-green bracts lasting for weeks over dark green leaves with white midribs. It is happy in sun or shade. All these spurges are at their best in fertile, well-drained soil, and can be increased by seed.

FESTUCA AMETHYSTINA

deciduous grass H 15cm/6in s 23cm/9in foliage
z 4–8

Festuca amethystina has hair-fine leaves of glaucous tone in which there is a hint of lilac. This fescue is a pretty companion for purple foliage, drifting among the boldly-lobed, metallic purple *Heuchera* 'Palace Purple' or themselves embroidered about with *Ajuga reptans* 'Atropurpurea' perhaps. It needs spring grooming to comb out the faded remnants of last year's blades, and is best divided and reset at fairly regular intervals, in spring. It has a tufted habit, with no tendency to run. Give it sun and a well-drained soil for best results.

FUCHSIA

shrubs H 90cm/3ft s 90cm/3ft
summer to autumn z 7–9

Whether or not your winters are mild enough to allow fuchsias to form a permanent woody framework, they adapt very well to a pseudo-herbaceous existence, growing away from below ground in late spring after last year's woody stems have been cut right down. On the new growths that form they bear a long succession of their dainty flowers – for in the border those with small and slender flowers seem more appropriate than the doubles, with their flouncing petticoats weighing down the stems. Thus my choice is for singles such as lilac and shell-pink 'Chillerton Beauty'. In 'Genii' typical fuchsia flowers of red and violet are allied to sharp lime-yellow foliage on red stems, an agreeably clashing companion with yellow or orange red hot pokers. The foliage is the point, too, of *Fuchsia magellanica* 'Versicolor', in dove-grey flushed with pink, and of the paler, cream-edged *F. m.* var. *gracilis* 'Variegata' (with red and purple flowers) or *F. m.* var. *molinae* 'Sharpitor' (with palest pink flowers). Fuchsias are at their best in a well-nourished soil, and are perfectly happy in shade. Where winters are too cold for them to survive even in herbaceous mode, they can be lifted, their stems cut half back, and buried in a deep trench; but this is obviously more trouble than leaving them undisturbed, with a thick mulch around the stems in case of unusually sharp frost. They root from cuttings with the greatest of ease at any time of the year.

From the vivid lemon-green of the bracts around the tiny orange flowers to the velvety green of the foliage, Euphorbia schillingii *is a reminder that green is a colour.*

geranium

butterfly blooms

DETAILS FROM TOP:
Geranium cinereum *'Lawrence Flatman' is ideal for the front of a small border, flowering for weeks on end.*

Accompanying a ceanothus in late spring flower, Geranium macrorrhizum *'Album' makes an aromatic carpet all year.*

In autumn the leaves of Geranium macrorrhizum *turn to russet and crimson.*

The subtly-coloured flowers of the mourning widow, Geranium phaeum, *are here partnered by the pale pink pokers of* Persicaria bistorta *'Superba'.*

MAIN PICTURE:
The sombre, nodding flowers of the mourning widow are complemented by its pretty foliage.

GERANIUM

herbaceous perennials H 15cm–1.2m/6in–4ft
S 23cm–1.2m/9in–4ft
early summer to early autumn Z 4–8 [unless indicated]

The cranesbills are a splendid race of (mainly) frost-hardy, undemanding and, withal, beautiful perennials to grace our borders. 'Grace' is the proper word, for little has been done to the cranesbills by breeders anxious for bigger, brighter flowers, so even cultivars, in the main, retain the elegance of the wild species. In early summer *Geranium himalayense* decorates the front of the border, its violet-blue, purple-veined flowers large for the size of plant, floating over finely cut leaves. It spreads by scuttling roots, but not so as to be a nuisance. It is at its best in the selection 'Gravetye', which has a tad more red-purple at the centre of the flower. 'Plenum' ('Birch Double') is quite sweet once you accept that its flowers are pinkish-mauve, not blue, and must be kept away from the clear yellow tints that so flatter 'Gravetye'. 'Johnson's Blue' is a somewhat taller hybrid of *G. himalayense* with *G. pratense*, full of large, porcelain-blue flowers in summer over deeply-cut leaves; it is an ideal companion for soft lemon-yellow shrub roses. Another species of modest size is *G. renardii* [z 6–8], like 'Johnson's Blue' a clumper rather than a runner, and a plant you must caress, for its circular, lobed leaves of gentle grey-green have the texture of figured velvet, to which its pearly white, faintly purple-veined flowers are the perfect complement. Try it in a cool blend of colours with *Rosa glauca* and *Salvia officinalis* Purpurascens Group.

The wood cranesbill, Geranium sylvaticum *'Mayflower' flowers earlier than the meadow cranesbill,* (G. pratense), *and here lights up a late spring border, with the sky-blue spires of* Veronica gentianoides *and the white lace of a viburnum.*

Many geraniums make excellent ground-cover for the front of the border and drifting back among taller plants. The pink-flowered, free-spreading *G. endressi*, which has a number of different manifestations from salmon- to chalky pinks, will seed itself to make a decorative carpet of sharply-lobed leaves. *G. macrorrhizum* [z 3–8] is semi-evergreen and has strongly aromatic, softly clammy foliage. The flowers open early in the geranium season, typically a muted crimson-purple, but there exist colour-variants such as the intense magenta 'Bevan's Variety' [z 3–8], soft rose 'Ingwersen's Variety' [z 3–8], ➤

and 'Album' [z 3–8], in which the white flowers are held in pink calyces. Its leaves turn to crimson and orange in autumn. It grows in almost any soil, in sun or shade, and makes a dense, weed-suppressing carpet. All its forms assort well with other soft-toned flowers of late spring: *Dicentra formosa,* which comes in the same colour range (see page 197), Spanish bluebells in soft blue, white or mauve-pink, lily-of-the-valley, forget-me-not flowered *Brunnera macrophylla* (another good weed-beater with its big, bold leaves), and the like.

There is a hybrid, *G.* × *cantabrigiense*, smaller in size and in leaf, between *G. macrorrhizum* and *G. dalmaticum*; it also comes in mauve-pink or white ('Biokovo'). For small spaces *G. dalmaticum* itself is a pet, with shiny, rounded leaves and lilac-pink flowers, as happy in sun as in shade, or on the flat as growing vertically in a wall with tiny ferns. The bloody cranesbill, *G. sanguineum*, makes a wide mat of deeply cut, dark green leaves, with crimson-magenta, white or pink flowers; in the very prostrate var. *striatum* (var. *lancastriense*) the pale, clear pink flowers are veined with crimson; in 'Shepherd's Warning' they are deep rose-pink.

As summer advances, touches of fierce red-purple add pep to groups of subtle colouring, and for this three are geraniums small or large – *G. cinereum* for the front of the border, *G. psilostemon* (see page 132) further back. The first is a neat hummock of a plant with small, grey-green leaves and flowers that vary from white to the assertive magenta of *G. cinereum* var. *subcaulescens*, enhanced by blood-red veins leading to a near-black central blotch and black stamens. Its selections 'Giuseppe' and 'Splendens' are especially vivid in colour. *G. cinereum* 'Lawrence Flatman' is more muted, in mauve with murrey veining and a dark triangle at the apex of each petal; 'Ballerina' lacks the dark spot and is perhaps the more appealing as a result. All these are front-of-border plants. The bold *G. psilostemon* is a whopper, with large, deeply divided leaves, and big, brilliant magenta flowers with black veins that coalesce into a black eye. It is fit to assort with the big grey-mauve moss rose 'William Lobb', amid silvery foliage perhaps; or will hold its own against the strongest orange, vermilion and ochre tones in mixtures of ottoman richness.

The meadow cranesbill, *G. pratense*, a plant of European roadside verges and meadows, is a worthy garden occupant as well. In its typical violet-blue wildling manifestation it is often found with the creamy froth of meadowsweet and the magenta-pink spires of rose bay willow herb; it is a fallacy to suggest that colours never clash in nature, but in this case at least the old lady displays immaculate taste which could be emulated in the border, substituting the more refined *Epilobium dodonaei* for the rampant rosebay. The wood cranesbill, *G. sylvaticum*, is similar, though perhaps a little more muscular; 'Mayflower' is a lilac-flowered cultivar of especial merit. Among the cultivars of the meadow cranesbill are the opalescent 'Mrs Kendall Clarke', and white and blue streaked 'Striatum'. They have a slight tendency to flop and you may therefore wish to stake them. Its double forms in white, blue or purple their rosettes or pompons heavier with petals than the ethereal singles, are decidedly the better for support.

Flopping is exactly what is required of *G. lambertii,* a reclining plant with large, cupped, modestly nodding white flowers, exquisitely veined with crimson-pink seeping into a crimson stain at the base of the petals, between which the bright green sepals can be glimpsed; if you can contrive to plant it on a bank or at the top of a retaining wall, this can be achieved without lying on your stomach. It does not get under way until well into summer, but goes on into autumn. Another that flowers late and long is *G. wallichianum* 'Buxton's Variety', which bears its Spode-blue, white-eyed flowers on trailing stems. A smaller plant than *G. lambertii,* it will weave through neighbouring plants, its nemophila-like flowers popping up unexpectedly amid alien foliage; it is especially pretty with grey foliage. A billow of *Senecio viravira,* say, interwoven with the little geranium, would be the perfect ground-planting for *Clematis* 'Perle d'Azur', its flowers exactly matching the tint of 'Buxton's Variety'.

Its sombre slaty-maroon, wistfully nodding flowers earn *G. phaeum* [z 5–7] the nickname of mourning widow. In the wooded park surrounding the royal palace in The Hague, Netherlands, it grows massed with the clear yellow greater celandine in the green-washed light that filters through the trees. Extra-dark forms have been selected and given the cultivar name 'Mourning Widow'; there is also an alabaster-white form, 'Album', the warm mauve 'Lily Lovell', and a subtle slate-blue, *G. phaeum* var. *lividum*. All will grow even in deep shade, in any reasonable soil; the type can be increased by seed, and cultivars by division.

Almost any geranium, except the assertive violet-purple *G.* × *magnificum*, which fires all its barrels at once in early summer, is apt to flower for weeks or even months on end if regularly divided and replanted in soil enriched with good manure or compost; division is also the way to increase them, and if you grow the meadow cranesbill, you may find both the type and 'Striatum' will sow themselves freely, as will the mourning widow. *G. sanguineum* can also be increased by cuttings.

OPPOSITE FROM TOP:
The restrained colouring of Geranium renardii *calls for soft accompanying tints; here it grows with* Rosa *'Cantabrigiensis'.*

The double purple Geranium pratense *'Plenum Violaceum' is a grand old border plant.*

The meadow cranesbill itself, Geranium pratense, *is equally suited to the border or to growing in grass, as it does in the wild.*

Geranium phaeum *'Lily Lovell', is a selection of the mourning widow that wears the mauve of half-mourning.*

RIGHT:
The furred buds of Geranium himalayense *presage large, butterfly-veined flowers.*

Helictotrichon sempervirens is above all a foliage plant, with its wire-fine, blue-grey blades; but the pale, oat-like inflorescences make quite an impact in their season.

The broad, lobed, glaucous leaves of Macleaya are the perfect foil for the flowers of Hemerocallis 'Pink Damask', one of the first, and still the best, of the warm pink daylilies.

Hakonechloa macra

deciduous grass H 30cm/1ft S 45cm/1½ft foliage Z 4–9

Hakonechloa macra is a Japanese grass, valued in gardens in its two variegated cultivars, 'Alboaurea' in green and yellow overlaid with bronze, and the brighter yellow-striped 'Aureola'. Both form dense clumps of arching blades that, even in still air, evoke the movement of a wind-ruffled field of barley. They prefer a leafy soil and light shade; but too much shade mutes their bright tints. They are increased by division.

Helictotrichon sempervirens

deciduous grass H 1.2m/4ft S 30cm/1ft foliage Z 4–9

If you want an intensely blue-glaucous grass that will stay in its allotted place, opt for *Helictotrichon sempervirens*. It forms neat, dense clumps of blue stiletto blades topped, in summer, by narrow flower spikes of the same pale blue-grey, beautiful with smoky-purple foliage or matching in colour, but contrasting in texture, with the blue-grey Arizona cypress. Give it full sun and a well-drained soil, and increase it by division or seed.

Hemerocallis

herbaceous perennials H 90cm–1.2m/3–4ft S 60–90cm/2–3ft late spring, summer Z 3–9

I grew up with the old tawny daylily, *Hemerocallis fulva*, which grew and flowered lustily in sticky clay at the base of a shady wall, handsome from the moment its pale green blades speared through the soil in spring until the fading of the last of its light terracotta flowers in high summer. Obliging it may be, but the genus has far finer things offer, starting, in late spring, with the small-flowered *H. dumortieri* and *H. middendorfii*, warm, deep yellow in colour, opening from brown buds, whence 'Golden Chimes', in amber yellow with mahogany reverse, or the sharper lemon 'Corky', may have inherited their colouring, their branching heads of dainty flowers, and their delicious fragrance (see page 92). Quick to follow these early species is the lemon lily, *H. lilioasphodelus* (*H. flava*), in which the larger flowers are a uniform shade of pure, soft yellow, and endowed with an even more wonderful perfume. Daylilies are a cult plant with hundreds of cultivars, old and new, from which I will mention just one, conscious that I am excluding, along with the modern wide, frilled confections in which all purity of line has been sacrificed to novelty, others that are almost as beautiful as the lemon lily. That one is 'Pink Damask', its elegant flowers of an alluring shade of peach with intimations of terracotta.

Most daylilies, other than some developed for mild southern US climates, are adaptable and easy, growing in any fertile soil in sun or part shade. They can be increased by division of the more or less swollen, more or less running roots.

A border need not be rich in flowers to be beautiful, as this sweep of diverse late-spring foliage shows. Its components include silvery Stachys byzantina *'Big Ears',* Bergenia crassifolia *and clipped box in the foreground, iris leaves and the pale spikes of* Veronica gentianoides *'Pallida', violas, and in the distance, the sugar-pink pokers of* Persicaria bistorta *'Superba'.*

hosta

leafy calm

DETAILS FROM TOP:
Little Hosta undulata *var.* undulata, *long grown in gardens, retains its popularity on account of its intriguingly twisted, white-splashed leaves.*

Of the many blue-leaved hostas introduced during the last quarter century, 'Halcyon' remains one of the finest, with its ribbed leaves of substance.

Hosta crispula *is another old favourite, with assertive, white-margined leaves, ideal for cool colour schemes in shady places.*

'Gold Standard' displays its broad chartreuse-yellow leaves in a clump of ample proportions.

MAIN PICTURE:
Of all the recently-introduced yellow-leaved hostas, 'Piedmont Gold' has proved one of the finest among large-leaved culitivars.

HOSTA

herbaceous perennials H 30cm–1.5m/1–5ft S 30–90cm/1–3ft
summer/autumn Z 3–9 [unless indicated]

Few perennials so nobly furnish the garden as a mature, well-nourished clump of Hosta sieboldiana *var.* elegans.

With the hundreds of hostas now available, the genus has come a long way since the days when there was little to choose from but the blue-leaved *Hosta sieboldiana* var. *elegans*, *H. fortunei* in plain green with flowers of clear lilac on taller stems, yellow-splashed *H. fortunei* var. *albopicta* and the all-yellow *H. fortunei* var. *albopicta* f. *aurea* which so soon fades to two tones of jade green, *H. ventricosa* with its fine, violet bells in late summer and rich green leaves, and a handful of white-variegated hostas: white-edged *H. undulata* var. *albomarginata* (*H.* 'Thomas Hogg') or the bold *H. crispula*, and little *H. undulata* var. *undulata* with its twisted leaves, white at the centre. These have been joined by many other good things that broaden the range of possibilities. If you want a distinctly glaucous-blue hosta of modest dimensions, there are the splendid 'Halcyon' and the range of Tardiana hybrids. In the tall 'Krossa Regal' the upstanding blue leaves are white-backed. There are now a great many cultivars, with leaves – large or small, pointed or rounded – that emerge in tender lime-yellow tones, retaining their colouring all season; one of the most magnificent is 'Sum and Substance'. *H. tokudama* is like a smaller *H. sieboldiana*, with blue-grey, puckered, circular leaves; it has two yellow-hazed forms, and has given rise to all-gold cultivars like 'Golden Prayers'. If a narrower leaf appeals, there is *H. lancifolia*, with its deep green leaves and violet flowers in early autumn. Substantial 'Tall Boy' has rich lilac-purple bells almost at head height, over heart-shaped, pointed leaves of clear green.

Hostas decorate shady places admirably, especially in rich, moist soils, but they also do well in sun, and some of the newer yellow-leaved kinds develop their best colour in full light. Only the white-edged kinds are apt to burn in hot sun or drying winds. Hostas are also surprisingly drought-tolerant once established. They can be increased by division: cut slices out of an old clump as though from a cake, best done in spring as the new shoots are becoming visible. Fill in the gap with enriched soil, and the old clump will be all the better.

IMPERATA CYLINDRICA *'RUBRA'*

deciduous grass H 60cm/2ft S 30cm/1ft foliage Z 5–7

The blades of *Imperata cylindrica* 'Rubra' emerge conventionally enough in green, but turn to blood-red as spring passes into summer. Give it a sunny place in well-drained soil, and increase it by division.

The ethereal colouring of Iris *'Florentina', pearled with dew, is enhanced by its broad, rich green sword leaves.*

IRIS

deciduous and evergreen perennials H and S 23–45cm/9in–1½ft summer Z 5–9 [unless indicated]

If choosing hostas is difficult because of the huge number of cultivars on offer, with irises it is the inherent diversity of the genus itself which challenges the discerning gardener. Granted that every iris has sword leaves (varying from rapier to broadsword, from stiffly erect to arching) and flowers which more or less closely conform to the classic fleur de lis outline, there are still many variations on the theme. If pressed, perhaps I might admit to loving the Californian (Pacific Coast) hybrids most of all. Here is a race of low-growing, neat-leaved irises easily raised from seed, and every seedling enchanting. Deriving from the buff-yellow, amber-veined *I. innominata* [Z 6–9], lilac or white *I. douglasiana* [Z 6–9] and coppery brick-pink *I. fulva* [Z 7–9] and other species of the west coast of North America (all of them beautiful in their own right), they range from alabaster-white through all the tenderest shades of Chinese and Naples and amber yellow, amethyst and aquamarine, lavender, violet, tan, and tawny madder, all exquisitely pencilled, scribbled and thumb-printed with deeper or contrasting shades, and poised like flights of butterflies. Give them sun or dappled shade, in leafy, gritty, lime-free soil for preference, setting the smaller seedlings in the choicest corners and drifting the taller ones among shrubs. You may wish for another hectare or two of land to line out all the seedlings you raise from them; individual seedlings to which you irrevocably lose your heart can be divided.

All that the Californian hybrids lack is fragrance; but that you can have from *I. graminea* [Z 5–8], the plum tart iris, so called because its modest little red-purple and violet flowers smell just like stewed plums, or indeed like the open tarts of Fellenberg plums, aromatic and dripping with red juice, which we make in Switzerland every autumn. Narrow leaves entirely conceal these flowers, which open in summer, so it is a treasure to tuck away in an odd corner, and strictly speaking does not belong in this chapter at all.

The old purple and violet bearded *I. germanica* is seldom seen nowadays, having given way to a range of cultivars classified as tall bearded, intermediate bearded, dwarf bearded, and variants thereon. It remains a good border plant, showy without vulgarity, retaining the classic profile, and I like its inky fragrance. Another bearded iris of great antiquity is 'Florentina', of which the roots, dried, are the orris root of pot pourri; it has grey-white flowers, greyish leaves, and an agreeable perfume, and grows in Tuscan orchards and among Muslim graves, flowering in late spring or early summer. *I. pallida* [Z 6–9] makes, in its most popular variants, a virtue of its leaves, which last longer than most beardeds' before turning tatty. *I. pallida* subsp. *pallida* (*I. pallida* var. *dalmatica*) has fine, broad, blue-grey blades and perfumed flowers of pure outline and clear lavender-blue colour; *I. pallida* 'Argentea Variegata' is less fine in flower but the leaves are striped with ivory, and in 'Variegata' the stripes are primrose to butter-yellow, accompanied by flowers of good quality. All these, together with any of the ruffled or frilled bearded cultivars in self or contrasting colours that you may fancy, are at their best in full sun, in fertile, drained soil, and are increased by division of the stout rhizomes, which should not be covered with soil when you replant them but left exposed to the sun for a good baking in summer.

And so, as summer advances, we come to *I. orientalis* (*I. ochroleuca*) [Z 5–7], a proud iris with stiffly upright leaves and tall stems of large, incisive flowers, white with a canary yellow flash on the curving falls which give it the perfect *fleur de lis* outline. Any fertile, drained soil suits it, in sun or part shade. It can be increased by division or seed.

KNIPHOFIA

herbaceous perennial H 60–90cm/2–3ft
S 45cm/1½ft early autumn Z 6–9

If you succumb to collector's mania, it is not hard to have red hot pokers in flower all year, in mild climates at least; in sizes from knee- to over head-high; and in a range of colours which belies the tag 'red hot', for they come in lemon-white and ivory, every shade of yellow from palest primrose through lemon and gold to deep amber, foody tones of unripe apricot, tangerine, blood-orange, toffee, biscuit, and peach, shades of red from terracotta and coral to grenadier scarlet, cherry, and cinnabar, and even soft green. Frequently, the buds are of contrasting colour, giving the familiar bicolor, red and yellow poker effect as well as subtler combinations of caramel and biscuit, or peach and lemon-ice. Having whetted your appetite, I shall name one cultivar in particular, 'Little Maid', a small, slender poker opening from cream buds to lemon-white. She has proved durable so far, while other cultivars come and go, which only adds to the fun of the chase.

Though they are streamside plants in the wild, kniphofias dislike the combination of cold and wet in winter, especially in stodgy soils; give them, then, a well-drained soil, and a place in the sun. They can be increased by division; seed is a lottery, though a good cultivar just might give you some interesting seedlings. One such, introduced a good many years ago and still with us, is 'Bressingham Comet', a child of *Kniphofia triangularis*, an autumn-flowering species with slender flames of vivid scarlet and narrow, grassy leaves, commonly seen in gardens under the name of *K. galpinii*. 'Bresingham Comet' is of softer orange-flame tint.

A late summer scene with all the freshness of spring: blue Borago officinalis *and creamy* Aconitum *'Ivorine', white* Anemone × hybrida *'Honorine Jobert' framing a clipped pryamid of golden privet* (Ligustrum vulgare *'Aureum'*) *and the white pokers of* Kniphofia *'Little Maid'. Only the tarnishing sprays of* Alchemilla mollis *convey the sense of summer passing into autumn.*

The tree lupin, Lupinus arboreus, *is the centrepiece of this planting in which verticals dominate, drawing the eye upward. With it grow delphiniums, tawny irises and a blue geranium.*

Lavandula

evergreen shrubs H 45–75cm/1½–2½ft S 45–75cm/1½–2½ft summer Z 5–8 [unless indicated]

Fragrant in flower and aromatic in leaf, lavender is a native of the Mediterranean region, where it has long been cultivated in selected, extra highly scented strains for the perfume industry. The hardiest of lavenders are not necessarily the most attractive in the garden, though I have a soft spot for the old-fashioned Dutch and Old English lavenders, forms of *Lavandula* × *intermedia* [Z 5–7](see page 73), with their good grey foliage and pale spikes (and a corresponding faint aversionto the thin-leaved, dark-flowered selections of *L. angustifolia* such as 'Hidcote'). The best foliage belongs to the Spanish *L. dentata* var. *candicans* [Z 8–9], its name testifying to its platinum-pale, finely-toothed leaves, and to *L. lanata* [Z 8–9], woolly-white in leaf and strongly perfumed. Both need a warmer place than the Dutch and Old English lavenders, in full sun and drained soil, and can be increased by cuttings. All lavenders are the better for a good trim back as the flower spikes fade, or in spring.

Lavatera maritima

soft-wooded shrub H 1.5m/5ft S 90cm/3ft autumn Z 8–10

Lavatera maritima (*L. bicolor*), a shrubby mallow, has flowers of almost translucent ice-mauve veined, and flooded at the centre, with madder-crimson, set off by softly grey-felted, lobed leaves. It looks wonderful with pale pink osteospermums flopping about its feet. Give it a place in the sun, with shelter from wind, in well-drained soil. It can be cut hard back in spring to keep it compact and to remove frost-damaged wood, and is easily increased by cuttings.

Lupinus arboreus

semi-evergreen shrub H 1.5m/5ft S 1.5m/5ft summer Z 7–9

The Californian tree lupin is a disorderly but endearing shrub, quick-growing from seed, with fingered, fresh green leaves and spikes of tender lemon- or primrose-yellow flowers endowed with a delicious bean-field fragrance. It is just the thing for giving an air of instant maturity to a new border, or for rapidly filling a gap, but may just as quickly leave one; it does very well by the sea, with no fear of wind and spray. As well as the typical yellow, it can be had in lilac or white; named or colour forms are increased by cuttings rather than seed. Give it full sun and a well-drained soil and do not hesitate to cut it hard back in spring to restore some sort of order to its gangly limbs.

MACLEAYA

herbaceous perennials H 2.1m/7ft
S 60–90cm/2–3ft summer Z 4–9

The plume poppies earn their nickname from the tall, airy spires of many tiny ivory or skin-pink flowers; but it is their foliage that gains them a place in this chapter. Bold, rounded, deeply lobed leaves, glaucous-grey above and white on the reverse, are held on strong white-bloomed stems. The ivory-flowered *Macleaya cordata* is the better-behaved, whereas pale coral *M. microcarpa* has running roots and will quickly fill and overspill its allotted patch. Both are easily increased by division or root cuttings, and grow best in drained soil, in sun.

MELIANTHUS MAJOR

shrub H 2.4m/8ft S 1.8m/6ft
spring to summer foliage Z 8–10

Among the noblest of foliage plants, *Melianthus major* looks as though it has borrowed its plumage from some huge bird, the prehistoric Archeopterix perhaps. Each great leaf is composed of saw-toothed leaflets, pale jade-primrose when they unfurl in the spring, slowly turning to distinctive glaucous-blue. Though woody-stemmed, the plant adapts well to herbaceous mode in areas slightly too cold for its topgrowth to survive, so long as the roots are protected from freezing by a generous mulch. In any case, surviving stems can be cut right back in spring, after the risk of frost has passed, to generate the finest foliage; undamaged and unpruned stems may well produce spikes of maroon flowers with a strange, peanut-butter smell. A sheltered place in the sun is needed; a well-drained, fertile soil ensures good foliage.

ABOVE *Against the sombre backdrop of a purple filbert* (Corylus maxima *'Purpurea'*), *the large glaucous leaves of* Macleaya cordata *seem even paler. The strong yellow of* Ligularia stenocephala, *lemon* Lysimachia ciliata *and a butter-yellow daylily yield to primrose* Digitalis lutea *and white* Tanacetum corymbosum *and, in the foreground, white* Viola cornuta *Alba Group.*

BELOW Melianthus major *is growing here with purple* Ricinus *and red canna lilies.*

The autumn sun lights up the silky plumes of Miscanthus sinensis *and the broad purple blades of orange-flowered* Canna *'Assaut', with* Aster lateriflorus *'Horizontalis' in the foreground and the narrow-leaved* Helianthus salicifolius *to the left.*

Miscanthus sinensis

grass H 1.5–1.8m/5–6ft S 60cm/2ft
late summer to autumn Z 5–10

The maiden grass forms clumps of gracefully arching blades with pale midribs, topped – at least in regions where the summers are reliably warm to hot – by silky, rippling plumes of flower which age to ivory fluff. *Miscanthus sinensis* comes in several cultivars, including white-striped 'Variegatus' and the yellow-banded tiger or zebra grass, 'Zebrinus', which is at its brightest after midsummer and can be relied on to flower freely in autumn; the elegant, narrow-bladed 'Gracillimus'; 'Morning Light', another smaller cultivar, free-flowering, with narrow, white-edged leaves; and *M. sinensis* var. *purpurascens*, which has stems flushed with purple and blades turning to orange, buff and amber in autumn (whereas the others tend to fade to a modest parchment). 'Silberfeder' ('Silver Feather') is one of the finest in flower, producing shimmering tan-pink, arching flower plumes even in cool climates; they open earlier than those of 'Zebrinus'.

Unlike many grasses, *M. sinensis* is not invasive, but increases slowly at the root; it grows in any fertile soil, moist or dry, in sun or shade, and can be propagated by division.

Nepeta govaniana

herbaceous perennial H 90cm/3ft S 60cm/2ft
summer Z 4–8

The lavender-blue and grey haze of catmint, *Nepeta* × *faassenii*, is well known, and a pretty thing it is for sunny places, or as a classic companion for roses, or a place of repose for cats intoxicated by chewing or rolling in it. But *N. govaniana* is a very different thing, a plant for cool, shady places in

RIGHT *With its delicate spires of primrose yellow flowers,* Nepeta govaniana *is quite distinct from the sun loving, blue-flowered catmints. Here it grows against a backdrop of purple* Atriplex hortensis *var.* rubra, *with the daisy-flowered* Argyranthemum *'Vancouver',* Achillea millefolium *'Cerise Queen', pink roses and a few stray blooms of* Lavatera *'Rosea'.*

soil that does not dry out, with foliage of tender green and airy sprays of soft lemony-primrose flowers over a long summer season. It is increased by division, cuttings or seed.

OENOTHERA

herbaceous perennials H 23–45cm/9–18in S 30–60cm/1–2ft summer Z 4-8

Evening primroses are not primroses at all, but the name is here to stay. The day-flowering species are sometimes called suncups or sundrops, which is far more appropriate for *Oenothera macrocarpa* (*O. missouriensis*), the Ozark sundrops. Here is a plant with trailing stems set with long, narrow, dark green leaves enhanced by white midribs, and immense, pure yellow cups in red calyces over a long summer to autumn season. It is best increased by seed. *O. fremontii* is similar, its flowers perhaps of sharper yellow tint. These sprawling sundrops look their best at the border front, spilling over stone edging perhaps. Of stiffly upright habit, *O. fruticosa* (*O. tetragona*), the common sundrops, has bright yellow flowers opening from red buds, and darkish foliage, mahogany-tinted in spring in subsp. *glauca* (*O. tetragona* var. *fraseri*). 'Fyrverkeri' ('Fireworks') is a fine selection. These upright-growing sundrops are propagated by division. All species demand sun and well-drained soil.

OLEARIA

shrubs H 90cm/3ft S 90cm/3ft early summer Z 9–10

The antipodean daisy bushes include a little group of softish shrubs with grey foliage, the outline of a cumulus cloud, and an abundance of bright daisies, snow white or lavender-blue or lilac-mauve, like a small-flowered, out-of-season Michaelmas daisy. This gives them a very different character from the essentially foliage shrubs that are described on page 49. Their naming is a little confusing: what was usually known as *O.* × *scilloniensis* has been officially renamed *O. stellulata* De Candolle but anything bearing the tag *O.* × *scilloniensis* is worth snapping up. Typically it comes in pure white: *O.* × *scilloniensis* 'Master Michael' has intense lavender blue daisies.

They do not share the resistance of many daisy bushes to wind, but need a warmish place in well-drained soil. They can be increased by cuttings.

ABOVE *Like long, slender fingers, the narrow leaves of* Oenothera macrocarpa *set off the huge, clear yellow blooms.*

LEFT *The flowers of* Olearia stellulata *De Candolle* (O. × scilloniensis) *completely mask the foliage in their season, transforming a discreet, grey-leaved shrub into a cloud of starry white daisies.*

Framed in the rain-spangled blades of a daylily, the scarlet blooms of this Paeonia officinalis *'Rubra Plena' stand proud above the substantial, dark green foliage, a study in complementary colours.*

Paeonia

herbaceous perennials H 45–90cm/1½–3ft
S 45–60cm/1½–2ft late spring
Z 4–8 [unless indicated]

The double crimson cottage peony, *Paeonia officinalis* 'Rubra Plena', is a grand old plant, easy and long-lived. The more refined *P. veitchii* var. *woodwardii* [Z 7–8] has fresh green foliage to accompany its nodding saucers of clear pale pink with cream anthers and pink filaments. In *P. peregrina* we find the alliance of complementary colours, bright glossy green foliage and flowers of intense pure scarlet, or paler vermilion with a silken sheen in 'Otto Froebel' ('Sunshine'). Unlike the other species, which are clump-formers, the tuberous roots of *P. peregrina* [Z 6–8] will increase quite rapidly if suited. What they all appreciate is a fertile, humus-rich, well-drained soil, in sun or light shade. Division is an easy means of increase, and if your peony flowers begin to dwindle in number, it may be that the plants are starved, needing to be lifted, divided and replanted in fresh, enriched soil; or they may have become too deeply buried, for if the crowns are more than a whisker beneath the soil surface the plant will sulk. Again, if carefully teasing away the soil that has accumulated does not produce flowers next season, lifting and replanting at the proper depth should do the trick.

Papaver

herbaceous perennials H 45–60cm/1½–2ft
S 30–45cm/1–1½ft summer Z 3–7 [unless indicated]

Oriental poppies are included in the chapter that follows this, for although they are substantial and showy plants they flower early, die down at midsummer, and leave such a gap that I count them as fleeting effects in the border. Less bulky, but considerably more refined and longer-lasting are a group of poppies with flowers of the typical crumpled silken texture, varying from clear apricot to tangerine in colour. The nearest to commonplace is *Papaver atlanticum* [Z 6–8], especially in its untidy double form; the single is greatly superior, with a long succession of nodding, clear orange flowers on long stems over green basal foliage. It seeds itself freely. *P. pilosum* [Z 6–8] is similar, though leafier. *P. rupifragum* [Z 7–8] has flowers of tangerine-apricot over blue-glaucous, hairy foliage, and *P. spicatum* (*P. heldreichii*) [Z 6–8], the most frost-resistant of the four, is also the most beautiful, its wide, soft apricot flowers on short stalks opening top-down from white, hairy buds, over good, thickly-furred blue-grey basal leaves. All like sun and well-drained soil and are more easily increased from seed than by division, in my experience.

PARAHEBE PERFOLIATA

evergreen subshrub H 60cm/2ft S 75cm/2½ft
summer Z 8–10

Parahebe perfoliata (*Veronica perfoliata*) looks remarkably like a tuft of eucalyptus until it flowers, for the stem-clasping, broad-based, pointed leaves are glaucous-blue in maturity – on first emerging, they are tinted with plum-purple. As the season advances the deception is unmasked, for the digger's speedwell bears loose, arching sprays of speedwell flowers of tender lilac-blue with cream stamens.

It creeps inoffensively underground, and looks its best if the old stems are cut out each year to leave the way clear for the new growths to emerge uncluttered. It enjoys sun and a well-drained soil, and is increased by cuttings taken in summer, or seed.

PENNISETUM

deciduous grasses H 45–90cm/1½–3ft
S 45cm/1½ft summer/autumn
Z 5–10 [unless indicated]

Most of the grasses described in this book are valued more for their foliage than their inflorescences; but the pennisetums compensate for their undistinguished grassy blades with their endearing bottle-brush spikes. In the tall *Pennisetum alopecuroides* these are of an unusual slaty-indigo colour tufted with white, appearing in autumn; 'Woodside' is a selection of free-flowering character. Some people like the effect of the parchment-pale blades in winter; to me they look merely dead. Another autumn-flowering species is *P. villosum* [Z 7–9], which has white, fluffy bottlebrush spikes, nodding from arching stems. *P. orientale* [Z 7–9] bears its grey-pink, furry-caterpillar spikes in summer; the long hairs that give the spikes their fuzzy outline are mauve-purple at first, fading to greyish-buff. They all have to a marked degree the tactile quality which impels so many of us to run our hands along the stems of grasses and over the inflorescence, usually to strip it; but these are too pretty to strip, though irresistible to stroke. They do best in sun, in well-drained soil, and are ncreased by division or seed.

The fluffy, pinkish-cream bottlebrushes of Pennisetum alopecuroides *make a broad sweep around the rosettes of soft shield fern* (Polystichum setiferum) *and the giant oat,* Stipa gigantea. *In the distance blue* Festuca glauca *frames a clump of* Miscanthus sinensis *'Variegatus'.*

The waxy, blue-grey leaves of Parahebe perfoliata *add as much to this gentle harmony of pink and violet as do its sprays of tiny Spode-blue veronica flowers. With it are growing a viola,* Campanula persicifolia, *and the Old Blush China Rose,* Rosa × odorata *'Pallida'.*

The elegantly-poised trumpets of penstemons have prompted many breeders to select seedlings for a colour of special clarity, or strongly defined throat markings. The red cultivar is 'Fire Dragon'; the pink could be 'Apple Blossom' or the closely similar 'Hidcote Pink'.

Penstemon

evergreen perennials H 30–90cm/1–3ft s 30–60cm/1–2ft summer to autumn z 6–9 [unless indicated]

The jewel colours and long-flowering season amply justify the small amount of management that penstemons need if they are to give of their best: young plants flower for much longer than older ones, and an easy routine of autumn cuttings, overwintered in a frame and planted out in spring, is also a valuable insurance against winter losses of the more tender varieties. As a general rule, the larger the leaf and flower, the more tender.

Having said that, *Penstemon campanulatus* is not one of the hardiest, despite its narrow leaves and small flowers. A probable, and hardier, derivative is the soft pink 'Evelyn'. 'Hidcote Pink' leans more towards coral pink, with red striations in the throat. 'Apple Blossom' describes itself, as does 'Mother of Pearl' (which is streaked crimson in the throat). Penstemons rather go in for opalescent, tender lilac-mauves, as in 'Alice Hindley', or 'Stapleford Gem' in cream and blue-lilac, often miscalled 'Sour Grapes' – the true 'Sour Grapes' has blue-purple bells with a bloomy finish, nearer to ripe than to sour grapes.

As well as these pastel shades, there is a range of rich colours to choose from. *P. hartwegii* [z 8–9] has tubular, scarlet flowers, and has bequeathed this colour to bright red cultivars such as the pure-toned 'Schoenholzeri' ('Firebird'). 'Port Wine' is an appropriately bibulous colour. For fairly evident reasons most English-speakers still call 'Andenken an Friedrich Hahn' [z 7–9] by its more descriptive name of 'Garnet', a splendid plum red.

P. heterophyllus is a smaller plant than all of these, and exquisitely coloured, its narrow tubular bells varying from lilac-blue to the pure turquoise of 'Blue Springs', set off by darkly glaucous, narrow leaves, often flushed with muted purple. It is subshrubby, as is the taller 'Catherine de la Mare', which is very free with its lilac-blue spikes, and more frost-resistant than 'Blue Springs'.

All penstemons are at their best in sunny places, in fertile, well-drained soil, with shelter from cold winds.

Perovskia

deciduous shrubs H 1.2m/4ft s 45–60cm/1½–2ft late summer z 5–9

The grey, white-backed, dissected or toothed leaves of the Russian sages are endowed with a powerful turpentine aroma, and form the plinth for tall, slender spires of small flowers on white stems, making a haze of lavender-blue for many weeks. This bright, clear tint is succeeded by the winter effect of the grey-white stems; in spring these are best cut hard back, fuchsia-fashion. *Perovskia atriplicifolia* is a mouthful of a name, but easier to say and probably more beautiful still is *P.* 'Blue Spire'. They need a sunny, open place and well-drained soil, and are increased by cuttings.

PERSICARIA

herbaceous perennials H 60cm–1.2m/2–4ft s 60cm–1.2m/2–4ft early summer/summer to autumn Z 3–8 [unless indicated]

Amid the cloudy or rounded shapes of so many broadbrush prennials, the pokers and spikes of *Persicaria* (*Polygonum*) are invaluable for contrast in the border. The knotweed season opens in early summer with the bistort, *P. bistorta*, of which 'Superba' is the cultivar to go for, on account of its pale chalky-pink poker spikes over a weed-excluding mat of blunt-ended, dock-like leaves. Of the same style, but neater and later, *P. millettii* [Z 5–9] has crimson pokers over a long summer season. In *P. amplexicaulis* [Z 5–9] (see page 91) the flowers are narrow, tapering spikes rather than pokers, lasting from midsummer until autumn. 'Atrosanguinea' is deep ruby-crimson, 'Firetail' is a brighter red, and *P. amplexicaulis* var. *pendula* ('Arun Gem') has arching, vivid pink tassels. With the same long season but of different style is *P. campanulata*, which rapidly spreads a mat of soft-textured, ribbed, fawn-backed leaves over which are held tall stems with branching heads of many dawn-pink or blush-white bells.

All these knotweeds thrive in ordinary to moist soils, in sun or light shade, and can be increased by division of the clumps while dormant.

The dock-like leaves of bistort, Persicaria bistorta, *are said to make quite good eating in times of dearth; but it is for its chalky pink pokers, appearing in late spring, that the selection 'Superba' is grown.*

PHLOX

herbaceous perennials H 90cm–1.2m/3–4ft s 45–60cm/1½–2ft summer/late summer Z 4–8

The flowery borders of an English garden in high summer are incomplete without the warm, peppery fragrance of phloxes, and their pastel or rich shades and billowy outlines. *Phlox maculata* begins its display of tall, cylindrical spires earlier than the more familiar *P. paniculata*, which has dome-shaped heads and runs to brighter colours. The first is typically mauve or white; 'Alpha' is lilac-pink, 'Omega' white with a lilac eye. There is nothing quite like a pure white phlox; *P. paniculata* 'Fujiyama' ('Mount Fujiama') is outstanding, tall and late-flowering, into autumn. For the rest, there is a great choice of colours ranging from white with a pink eye through shades of pink to crimson, ice-mauve through lilac to purple and claret-red. Of

Candy pink Phlox paniculata *is accompanied by the sultry purple leaves of* Atriplex hortensis *var.* rubra, Verbascum chaixii *'Album'*, Rosa × odorata *'Pallida'*, *and* Physostegia *subsp.* speciosa *'Bouquet Rose'*.

special note are two cultivars of *P. paniculata* with cream and green leaves: 'Harlequin' with purple flowers and 'Norah Leigh', in pale lilac-mauve.

Phlox need a rich soil that does not dry out, in sun or light shade; little looks more miserable than a phlox wilting in the heat of summer because it has nothing at the root to draw on. The other threat is eelworm; infected shoots are swollen, with scraps of twisted leaf attached. The remedy is to burn them, to replant something else in that patch; and to buy stock that is disease-free. Propagation by root cuttings from plants grown in clean ground is the safe way to ensure the infection is not passed on.

A low sun enhances the dramatic colouring of this purple phormium belonging to the 'Maori' series, each blade striped in sunset colours.

Phormium

evergreen perennials
H 1.2–3m/4–10ft S 60cm–1.2m/2–4ft
summer Z 8–10

The New Zealand and mountain flaxes, especially in their largest manifestations, have considerable presence, with their fans of broad blades (by contrast, the narrower blades of cordylines are arranged in symmetrical rosettes). *Phormium tenax*, the New Zealand flax, the larger of the two species, has tall spikes of blood-red flowers on plum-coloured stems and holds its grey-green sword leaves stiffly upright, while *P. cookianum*, the mountain flax, has arching blades and is more subdued in brownish flower. Among cultivars of *P. tenax*, and boasting its guardsman's posture, are the bloomy purple Purpureum Group, and yellow-margined 'Variegatum'. *P. cookianum* subsp. *hookeri* offers 'Tricolor', with restrained red and yellow stripes on its green leaves, and 'Cream Delight' with boldly cream-edged, cream-striped leaves. Cultivars which seem to have the blood of both the New Zealand and the mountain flax, and which have more or less arching blades, range from sombre or intense oxblood-red and grape-bloomed purple to the brilliance of 'Yellow Wave' and a clutch of rainbow-toned confections coloured in shades of orange, apricot and peach, chocolate, tan and scarlet, such as the 'Maori' series and the muscular 'Sundowner'. To give their upstanding or arching blades full value, keep the planting around them low. Their varied colours give scope for endless harmonizing or contrasting associations – the silver filigree of *Anthemis punctata* subsp. *cupaniana* around 'Sundowner', say or *Helichrysum petiolare* 'Limelight' embracing 'Yellow Wave'.

Phormiums will grow in any fertile, well-drained soil, in sun or light shade. They can be increased by seed, though anything may result – the Purpureum Group are may produce a range of tones. Cultivars must be propagated by division to ensure identical offspring. As a general rule, the brighter the leaf colouring, the less frost-resistant the cultivar; a generous mulch to protect the crown is advisable in borderline hardiness zones. Remove tattered and discoloured blades in spring.

Phygelius

soft-wooded shrubs H 90cm–1.2m/3–4ft
S 60–75cm/2–2½ft summer to autumn
Z 7–9 [unless indicated]

The Cape figwort, *Phygelius capensis*, bears its curving, narrow trumpets of clear bright red with yellow throats over a long summer season in a one-sided spike; *P. aequalis* [Z 6–9] is softer in colour, its flowers muted coral-red with pale citron throat and dark lip. It has an irresistible lemon-primrose variant ineptly called 'Yellow Trumpet'. One of the first hybrids between the two, collectively known as *P.* × *rectus*, was 'African Queen', in vivid red. It has been more recently followed by 'Devil's Tears', in deep pinkish-scarlet with orange-red lobes, dusky pink 'Winchester Fanfare', soft salmon 'Salmon Leap', 'Pink Elf', a dwarf cultivar with narrow trumpets of pale pink with deeper streaks and crimson lobes, and the wholly lovely 'Moonraker' in creamy primrose.

Phygelius are subshrubby and adapt happily to a herbaceous existence; they are easily increased by cuttings or division and thrive in fertile, well-drained soil in sun.

Once it became available, Phygelius aequalis *'Yellow Trumpet' was quick to spread among discerning gardeners, and no wonder, for it bears these gracefully hanging primrose tubes over a long season.*

PLEIOBLASTUS AURICOMUS

bamboo H 90cm/3ft S 90cm/3ft foliage Z 5–10

Easily the best of the smaller variegated bamboos, *Pleioblastus auricomus* (*Arundinaria viridistriata*) has wide, soft-textured blades generously striped with canary yellow, on slender canes. It develops its best colour in sun but will also thrive in light shade; it prefers moist soil. It is also the better for having the old canes cut to the ground each spring, allowing new canes to grow uncluttered. It is increased by division of the slowly spreading roots.

PROSTANTHERA ROTUNDIFOLIA

deciduous shrub H 90cm/3ft S 90cm/3ft
early summer Z 9–10

The Australian mint bush, *Prostanthera rotundifolia*, with its aromatic foliage, is a pretty creature with clouds of labiate flowers, typically soft lavender blue, sometimes mauve-pink, and occasionally white. I like to pair them with like-coloured daisy bushes, the blue mint bush with *Olearia* × *scilloniensis* 'Master Michael', for they match almost exactly in colour but are very different in flower shape; and they like similar conditions of well-drained soil, shelter and sun. Cuttings root easily.

The mint bush, Prostanthera rotundifolia, *is endowed with aromatic foliage – hence its common name – and is very free with its small, lipped flowers in violet-blue or lilac-pink.*

In this summer border Salvia verticillata *and the Vatican sage,* Salvia sclarea *var.* turkestanica, *are joined by delphiniums, astrantias, the pale cumulus spires of* Campanula lactiflora *and creamy plumes of* Artemesia lactiflora.

Ranunculus

herbaceous perennials H 25–90cm/10in–3ft s 25–30cm/10–12in late spring/early summer z 4–8

In the days when buttercup meadows were a common sight in northern Europe, the idea of growing – as opposed to trying to exterminate – buttercups in the garden might have seemed akin to madness, beautiful though they are, with their burnished, rich yellow petals. Even now, it is the doubles that are likely to find a welcome: the tall bachelor's buttons, *Ranunculus acris* 'Flore Pleno' [z 3–7], and the double creeping buttercup, *R. repens* var. *pleniflorus* [z 3–7]. I am not aware of a double form of *R. gramineus*, but the single is in any event a delight, with its comparatively large buttercups over grassy, blue-glaucous foliage. It is a slighter, shorter plant than the others, and is happier in sun; the others are equally at home in sun or shade, in fertile soil that does not dry out. All can be increased by division.

Rudbeckia fulgida

herbaceous perennial H 60cm/2ft s 30cm/1ft summer to autumn z 3–9

My ability to accept yellow daisies is distinctly limited, but I gladly make an exception for the black-eyed Susan, *Rudbeckia fulgida* var. *deamii* on account of the thimble-sized, velvety black central cone which gives such character to its many-rayed, bright canary yellow flowers, which it bears with generosity over a long season. Furthermore, it is happy in conditions that many plants would resent: sticky, stodgy soil, in sun or shade. There is more than one variant on offer, but one is probably enough in the average-sized garden; you can choose from var. *speciosa* or the very fine var. *sullivantii* 'Goldsturm'. They slowly spread into leafy clumps which can be increased by division.

Ruta graveolens

evergreen shrub H 60cm/2ft s 60cm/2ft foliage z 4–9

The finest form of rue or herb of grace is the cultivar known as 'Jackman's Blue', in which the sea-green foliage of the type is transmuted into a steely blue-glaucous tint. A severe pruning each spring will maintain the desired domed shape and reduce or eliminate the yellowish flowers, which are only a distraction. Wear gloves while doing this, for some people are allergic to this strongly aromatic shrub. Full sun and well-drained soil, to recall its Mediterranean origins, help to keep it compact and bright in leaf.

SALVIA

herbaceous perennials/evergreen shrub
H 60cm–1.5m/2–5ft S 60–90cm/2–3ft
summer, autumn Z 5–9 [unless indicated]

The conventional sage of hardy flower borders is *Salvia nemorosa*, and a good thing it is too with its branching heads of long-lasting violet-blue flowers in purple bracts, which themselves extend the season for several weeks after the flowers have fallen. But for all its qualities, and its easy temper in any reasonable soil, I do not find it particular lovable. *S. argentea*, on the other hand, fickle though it can be if you allow it to get wet feet in winter, is wholly endearing, with its rosettes of broad, woolly-white leaves that feel as if they have been composed of closely-massed cobwebs. The flowers that overtop these strokeable confections in the second year are white, in pewter calyces, the whole making a ghostly colour scheme. Give it full sun and sharply-drained soil for best results, and increase it by seed. By contrast, *S. uliginosa* [Z 6–9] spreads freely at the root in dampish soils, and is easily divided. Its smallish leaves are rich green; in autumn it bears many slender, mobile stems topped by spires of pure blue flowers.

One of the best of sages for foliage effects in the border is the purple form of the culinary sage, *S. officinalis* Purpurascens Group [Z 5–8]. It is of softer colouring than the usual run of purple-leaved shrubs, more a gentle greyed purple than a strident mahogany. It assorts well, therefore, both with shades of pink and mauve and crimson, and with the softer yellows. I have seldom seen it waste its energies on flowering, whereas the more typical grey-leaved sage sometimes bears violet-purple spikes. Though evergreen, the purple-leaved sage can look disconsolate in cold, wet winters; a sheltered place in full sun, in a well-drained soil, suits it best. It can be hard-pruned in spring to keep it compact or to remove frost-damaged wood but if allowed to sprawl unchecked develops into a wide mound like an unmade duvet. Summer cuttings root easily.

When the grey leaves of common sage, Salvia officinalis, *become suffused with purple, the result is the tender colouring of the Purpurascens Group.*

SANTOLINA

evergreen shrubs
H 60cm/2ft S 60cm/2ft
summer Z 7–9

These, like the shrubby sage, are aromatic Mediterranean sun-baskers, most with grey or silvery foliage, as in the familiar lavender cotton, *Santolina chamaecyparissus* (*S. incana*). Despite the brightness of its tightly bobbled, silvery foliage, it is marred by brassy button flowers. Accordingly, my preference is for the ➤

In this immaculately groomed formal layout, the low, wide domes of Santolina chamaecyparissus *are maintained in their flowerless perfection by rigorous clipping in spring.*

more feathery, and greyer-leaved *S. pinnata* subsp. *neapolitana*, which has paler yellow flowers. Exceptionally, *S. rosmarinifolia* subsp. *rosmarinifolia* 'Primrose Gem' has bright, rich green foliage to set off its creamy sulphur button flowers.

All demand a well-drained soil and are the better for a severe pruning in spring, to make fresh new growths after winter has tarnished the old, and to remain compact. Tight domes lend themselves equally well to formal layouts or to making a solid foundation amid looser, more relaxed plantings. They are easy to increase from summer cuttings.

As summer yields to autumn, the stonecrops come into their own. Here the flat pink heads of Sedum *'Herbstfreude' ('Autumn Joy') are echoed by the pink tints on the leaves of* Fuchsia magellanica *'Versicolor'.*

SEDUM

succulent perennials H 10–60cm/4in–2ft
S 23–60cm/9in–2ft summer, autumn
Z 3–9 [unless indicated]

The stonecrops – with rare exceptions – are sun-loving succulents happy in well-drained soil, fertile or poor. They are doubly welcome on account of their season of flower, from late summer into autumn. For the front of the border there is a a trio flowering in late summer. *Sedum* 'Ruby Glow' [Z 5–9], glaucous of leaf and garnet-pink of flower, is the smallest; next up in size comes 'Vera Jameson' [Z 4–9], with more purple in the leaf and flowers of more muted pink; 'Sunset Cloud' is the largest, a sultry creature with wine-dark flowers. *S. cauticola* [Z 5–9] is another small sprawler, with circular, blue-grey leaves margined purple, and pink flowers flushing deeper rose with age. All these enjoy full sun and well-drained soils, surviving on the merest scrap of nourishment.

With its flat heads of dusty pale pink, starry flowers in late summer, the ice plant, *S. spectabile*, is another that belongs at the forefront, if only to admire with greater ease the butterflies that flock to sip its nectar. Its fleshy foliage is pale jade green. If you want more, go for its pink cultivar 'Brilliant'. Richer colouring also belongs to *S.* 'Herbstfreude' ('Autumn Joy'), which is taller, with thick, blue-grey leaves and wide, flat heads of deep pink turning to deeper russet tones with age and lasting through the winter. In the less rigidly upright *S. telephium* subsp. *maximum* 'Atropurpureum' the foliage and flowers alike are suffused with dark pigment, so that the leaves are purple with a grape-like bloom and the flowers little crimson stars. All these sedums can be increased by cuttings or division.

SISYRINCHIUM STRIATUM

evergreen perennial H 60cm/2ft S 30cm/1ft summer Z 6–9

The iris-like leaves of *Sisyrinchium striatum* are blue-grey, appealing with the narrow spikes of small, creamy-primrose flowers finely lined with slate-purple on the backs of the petals. Seedlings appear in great abundance.

After the stiffly upright flowerspikes of Sisyrinchium striatum *are over, the rosettes that bore them die away; but there is always a generous supply of successors, both from the roots and from the many seedlings they leave behind.*

STIPA

grass H 45cm–1.8m/1½–6ft S 90cm–1.2m/3–4ft summer to autumn Z 7–9

Stipa gigantea is like a huge oat, with tall, airy heads of flowers, each tipped with a long, slender awn, above a clump of arching, narrow blades; at first sheeny fawn-pink, the flower heads mature to rich wheaten gold, lasting long before finally losing their shape to the battering winds of autumn. It is especially fine when lit by a low sun to cast a long shadow. It can be increased by division or seed.

TEUCRIUM FRUTICANS

evergreen shrub H 90cm/3ft S 90cm/3ft summer Z 7-9

Here is a shrub of great refinement for warm, sheltered, sunny corners to remind it of its southern Mediterranean origins. Of open habit, with small, silver-felted leaves and white stems, it has little labiate flowers of tender sky blue, at their brightest in 'Azureum', opening over a long summer season. It can be increased by cuttings, and should be planted in well-drained soil.

THALICTRUM

herbaceous perennials H 90cm–1.5m/3–5ft S 30–60cm/1–2ft summer Z 5–8

The first of the meadow rues to flower, in early summer, is *Thalictrum aquilegiifolium*, which has pretty foliage like that of a columbine, of fresh pale green. The flowers, on branching stems, are a cloudy fuzz of warm lilac, varying to ivory-white in var. *album* and to sultry purple in the aptly-named 'Thundercloud'. The taller, later-flowering *T. flavum* subsp. *glaucum* is of similar character, though very different colouring, with divided, very glaucous foliage and frothy, acid lemon flowers. In *T. delavayi* the foliage is exiguous, but the individual flowers are more emphatic, being endowed with lilac-blue petals (or white in 'Album') around a fluff of cream stamens, and held in great open, airy panicles. They may look as though light enough to take flight, but their weight means you will need to stake the plants individually except in the most sheltered places. This is even more the case with the enchanting 'Hewitt's Double', in which each flower is a tiny formal rosette of clear lilac. The sudsy-headed meadow rues do well in any fertile, well-drained ➤

Pewter and gold combine in this planting of the giant oat, Stipa gigantea, *with apricot-yellow* Lilium henryi, Artemisia absinthium *'Lambrook Silver', and the metallic white bracts of the sea holly,* Eryngium giganteum.

soil, in sun or light shade, and are increased by division or seed; but *T. delavayi* needs rich living, shelter and fleeting shade. Ignore the usual rule about not burying the crown by planting too deep; this one is best set in a hollow which is filled in as it grows. It is increased by division or seed, or cuttings in the case of the double form.

In this early summer medley the foamy mauve-pink flowerheads of Thalictrum aquilegiifolium *float above the alabaster-white, ruffled pincushions of* Astrantia major, *with magenta* Geranium psilostemon *in the background. All three have handsome foliage too.*

Tulbaghia violacea

herbaceous perennial H 60cm/2ft S 20cm/8in summer to autumn Z 7–10

A poppet of a plant for warm, sunny corners in well-drained soil, *Tulbaghia violacea* has agapanthus-like heads of lilac-blue flowers over narrowly strap-shaped, grey-green leaves. In 'Silver Lace' these are heavily striped with white, making this a plant to cosset in some choice corner rather than to plant in quantity. Both are increased by division.

Veratrum

herbaceous perennials H 1.8m/6ft S 60cm/2ft summer Z 3–8

Both in flower and foliage the false helleborines are handsome plants for rich soil in shade, in a place sheltered from wind, so the bold, pleated leaves do not become tattered and torn. Forming a rich green pile, they are topped in late summer by bare stems bearing great branching plumes of flower, which in *Veratrum nigrum* are bitter-chocolate to maroon in colour. It can be grown from seed, but take a long time to reach a good size; or can be carefully divided while dormant.

Yucca

evergreen shrubs or perennials H 1.5–2.4m/5–8ft S 60cm–1.5m/2–5ft summer Z 5–10 [unless indicated]

The yuccas are plants of the arid regions of south-western North America, though several are surprisingly ready to adapt to the wetter climates of western Europe and elsewhere provided they are grown in well-drained soil, in sun. Of those that do not develop a trunk, *Yucca filamentosa* is characterized by smallish rosettes of grey-green leaves with thread-like white hairs along the margins; the flower spikes have erect sideshoots, making a compact spire of cream bells. 'Bright Edge' is yellow-margined, and 'Variegata' is yellow-striped. *Y. flaccida* [Z 7–9] is of similar stature, with leaves that are more lax, arching at the tips, and a more open, airy flower spike; best of all for flower is 'Ivory'. This species too comes in variegated mode: 'Golden Sword' has yellow-margined leaves.

In time the Spanish dagger or roman candle, *Y. gloriosa* [Z 6–9], develops several trunks, ending in bold rosettes of stiff, dull green, ferociously spike-tipped leaves. Tall spires of cream bells open in summer. These striking yuccas are best set off by the simplicity of stone paving – at the intersection of paths, perhaps.

Somewhat different in style is *Y. glauca* [Z 4–8], a hemisphere of very many, very narrow, blue-grey, white-edged blades topped by a narrow spike of ivory bells. Most striking of all in this mode is *Y. whipplei* [Z 8–11], our Lord's candle, intensely blue in stiletto-blade leaf. In time each dense rosette produces a soaring spire of hundreds of white, purple-tinged flowers, only to die of exhaustion thereafter. It can be increased from seed.

All yuccas are the better for being well-groomed, which involves removing old, withered or tatty leaves. Those that do not form trunks spread slowly at the root and can be increased by division; the branching kinds by removing side branches as cuttings, allowing them to form a callus (leave them in a cool, shady place for a few days) before inserting in sharply-drained compost.

This Yucca gloriosa *is perfectly placed, marking the angle of a path where it cuts through the border. Throwing into relief the spire of ivory bells is a dark backdrop of purple* Cotinus coggygria *and the softer, white-dusted purple foliage of the teinturier vine,* Vitis vinifera *'Purpurea'.*

ZAUSCHNERIA CALIFORNICA

herbaceous perennial H 30–45cm/1–1½ft
S 45cm/1½ft late summer to autumn Z 8–10

The California fuchsia is another plant that has had a run-in with the taxonomists; for a while it was considered to belong in *Epilobium* (as *E. canum*), and here you may find it in some books and catalogues. But now it is back in the familiar guise of *Zauschneria californica* subsp. *cana*. The flowers are vivid scarlet-vermilion trumpets, borne over green or silvery foliage, ideal as a contrast to yellow knipofias. *Z. californica* 'Solidarity Pink' is a pretty, pale shade; there is also a white, 'Albiflora'. All have a very long season, flowering until the first frosts of autumn. Sun and sharply-drained soil are a must; increase is by cuttings.

All summer long Zauschneria californica *'Dublin' is a mass of little trumpet flowers of clear, pure vermilion, a rare and welcome colour among hardy border plants.*

fleeting effects

annuals, bulbs & short-season perennials

The bones of the border are fleshed out with drifts and blocks of colour; it is time to add the finishing touches. Chaste snowdrops, squills blue as tropical skies pierce the cold soil as winter yields to spring; bright tulips and crown imperials prefigure summer's plenty, and poppies burst their buds, and flaunt, and die at summer's height, giving way to the paddle blades of cannas and fragrant gingers, swooningly perfumed spires of tobacco flowers and lilies, gladioli dainty as butterflies and tiger-striped Peruvian lilies, stately summer hyacinths and luminous nerines. Amid these short-lived delights are tribes of daisies – pastel-shaded Paris daisies, daisies of the veld in azure and royal purple, pink and glistening white – to deck the border for months on end. Plants with lax, insinuating stems interweave their silvery, feathery or softly felty foliage amid this profusion of bloom, emollient and conciliatory amid so much competitive colour.

Certain shades of pink, like this annual Cosmos *'Imperial Pink', glow with a particular intensity in the gloaming of early morning or evening. The lime-yellow foliage of* Robinia pseudoacacia *'Frisia', behind the floating cosmos flowers, is almost translucent in the low rays of the sun.*

Columbines (Aquilegia) *of varying hues, red oriental poppies* (Papaver orientale), *white lupins and the great globes of* Allium hollandicum *'Purple Sensation' combine into an idealized flowery mead, overseen by a silvery weeping pear,* Pyrus salicifolia *'Pendula'.*

It is their very evanescence which gives so many of these plants their charm. They are the polar opposite of the stalwart evergreens that frame the garden, and their display is the more keenly awaited for being so fleeting.

This chapter embraces an eclectic mixture of perennials, biennials and annuals, bulbs and subshrubs; plants chosen for their flowers or for their foliage, for their structure and outline, for their texture, or for their colour. What allies them is that, whether because they are evanescent in flower, spend part of the year below ground or are unreliably winter-hardy, they cannot be counted upon to form permanent visual elements of the border. Some of the hardier plants – foxgloves, honesty, forget-me-nots, even tobacco flowers – may become almost permanencies by seeding themselves, when they will need only to be thinned so as to grow strong and stocky, or hoed or pulled out where they are misplaced. Other plants that are annual or can be treated as such, flowering the same year from seed sown in spring, are best raised afresh each year: among them cleomes, castor oil plant, and mallows in all their diversity. The first two in particular have the look, the muscularity, of permanencies even though they need to be renewed each year. Other annuals, such as cosmos, though they may flower for

The lady tulip, Tulipa clusiana, *frail-seeming and slender compared with modern bedding tulips, is still unmatched for elegance and delicacy of colouring.*

Closely related to the ornamental onions (Allium), Nectaroscordum siculum *is fascinating at every stage from budburst to seedhead. These dusky, drooping bells will fade to parchment, turning their heads to the sky as they do so.*

several weeks with generous treatment, have a lighter structure that suggests impermanence; this is part of their charm. Some plants that need regular renewal by cuttings or seed are hardy and technically perennial, but apt to be short-lived; named pansies and violas, for example.

Perennials and subshrubs that are not frost-hardy (a relative term, of course; the cut-off I have chosen is, roughly, Zone 8) are included only if they are easy to keep going by taking cuttings, or perhaps by sowing seed, each year. Many of them are hardly fleeting in their visual impact, their flowers lasting over a long season or their foliage handsome from late spring to the frosts; but because they cannot be considered as part of the permanent planting of the border, I include them in this chapter. In frost-free climates, of course, plants such as osteospermums, nicotianas and dahlias, cannas, ginger lilies and Paris daisies, and all the gorgeous tribe of central and south American salvias can all be treated as hardy perennials or subshrubs.

Many bulbs count as finishing touches *par excellence*. They can be tucked in among, or even

The shaggy bark of the river birch, Betula nigra, *rises from massed forget-me-nots (a strain selected for the richness of their colour,* Myosotis *'Royal Blue'), which lie like pools of fallen sky lit by the spring sunshine.*

beneath, clumps of perennials that flower at a different season, and which, if rightly chosen, can perform the additional task of masking the dying foliage of those bulbs that do not fade away gracefully. They are, on the whole, slender in growth, with no tendency to elbow aside their companions in the border, and are gratifyingly quick to produce results, the very next flowering season after planting as a rule. Few plants wake up a summer border so well as bulbs – think, for example, of cardinal red tulips among the green shoots of spring. But though 'bulbs' and 'spring' are an almost instinctive association, their season runs in fact from the snowdrops, crocuses, scillas and tiny irises of late winter and early spring, through narcissi and grape hyacinths, the anemones of the Mediterranean and the tulips and fritillaries of Central Asia in later spring followed by a succession of alliums, lilies, gladioli and summer hyacinths, to colchicums, nerines and belladonna lilies in autumn.

Some of the perennials in this chapter die away soon after flowering – oriental poppies and Peruvian lilies, notably – to leave an ugly gap in the border. If you do not have adjacent a conveniently floppy plant – the perennial pea, *Lathyrus latifolius*, perhaps – to train over the empty space, you can instead tuck in a few potsful of 'in and out' plants between your poppy crowns or on top of your alstroemeria roots. Two or three each of *Helichrysum petiolare*

Iris *'Katharine Hodgkin' is one of the gems of early spring, its alabaster-pale flowers exquisitely pencilled and veined with mauve and leopard-marked with black on lemon around the saffron streak of the falls.*

White as the snow they pierce, snowdrops (Galanthus) *are one of the first signs that winter will yield at last to spring. Pick a bunch and bring them into the house to enjoy their discreet honeyed perfume.*

The flowers of Salvia cacaliifolia, *of no less an intense lapis lazuli blue, are smaller and more gracefully disposed on lax stems than those of the more familiar* Salvia patens.

and a trailer such as *Verbena* 'Silver Anne' (with the grey helichrysum) or *Bidens ferulifolia* (with *H. petiolare* 'Limelight'), to say nothing of *Tropaeolum tuberosum* grown horizontally rather than vertically, will fill a square metre or two with no trouble and at great speed.

The helichrysum and the bidens share with certain other plants – notably *Senecio vira vira* – the agreeable habit of weaving their lax stems among and through neighbouring plants, knitting them together rather than imposing on them. The silver and grey foliage of the senecio and helichrysum are emollient companions for vivid colours; while 'interweavers' that are grown for their flowers peer charmingly from among the foliage or flowers of their neighbours. They play an invaluable aesthetic role in softening contours and blurring joins, as well as the practical one of masking gaps.

It is possible, of course, to imagine a border without bulbs, or annuals, or tender perennials; but such a border would be the poorer for their lack. All that is needed is the small discipline of taking cuttings in autumn or sowing seed in spring; and a frost-free place where the cuttings can be overwintered, several to a pot of sharply-draining compost, plus a cold frame to harden the young plants for planting out after the risk of frost has passed.

LEFT *'Bishop of Llandaff' is an old dahlia cultivar, still valued for its fulgurent scarlet, almost-single flowers and metallic black-purple foliage, echoed here by* Heuchera micrantha *var.*diversifolia *'Palace Purple'. The double blood red dahlia is 'Arabian Night'. These sultry, burning colours are enhanced by silver* Artemisia *'Powis Castle' and white* Lilium regale.

LEFT *The colour of brick can be a difficult backdrop to flowers; but as this group shows, it can be met on its own terms to enrich red, orange and carmine flowers. Red valerian* (Centranthus ruber) *becomes almost subfusc behind the flame and terracotta alstroemerias.*

The fiery heat of summer in the arid Central Asian steppes seems to burn in the flowers of Tulipa praestans *'Fusilier', as though stored in the bulbs that bake in the sun, secretly forming next year's flowers that force through the rocky soil in spring after the winter rains.*

allium

rainbow starbursts

DETAILS FROM TOP:
The solid drumstick heads of Allium sphaerocephalum, *in garnet-red, are borne on stiff stems.*

The burgundy-wine heads of Allium cernuum *are composed of elegantly nodding flowers.*

The huge globes of Allium cristophii *are formed of many gleaming, lilac stars.*

The soft yellow Allium flavum *is among the most irresistible of small species, with its star-burst flowerheads and slender leaves.*

MAIN PICTURE:
After their flowers have faded, ornamental onions still adorn the border; Allium hollandicum *displays its pale seeds on pink stalks.*

Allium

bulbous perennials H 30cm–1.2m/1–4ft S 15–45cm/6–18in
late spring, summer Z 3–8 [unless indicated]

Alliums are good mixers; here Allium hollandicum *'Purple Sensation' pops up among iris and lavender in a harmony of purples.*

Among the ornamental onions are several species which have considerable impact in the border while taking up the minimum of space and disappearing obediently underground once their season is over – though a few have not only handsome flowers, but striking seedheads as well, to extend their season of impact. One of the smaller species, almost too exiguous for the border until it has sown itself into a generous drift, is *Allium flavum* [Z 4–8], with showerburst heads of small, nodding, clear lemon flowers; prettiest of all is its selection 'Blue Leaf', in which the stems and chive-fine leaves are blue-glaucous. *A. carinatum* subsp. *pulchellum* is much the same in lilac-purple, or better still in milk-white, f. *album*. Hardly taller is *A. cernuum*, its name indicating the spraying, soft wine-red flowers borne in summer on gracefully arching stems. Among mid-sized species, *A. sphaerocephalum* is unusual in the intensity of its maroon-crimson colouring. Its dense flowerheads are egg-shaped and last long in beauty.

Among the taller, bolder alliums, *A. hollandicum* 'Purple Sensation' [Z 4–7] opens the season in late spring, its drumstick heads of rich purple-lilac similar to those of the summer-flowering *A. giganteum* [Z 4–8]. *A. cristophii* [Z 4–8] is shorter in growth, but its flower-heads are the largest of all, football-sized confections of many metallic amethyst stars on slender spokes, like the model of a spherical molecule, a suggestion heightened when the flowers fade and the seeds form, dropping to germinate freely and leaving the parchment-pale scaffolding of the flowerhead to last well into autumn.

All these alliums are absurdly easy to grow given a well-drained, fertile soil and a sunny place. If they do not do the job for themselves, they can be increased by sowing seed or dividing the oniony bulbs.

Typically soft pink, the belladonna lily (Amaryllis belladonna) *has produced a number of selections of special intensity of colour. One of the finest is 'Johannesburg', which is endowed with the same apricot perfume as the type.*

ALSTROEMERIA

herbaceous perennials H 1.2m/4ft S 45cm/1½ft summer Z 7–10

The common Peruvian lily, *Alstroemeria aurea* (*A. aurantiaca*), is a handsome thing with its flaming orange, tiger-striped flowers. Although it looks like a sun-lover, it will do quite well in light shade; sometimes slow to establish, it can be invasive once settled. The seldom-seen *A. ligtu* has given us the *ligtu* hybrids (see page 14), which are especially valued for the range of colours, from shell and peach pink to shrimp, coral, and tangerine, all with delicate stripings of sepia and maroon. They are easily raised from fresh seed, broadcast where you want them to grow (any well-drained soil will do), or sown two or three in a pot the contents of which, to avoid damage to the fleshy roots, should be dropped undisturbed into the planting site once the seedlings have retreated into their high summer dormancy. This early dormancy means that alstroemerias leave a gap in the border after flowering, which can be filled by overplanting – yank out the stems and pop in some pot-grown annuals or tender perennials. This will do no harm to established clumps of alstroemerias.

AMARYLLIS BELLADONNA

bulbous perennial H 60cm/2ft S 30cm/1ft autumn Z 8–10

The belladonna lily flowers in early autumn, spurred into growth by the rains of late summer; in regions where summers are habitually dry, a good soaking from hosepipe or watering can must substitute. The other prerequisites are rich soil and plenty of sun to ripen the bulbs. The result is well worth the little effort, for the belladonna lily's clear pink trumpets, narrowly flared around an ivory throat, and borne as many as eight on each stout naked stem of contrasting maroon-purple, are not only beautiful; they have a delicious ripe-apricot perfume. The strap-shaped leaves follow in winter, so a place sheltered from frost is needed; in regions where the belladonna lily is of borderline hardiness, it appreciates a sunny wall at its back. If you ever come upon any of the named selections, such as 'Johannesburg', 'Kimberley' or rose-red 'Capetown', snap them up. Increase is by division in their dormant season, unless you are inclined to try your hand at hybridizing.

ANEMONE BLANDA

rhizomatous perennials H 10–15cm/4–6in S 7.5cm/3in spring Z 4–8

Anemone blanda is one of the flowers that colours the rocky places and open scrub of the eastern Mediterranean in spring, its wide-open, many-petalled flowers held over prettily divided foliage. It differs in colour from region to region – white or dark blue in Greece, sky blue in Turkey. In our gardens we can deploy, as well as the typical tender blue of commerce, drifts of the deep blue 'Ingramii', the fine, large-flowered 'White Splendour', lilac-pink 'Charmer' and 'Pink Star', and the potent magenta-pink, white eyed 'Radar'. Any well-drained soil, in sun or light shade, suits these anemones, which can be divided for increase, or allowed to spread naturally at their own pace.

Daintier than the broad-petalled De Caen anemones, yet more substantial than the frail wood anemone of shady places, Anemone blanda *is one of the least demanding and most rewarding of small spring flowers. This is 'White Splendour'.*

BIDENS FERULIFOLIA

perennial H 15cm/6in S 90cm/3ft summer Z 8–10

Not so long ago, *Bidens ferulifolia* was quite a rarity; then everyone seemed to recognize its qualities and it is now readily available. On trailing stems set with finely dissected, fresh green foliage, it bears an unending succession of vivid yellow lazy-daisy flowers from the first warmth of summer until the frosts of autumn. It weaves its long arms through any neighbouring plant; one year I had it with another arch-weaver, the soft-textured, lime-yellow form of *Helichrysum petiolare* known as 'Limelight', and another season it became the plinth for the clear yellow poker *Kniphofia* 'Sunningdale Yellow'. It is easily renewed each year from a potful of autumn cuttings, kept in a frost-free place, and I have also found self-sown seedlings. Any well-drained soil, in sun, suits it.

Bidens ferulifolia *epitomizes all that is best in frost-tender plants that can be over-wintered as cuttings, to be planted out again in spring: a long season of flower, clarity of colouring, appealing foliage, and ease of propagation.*

The spidery flowers and leaves of Cleome hassleriana *give both colour and form to this predominantly pink planting, with other fleetings, including* Cosmos bipinnatus *and white tobacco plants, along with* Salvia viridis *and a backdrop of pink Japanese anemones and* Campanula lactiflora *'Variegata'.*

Following hard on the heels of the first snowdrops, Chionodoxa luciliae *gleams with cold blue fire against the bare soil of the border as it awakens from winter.*

CANNA INDICA *'PURPUREA'*

herbaceous perennial H 1.2m/4ft S 90cm/3ft
late summer Z 8–10

Unlike some cannas, which have been selected only for the brightness of their scarlet, orange or yellow flowers, *Canna indica* 'Purpurea' is valued above all for its foliage. 'Assaut' is very similar (see page 120). The leaves are of the usual bold paddle shape, though somewhat narrower than many hybrids, and their colour is a rich coppery maroon; the clear scarlet flowers are not too large.

Give it a place in full sun, in rich soil, and protect the fleshy roots with a thick mulch, or by lifting them in autumn and overwintering them in a just-moist medium in a frost-free place.

Propagation is by division; canna seed, if set, is bullet-hard (cannas are sometimes called Indian shot) and must be abraded before sowing. I have found that a quick whizz in a coffee grinder does the job well, and with much less effort than filing each one individually.

CHIONODOXA

bulbous perennials H 7–5–15cm/3–6in S 5cm/2in
early spring Z 4–9

Both chionodoxas and the smaller species of *Scilla* (see page 165) that flower in early spring can be planted in generous drifts – to which they will soon add by self-sowing – to bring the colours of summer skies to the bare, cold soil. *Chionodoxa luciliae* is known as glory of the snow, because it flowers on its native Turkish hillsides amid the receding snows of winter; it has clear blue, white-eyed flowers, fewer to each stem than in the rich blue *C. sardensis*. Both species are easy to grow in sunny, open places in well-drained, fertile soil, and can be increased by division of the bulbs as well as seed.

CLEOME HASSLERIANA

annual H 1.2m/4ft S 60cm/2ft summer

The spider flower, *Cleome hassleriana* (often known as *C. spinosa*), has more substance than most annuals, with its bright green, horse-chestnut-like leaves and wide spikes of flower that open over a long season and are followed by long, cylindrical green seedpods held horizontally. It comes in pink or white ('Helen Campbell'). There is no need to sow the seed too early – not before late spring – but then the seedlings should be kept moving so as to make lusty plants, so do not allow them to become pot-bound. They look wretched if starved or checked. Plant them out in midsummer in a sunny place in good, fertile soil, providing each plant with a cane, and handle them with care to avoid being snagged by the hooked spines that give the plant its botanical epithet.

COLCHICUM

cormous perennials H 15cm/6in S 15cm/6in
late summer, early autumn Z 6–8

Colchicums are commonly known as autumn crocuses, though they are not even in the same botanical family as true crocuses (some of which do also flower in autumn). Colchicums are much pinker than any crocus, and their chalice-shaped flowers are borne on naked stems; the big, broad leaves come later, handsome in spring when green and glossy but rather obtrusive in their dying off. As with other bulbs, however, it is important not to cut the leaves off before they have faded, for in doing so they return nourishment to the bulbs for next season's growth. *Colchicum byzantinum* opens the season in late summer, its lilac-pink flowers characterized by long stigmas with crimson tips; later, in autumn, it is the turn of *C. speciosum*, which is also typically mauve-pink, but also comes in white, the superb *C. speciosum* 'Album'. They will grow in any well-drained soil, even in thin grass, in a sunny or lightly shaded place; I have seen great drifts of them in the grass beneath and between tall trees in public parks. They can be increased by division during the dormant season or seed.

The glowing amethyst-pink of Colchicum speciosum *is set off here, unusually and effectively, by the silky-soft foliage of* Stachys byzantina. *Care will be needed to avoid the colchicum leaves spoiling the stachys in spring.*

The velvety, chocolate-crimson flowers of Cosmos atrosanguineus *gather all the warmth of summer to their hearts, but their smell of hot chocolate strangely evokes winter firesides.*

Cosmos

annual and herbaceous perennial
H 75–90cm/2½–3ft S 45cm/1½ft summer Z 6–9

In both leaf and flower *Cosmos atrosanguineus* resembles a refined dahlia, with darkish foliage and deep chocolate-crimson flowers, endowed with a fragrance to match their colour, for they smell just like a cup of hot cocoa. Its roots are less plumply tuberous than a dahlia's, so it is not ideally suited to lifting and storing over winter, but instead should be given a good mulch to protect the roots – which should be planted deep – against frost. Even with this cosy blanket it is very late to start into growth, hardly appearing before midsummer; a memory-jogging cane or two is a wise precaution against planting something else in what looks like an empty space in late spring. It needs a sunny place in retentive soil.

The annual *C. bipinnatus* has very finely dissected foliage and gracefully poised flowers of clear pink, rose, or white, in 'Purity'; it is easy from seed and lovely for cutting, lasting long in water. Being very quick to grow to flowering size, it is valuable for filling gaps from a sowing in late spring, perhaps to follow on from early-flowering biennials. So long as it is not starved, it will then flower until the first frosts. Any reasonable soil in sun or light shade suits this easy-going annual.

The orange stigmas of Crocus speciosus *echo the fallen beech leaves that lie around the brave little violet flames of each frail flower.*

Crocus

cormous perennials H 7.5cm/3in S 5cm/2in
late winter/spring, autumn Z 4–9 [unless indicated]

Anyone who has grown the choicer crocuses will know that mice seem to have a nose for the most expensive corms. The little 'tommies' – *Crocus tommasinianus* – seem to be left alone, and so willing are they to spread that you can soon have a drift of them among your border shrubs. Very early in the year their slender flowers emerge, buff on the exterior and opening wide to the sun to display their lavender-mauve inner segments. There are variants in deeper purple, red-purple and white, but none is so pretty as the pale type. There is a wider range of colour to be had from little *C. chrysanthus*, which has chubbier flowers and, in some cultivars at least, a distinct perfume, reminiscent of the kind you pay dearly for in small designer flasks. To my nose, this is especially so of 'Cream Beauty' and the white 'Snow Bunting'.

'Blue Pearl' is a fine lavender-blue, 'Ladykiller' is violet-striped on white, and if you prefer the warmer shades there are 'Zwanenburg Bronze', copper without and saffron within, and mahogany-striped 'Gipsy Girl'. Another assertive little person is *C. ancyrensis* [Z 3–9], with bright golden-orange flowers. There are many more early spring crocuses to tempt you and the mice, but I will pass straight to autumn and the blue-violet of *C. speciosus*, with its showy orange stigmas. It does tend to flop, but its colour is so appealing amid the falling leaves of autumn, or in thin grass, that it is easily forgiven. Any fertile, well-drained soil suits these crocuses, which can be increased by division or seed.

Dahlia

tuberous-rooted perennials H 90cm/3ft S 60cm/2ft
summer to autumn Z 7–9

Amid all the pompon, decorative and cactus dahlias on offer, there is the barest handful of species and cultivars that outlast fashion and surmount virus debilitation. One of those indispensables is the old 'Bishop of Llandaff', in which well-formed flowers of the most potent scarlet you can imagine are allied to deeply cut, metallic black-purple foliage (see page 140). *Dahlia merckii* is more refined, with its wide, branching heads of many small, clear lavender-lilac, single flowers, some with dark disks and a hint of maroon on the reverse, often with a dusky flush to the foliage too; others are pale-faced and green of leaf. Both need rich, well-drained soil in sun, and can be increased by division or cuttings; *D. merckii* can also be increased by seed. Like the familiar bedding dahlias, they can be lifted and stored in a frost-free place until it is safe to plant them out again in spring.

Dahlia merckii *has all the elegance and poise of a wildling, that – as so often when plants are intensively bred for bigger and brighter flowers – has been lost in many of the cultivars. The dark buds and stems add to its charm*

White foxgloves, Digitalis purpurea *f.* albiflora, *echoed by the white margin of the ground planting of hostas, soar like steeples amid the mauve foam of* Thalictrum aquilegiifolium, *white honesty* (Lunaria annua) *and a pink rose.*

DIGITALIS

perennials or biennials H 90cm–1.5m/3–5ft S 30cm/1ft early summer Z 4–8 [unless indicated]

The difficulties of typecasting plants by function and thereby persuading them into the chapter-by-chapter organization of a book are well illustrated by foxgloves. The common foxglove of woodland margins and copses, *Digitalis purpurea*, and its lovely manifestations in white or cream, with or without maroon freckles and spots, and the peachy 'Sutton's Apricot', could go into the woodland chapter; but as biennials ideally suited to add drifts of early summer colour and stately form to the border, they equally belong here, or – by virtue of their self-perpetuating nature – even in the main border chapter along with other permanencies. *D. lutea* has small, creamy yellow flowers similar in colour to those of the perennial *D. grandiflora* (see page 98). So here they are, but please think of them if you have a copse or wooded area to beautify as well. The trick to maintaining stands of white or peach-pink foxgloves unsullied by the common purple-pink, by the way, is to bring a critical eye to bear on the seedlings when thinning them out, which they will certainly need if they are to make well-developed plants for next season: any with a purple flush on the petiole will have purple flowers, while those with plain green leafstalks will come white or apricot.

Although it is a true perennial, I include *D. parviflora* [Z 5–8] in this chapter also, for it is a slender creature of which just a few plants suffice for you to admire its narrow pokers of many tiny, close-packed 'gloves' of chocolate-brown tint. *D. ferruginea* is of similar style, but taller, paler-toned in buff with tan interior, and more open of spike. These two thrive in well-drained soil in sun, and like the common foxglove can be increased by seed.

FELICIA AMELLOIDES

evergreen perennial H 15–23cm/6–9in S 15cm/6in
summer to autumn Z 9–10

South Africa is rich in irresistible daisies – osteospermums and dimorphothecas and the muscular gerberas, and also this little plant with its innocent, azure-blue daisies borne on neat little bushes over a very long season. *Felicia amelloides* 'Santa Anita' is an especially fine selection, a little larger in flower, without however any hint of coarseness; for this reason it wins my vote rather than *F. amoena* (*F. pappei*), even though the latter has more attractive foliage, fresh green and needle-fine. There is a rather horrid cream-variegated form of *F. amelloides* (see it for yourself, however, before you take my word for it).

Whether you prefer the purity of 'Santa Anita' or the kitsch of the variegated kind, give your felicia a warm, sunny place in well-drained soil. It is a simple matter to take cuttings each autumn as a precaution against winter loss.

FRITILLARIA

bulbous perennials H 90cm–1.2m/3–4ft
S 30–45cm/1–1½ft spring Z 5–9

The legend is told of the crown imperial that its flowers used to be white and held proudly erect over the ruff of fresh green foliage; but that it refused to bow its head when Jesus entered the Garden of Gethsemane, for which it was reproved by the Almighty, and has ever since blushed with shame and hung its head, five teardrops of repentance glistening unshed at the base of each bell. *Fritillaria imperialis* is typically rust-red in flower, deeper in 'Rubra', and there is a clear yellow, 'Maxima Lutea'. The bulbs have a strong foxy smell and can be increased by breaking off the outer scales, which will make new bulbs if set in drained compost in a pot or frame; or simply by division of old clumps, best done during summer dormancy. *F. persica* 'Adiyaman' is even more beautiful, with its pointed, glaucous leaves in whorls up the stems, and tall spires of nodding bells, smaller than those of the crown imperial, and far more subtly coloured in muted chocolate-purple with a pale bloom on the exterior. It too can be increased by division, or from seed. Both species need a well drained, fertile soil; the crown imperial will do equally well in sun or light shade, whereas the eastern Mediterranean species needs a sheltered, sunny place.

For other species of fritillary that are at their best in cooler conditions, or more informal settings of dappled shade or meadow, see page 184.

The azure daisies of Felicia amelloides *surround the gold-striped leaves of a canna lily. This grouping is typical of the long-lasting summer effects of plants that need resetting each year in all but frost-free zones.*

Its stately carriage, and the brilliance of its whorls of hanging blooms, have earned Fritillaria imperialis *the name 'crown imperial'. Despite its aristocratic looks, it is an easy plant that can be used in generous drifts to light up the spring border or woodland.*

fleeting effects

Snowdrops and snowflakes in the early spring border – the broad leaved Galanthus caucasicus *and* Leucojum vernale *– are set off by the marbled winter foliage of* Arum italicum *subsp.* italicum *'Marmoratum'.*

Galanthus

bulbous perennials H 15–30cm/6–12in S 7.5cm/3in late winter/spring Z 3–8 [unless indicated]

The common snowdrop, *Galanthus nivalis*, is enchanting beneath a light tree canopy or drifting among shrubs (see page 139); and its double form, 'Flore Pleno', is even more effective when massed, though its individual flowers, with their ragged edges and untidy centres, lack the simple charm of the wildling. If the elegance of a single snowdrop, with its three curvaceous outer segments and green inner markings, appeals to you, there are several fine cultivars that can be tucked in odd corners of your borders in fertile soil that is not too dry, among slate-dark hellebores perhaps, or between the emerging crimson-mahogany shoots of herbaceous peonies. 'S. Arnott' has large, beautifully-shaped flowers. The very ample flowers of 'Magnet' are borne on long pedicels, so that it moves in the least whisper of a breeze. *G.* 'Straffan' is another good, late kind. In *G. elwesii* [Z 4–8] the leaves are markedly glaucous; the flowers are large, with dark green marks on the inner segments. It prefers sharper drainage than the others. *G. caucasicus* [Z 4–8] is similar, with a long season of flower. All can be increased by division, which is best done after the flowers fade but before the leaves have died away. The common snowdrop, single or double, can quickly be made into generous drifts in this way; tuck a few bulbs into every little space among shrubs or between clumps of perennials.

Galtonia

bulbous perennials H 90cm–1.2m/3–4ft S 30cm/1ft late summer Z 7–9

The summer hyacinths are stately plants, slender enough in growth to tuck in among earlier flowering perennials to give a second display from the same patch of ground. The tall spires of fragrant, hanging bells are white in *Galtonia*

For snowy white bells in the summer border, turn to Galtonia candicans, *the summer hyacinth. Here its steeples of bells are framed in grasses (*Miscanthus *and pampas grass) and ferns.*

candicans, and pale peridot green in *G. viridiflora*, which is rather shorter in growth They should be planted deeply, in rich soil, in sun, and can be increased by division or seed; indeed, they may well seed themselves freely if suited.

Gladiolus

cormous perennials H 45–90cm/1½–3ft
s 30cm/1ft early summer, autumn Z 5–10 [unless indicated]

The big, stiff, brightly coloured gladiolus hybrids always make me think of station buffets at the end of trans-European railway journeys; but as well as these monsters, there are some delightful small-flowered gladioli to be had. These need no staking to support oversized spikes, and their dainty, butterfly blooms add colour and grace to the border without demanding much space. The corn flag of southern Europe, *Gladiolus communis* subsp. *byzantinus* [Z 7–10], could indeed belong equally in the chapter on woodland and orchard gardening, for it grows in the wild in fields and scrub. In the garden its open spikes of elegant, magenta-purple flowers, enlivened by cream flashes on the lower segments, light up the early summer border, where they can be set off by the pale blue spires of camassia, with pale pink and 'Hensol Harebell' blue columbines. The corn flag spreads freely by seeds and stolons, especially in light soil, but is slender enough not to present much threat to neighbouring plants.

At the same early summer season the flowers of the Nanus hybrids [Z 4–9] are borne. Their flowers open wider than those of the corn flag, and come in a wider range of colour, from the pure white of 'The Bride' or 'Nymph', in white with a faint pink stain outlined with carmine on the lower segments, through deepening shades of pink from peach and blush to cherry, and including lilac and salmon-orange. The narrow leaves begin to grow in autumn, so a sheltered place is advisable. They are best left alone once planted, since their winter-growing habit is not conducive to lifting and storing during frosts. Increase is by division of the corms.

Gladiolus *'Nymph' is one of the loveliest of the Nanus hybrids, exemplifying all their poise and daintiness. The lipstick smudge markings on the lower segments are one of the charms of this group.*

Hedychium coccineum *'Tara' is both among the most frost-hardy and one of the most beautiful of ginger lilies.*

HEDYCHIUM

rhizomatous perennials H 90cm–1.5m/3–5ft s 60–90cm/2–3ft late summer Z 7–10

The ginger lilies are related to culinary ginger, and their knobbly roots have the authentic ginger smell, as you will find when you come to divide them. But it is for their flowers, in the main, that they are valued in the garden. The tall, airy columns of *Hedychium gardnerianum* appear in late summer over broad green leaf blades; whether in warm yellow or cooler primrose, the spidery, powerfully fragrant flowers are decorated with long, red stamens. White-flowered *H. spicatum* is probably a touch hardier, while in *H. coccineum* the flowers are bright orange-scarlet. In areas where they are of borderline hardiness, the ginger lilies can be lifted and stored in a just-moist medium in a frost-free place for the winter. If suited they increase fast, to the point of threatening native vegetation in some areas. And what suits them, apart from a warm-temperate to subtropical climate, is rich, moist soil and sun.

HELICHRYSUM PETIOLARE

evergreen subshrub H 45cm/1½ft s 90cm/3ft foliage Z 5–9

Helichrysum petiolare and its cultivars are plants that I am inclined to use again and again, for they are unusually versatile. If allowed to grow free they form loose mounds of arching stems which spray outwards here and there in a pleasantly anarchic way, or weave through neighbouring plants; or they can be tamed by handcuffing the main stem to a cane, when they will develop a more formal, pyramidal outline with horizontal branchlets. The rounded to heart-shaped leaves are softly felted, platinum-grey in the type, chartreuse-green in 'Limelight', cream on grey in 'Variegatum'. *Plecostachys serpyllifolia* (hort. *Helichrysum microphyllum*) is effectively a miniature version in silver, with tiny leaves and the same sprawling habit. *H. petiolare* 'Limelight' is ideal for softening the stark lines of yellow-variegated phormiums, or to combine with clear yellow flowers, in one-colour groupings, but its gentle tones mix with almost anything. It needs a fertile, well-drained soil and burns easily in full sun; a touch of shade helps to keep the tender colouring. If kept dry at the root, all forms will survive surprisingly low winter temperatures; but they succumb quickly to soggy soil and cold weather. Cuttings root easily in sharply draining compost, and if taken in autumn can be overwintered in a frost-free place for planting out in spring after risk of frost has passed.

HERMODACTYLUS TUBEROSUS

tuberous-rooted perennial H 35cm/15in
S 10cm/4in spring Z 6–9

Nothing gives me greater pleasure in spring than the subtly-coloured flowers of the widow iris, with their pale khaki-green standards and velvety, deepest umber falls. They are flowers to pick in bud and to linger over as they open, releasing their strange, cool, green-spicy fragrance. What matter if they are followed by a floppy mass of narrow, grassy leaves? They increase freely in well-drained soil, preferring a sunny place.

IRIS

bulbous perennials H 15cm/6in S 5cm/2in
early spring Z 5–9 [unless indicated]

Almost before winter is over, the stocky little flowers of *Iris histrioides* push through the cold soil; the one to choose is 'Major', in rich blue with just a touch of violet, discreetly crested with gold on the falls. At much the same season the more slender *I. reticulata* flowers in a range of colours from azure ('Cantab', or 'Clairette' in which the falls are violet and white) through mid-blue (two-tone 'Joyce', 'Harmony', blue and violet 'Springtime') to violet and red-purple ('Pauline', orange-crested 'J. S. Dijt'). Some forms have a distinct fragrance of violets. They may succumb to ink disease, in which infected bulbs are darkly stained; but are so cheap to replace that it is worth buying fresh each year. Their equivalent in bright lemon yellow, *I. danfordiae* [Z 4–9], needs to be bought fresh each year for a different reason: it tends to break up into tiny rice-grain bulblets after flowering. A very deep planting may help to prevent this tendancy to break up. The ethereal *I. winogradowii*, in primrose-yellow, has crossed with *I. histrioides* 'Major' to produce 'Katharine Hodgkin', which has wide-falled flowers of alabaster-white veined and flecked with lemon and khaki (see page 139). This is a gem to cherish as you would a Fabergé original, rather than brave little flames of blue or citron to light up the early spring border at minimal effort for the return they give. All need a well-drained soil in sun, or light, open-skied shade.

Amid the sultry foliage of Viola riviniana *Purpurea Group* (V. labradorica), *the glowing ultramarine blue flowers of* Iris reticulata *mark the turn from winter's chill to spring.*

White on white – Lavatera trimestris *with the papery daisies of* Helichrysum bracteatum, *the green umbellifer* Ammi majus, *and white* Limonium sinuatum.

Lavatera

annual H 60–90cm/2–3ft S 60–90cm/2–3ft summer

Lavatera trimestris has typical flared trumpet-shaped mallow flowers, white, pink or rose-red, and a more substantial air about it than many annuals. In 'Mont Blanc' the brilliant white flowers are set off by dark green foliage, but the effect is somewhat spoiled by a rather dumpy habit; the taller 'Silver Cup' is soft pink, and another, more assertive pink is 'Loveliness'.

They are ideal as long-flowering follow-ons to early-flowering biennials, thriving in most fertile, well-drained soils in sun, and standing up well to spells of drought. Sow seeds in mid to late spring, and keep the seedlings well nourished, potting them on if need be so they do not become starved before planting out. Well grown plants not only fill more space, so you need fewer of them, but also flower more generously and for longer.

Like all lilies, the martagon lily (Lilium martagon) *has rich orange pollen, colouring the anthers that*

Lilium

bulb H 90cm–1.5m/3–5ft S 30cm/1ft summer z 3–8 [unless indicated]

Whether trumpet-flowered or turk's cap, lilies have an exotic air, with their waxen petals and their poise; some have a rich, swooning fragrance that evokes tropical nights. Yet many are as easy to grow as the most humdrum daffodil, so long as they are planted while the many-scaled bulbs are fresh and plump. Most need a free-draining, leafy soil, with some bonemeal for nourishment, and prefer sun to shade. Once they are settled in the garden, the clumps are best divided soon after flowering, so they can re-establish before the soil becomes cold and wet in winter.

The martagon lily, *Lilium martagon*, is a plant of subalpine meadows, where it is apt to be scythed down as part of the hay crop; in gardens, it deserves better treatment, in open places among shrubs or popping up between clumps of perennials in the border. Its turk's cap flowers, opening in early summer, are typically dusky pink; there is a delicious white form, var. *album*, very pretty amid white-variegated hostas to follow white dicentras;

and a rarity with dark plum-purple flowers opening from white-hairy buds, *L. martagon* var. *cattaniae*.

Just as easy as these, and quick from seed, is *L. regale*, from China. It comes into growth early in spring; a planting of low shrubs around it helps to protect the tender shoots from late frosts. In high summer its tall spires of maroon-budded trumpets, each white petal with a mahogany-pink stripe along its outer spine, fill the air with rich, sweet perfume. It is dramatic against a backdrop of *Cotinus coggygria* 'Royal Purple'. *L. regale* 'Royal Gold' is identical but for its clear yellow colouring. Both have the rich orange-tan pollen typical of lilies, which stains clothes (and noses, when you come too close to inhale their fragrance).

The elegantly poised, soft citron trumpets of *L. monadelphum* (*L. szovitsianum*) [z 5–8] are sometimes freckled inside with maroon. It is long-lived, but can be slow to establish. Unlike some lilies, it tolerates heavy, limy soil, if well-drained.

All white flowers gleam at dusk long after other colours have receded into the darkness, and *L. candidum* [z 4–8], the pure white Madonna lily, is no exception. Its crystalline flowers have golden pollen and a sweet perfume, more innocent and less cloying than the regal lily's. It has the reputation of preferring humble cottage gardens to grand ones, perhaps because, as a sterile plant increased over centuries by division of the scaly bulbs rather than regularly renewed from seed, it is susceptible to virus infections carried by aphids from other lilies, and would ordinarily have been spared that risk by virtue of being the only lily in a cottage garden. Unlike other species, the new basal foliage emerges in early autumn and remains green throughout winter, making late-summer planting an imperative.

Lilies can be quickly increased either from seed, in the case of species, or by scaling. This involves separating the outer scales from the bulbs (discarding any that are damaged or shrivelled) and keeping them damp, but not wet, in a warm place. Putting them in a plastic bag of damp vermiculite or similar sterile medium works well. A dusting of fungicide is a wise precaution. Tiny new bulbs will form at the base of the scales, to be detached and potted individually as soon as they are large enough to handle.

LUNARIA ANNUA

biennial H 90cm/3ft S 30cm/1ft spring/autumn
Z 6–9

Not only because it reminds me of my childhood garden, but also because it is a plant of two seasons and beautiful in both, money-plant or honesty finds a place in my garden. In late spring the lilac-purple or white flowers open, and in autumn the green seedheads ripen and dry, turning into the silky-papery, moon-pale 'honesty money'. *Lunaria annua* seeds itself, so that once in the garden, it will reappear year after year. There are variegated forms, with white flowers ('Alba Variegata', and the striking 'Stella' with very white leaves) or with the more usual lilac-purple flowers over cream and green leaves (*L. annua variegata*); do not throw out seedlings that are all-green, as the variegations take time to develop. Variants with deepest purple flowers have green leaves. 'Munstead Purple' is the name I used to grow these under, but seed of any richly-coloured honesty should produce more of the same, provided – and this holds good for the variegated ones, too – the parent plants have been grown in reasonable isolation from other honesties. Any fertile soil suits honesty, in sun or shade.

As the seedheads of honesty (Lunaria annua) *ripen from green to papery parchment, they pass through subtle shades of purple or muted red, seen here among meadow flowers – yarrow, plantain and mullein.*

Spring is rich in small, valiant flowers of sultry or pure blue. The grape hyacinth, Muscari armeniacum, *is one of the most dependable; 'Blue Spike' is a fine selection.*

Muscari

bulbous perennials H 7.5–15cm/3–6in S 3cm/1in spring Z 4–8 [unless indicated]

In the garden where I grew up, there is a river of blue grape hyacinths at the foot of a clipped lonicera hedge, filling the awkward gap between the hedge and a gravel path. The tight-packed spikes of prim little blue bells with their white, pursed mouths have never failed in half a century, and their fragrance is one of the delights of spring, even though you have to bend low, or pick a bunch, to enjoy it. So densely packed are the bulbs that the fresh green, chive-like leaves that follow form a solid, weed-excluding carpet before dying down for the summer. This is a form of *Muscari armeniacum*, its blue just tinged with violet; *M. azureum* [Z 7–8] and *M. aucheri* (*M. tubergenianum*) [Z 6–8] are a clearer shade of sky blue, and *M. neglectum* is deep indigo blue, paler in bud, with the same white-margined 'grapes'. Smaller than these is *M. botryoides* [Z 2–8], of which the white form is especially appealing. All grow in any well-drained, fertile soil, in sun, and can be increased by division of the clumps of bulbs.

Myosotis

biennials or perennials H 10–35cm/4–15in S 10–30cm/4–12in spring Z 4–8

Forget-me-nots are versatile, variable, and indispensable. In their smaller manifestations as neat little clumps set with flowers of lapis blue, most intense in the selection 'Royal Blue' (see page 138) – or, if you must, pink or white – they will tuck into the smallest corner; but they come also as casual, branching plants for making drifts of sky blue amid shrubs or under orchard trees. They are often used as spring bedding, with tulips, and for such formal occasions seed of the selected strain should be sown in late spring or early summer, the plants set in their flowering positions in autumn when the bulbs are planted. In wilder quarters they can be left to self-sow, which they will do freely – too freely, perhaps, but the seedlings are easy enough to tweak out where they are not wanted.

Narcissus

bulbous perennials H 15–35cm/6–15in S:7.5cm/3in spring Z 4–9 [unless indicated]

The place for big trumpet and large-cup daffodils is the showbench, in my view, not the garden: with rare exceptions they look equally gross and misplaced in grass or in the border. Among the exceptions I include the original pink daffodil, *Narcissus* 'Mrs R. O. Backhouse', for she is modest in size and thanks to her colouring – peach trumpet, ivory perianth – the perfect accompaniment to the apricot and pale copper tones of unfurling epimedium foliage. I have a weakness, too, for 'Binkie', a reverse bicolor in cool chartreuse green paling to lemon-sorbet with an ice-white cup. But even these are large compared with the half-height daffodils, which are more elegantly proportioned, and consequently more appealing in the border than the large flowered kinds: 'Dove Wings', 'Charity May' and 'Jenny' [Z 6–9] in white and primrose, and the ivory and cream miniature trumpet 'W. P. Milner' which I once grew with the black-leaved ophiopogon. 'Tête-à-Tête' [Z 6–9] is a neat little bunch-headed, short-trumpeted daffodil, citron and yolk-yellow. There are half-height trumpets in brighter yellow too – 'February Gold', and 'Peeping Tom' [both z 6–9] with his very long, slender trumpet. They will grow in any fertile, well-drained border soil, and if you set them between clumps of hostas or peonies, say, their dying foliage will be masked.

Daintier still are *N. triandrus* var. *triandrus*, the angel's tears, and derivatives such as ivory 'April Tears' and soft lemon 'Hawera', with their small, nodding flowers, several to a stem, and narrow, discreet leaves, so unlike the floppy, obtrusive foliage of big trumpet daffodils. The hybrids are happy in light shade, but the angel's tears needs a warm, sunny place. The taller *N. tazetta* [z 8–10] also has several small, short-cupped flowers to a stem, that look at you immodestly; its derivatives in yellow, 'Grand Soleil d'Or', and the very similar white *N. papyraceus* ('Paper White') [z 8–10] are familiar as bulbs for winter flowering indoors, but can also be grown in warm, sheltered places outside. They all have a delicious fragrance, with something of the poignancy of wintersweet to it.

All these narcissi can be increased by division, and indeed as the clumps become congested and flowering correspondingly reduced, they will be all the better for lifting, splitting and replanting.

Narcissi and hostas make ideal companions, the leaves of the hostas expanding to conceal the dying narcissus foliage. 'Hawera', with its dainty nodding blooms and fine grassy foliage, is set off here by Hosta fortunei *var.* hyacinthina.

The crinkled, glistening petals of Nerine bowdenii *seem all the brighter for being set against the rich mauve-pink goblets of* Colchicum speciosum.

NECTAROSCORDUM SICULUM

bulbous perennial H 90cm/3ft S 30cm/1ft
late spring Z 4–10

More familiar perhaps as *Allium siculum*, this is a striking plant with tall heads of dusky reddish bells that nod at first, turning upright as they develop into parchment-coloured seedheads, at which point they look like Bavarian castles, all towers and turrets (see page 137) The bulbs increase fast by stolons,which can be divided; seed is another easy method of increase. Any fertile, well-drained soil, in sun, is suitable.

NERINE

bulbous perennials H 60cm/2ft S 15–23cm/6–9in
autumn Z 7–9

Nerines flower in autumn, but they have the soul of summer in their clear, lovely colours. Their petals are covered with tiny, pearl-like cells that glisten and sparkle in the light. In *Nerine bowdenii*, the narrow segments, which vary in colour from pale to rich candy pink, are markedly crinkled. Accompanied by the strong pinks and magentas of *novi-angliae* Michaelmas daisies, the bright mauve-pink of colchicums and the clustered violet berries and pink autumn foliage of callicarpas, these nerines give the lie to the notion of autumn as a season of flaming scarlets and golds. They are somewhat frost-resistant, but need a sheltered place in well-drained soil in the sun, for the bulbs need a good baking in the summer to flower freely; furthermore, they prefer to grow with their snouts at or just above soil level, and the leaves, appearing after the flowers, are also vulnerable to winter frosts. Slight damage is unsightly, severe damage deprives the bulbs of nourishment for next season's flowers. Increase is by division while the bulbs are dormant in summer.

NICOTIANA

annuals/perennials H 60cm–2.1m/2–7ft
S 30–90cm/1–3ft summer to autumn
Z 7–10 [unless indicated]

Tobacco flowers come in many variants, and of the modern hybrids, too few, especially among the coloured or day-awake strains, are endowed with the wonderful perfume that floats on the air of warm summer evenings. Rich crimson tobaccos are superb in all-red plantings, with purple foliage, or contrasted with silver leaves; the coloured strains also include the famous *Nicotiana* 'Lime Green' and a delicate pale, slightly peachy pink.

For the real, voluptuous perfume, you must forgo colour and lay hands on the plant whose name I have never managed properly to ascertain, but which aficianados call *N. alata* 'Grandiflora'. Its white flowers are backed with khaki and stay folded into camouflaged anonymity until evening, when they expand their petals and pour out their fragrance. If you have ample space, you can also enjoy the terrific presence and potent night-time perfume of *N. sylvestris* [Z 8–10]. Here is a plant that will easily overtop you, its great, clammy, pale green leaves spreading a weed-excluding blanket almost a metre/yard wide in the rich, leafy soil it likes, while above you towers a pyramid of many long-tubed white flowers, gleaming in the dusk. Even a single plant is substantial enough, and generous enough with its perfume, to earn its keep. Its expansive ways make it ideal to plant where spring bulbs or early-flowering, early dormant perennials are grown and would otherwise leave an unsightly gap. A well-fed *N. langsdorfii* [Z 8–10] is no more than shoulder-high, tall enough to peer into the small, lime-green flowers, their little frilled lobes flaring around azure anthers. These have no pretensions to fragrance, but great charm, especially when massed in an airy green cloud.

All these tobaccos are perennial in mild climates, developing more or less fleshy roots, but are easily raised afresh from seed each year in colder regions, often even sowing themselves. They grow well in light shade.

OSTEOSPERMUM

evergreen perennials H 15–60cm/6in–2ft
S 30–60cm/1–2ft summer Z 9–10

Alluring daisies for mild climates or for summer bedding, the osteospermums vary in habit from trailing to upright. One of the most frost-resistant is *Osteospermum* 'Prostratum', a spreader as its name implies, with large, glistening white ray-florets around an inky blue disk, the slaty tones of which are echoed on the reverse of the rays. 'Silver Sparkler' is similar in flower, not quite so flat in habit, and distinguished by its cream-margined leaves, the whole thing very pale and fresh-looking. Then there are two cultivars with crimped petals, giving each ray floret the outline of a spoonbill's beak and revealing the contrasting inky blue of the reverse: 'Pink Whirls' and white 'Whirligig'. Both are of upright habit. All the osteospermums can be easily maintained in frosty areas if you take cuttings in autumn, overwintering them in a frost-free place and planting them out in a sunny position in well-drained soil after the last frosts.

The dark backdrop, and the immaculately clipped yews to right and left, are the perfect setting for the huge, pale leaves and soaring flowerheads of Nicotiana sylvestris, *grandest of the tobacco flowers. It is surrounded by* Salvia farinacea *in blue and white forms.*

At its best, Osteospermum *'Whirligig' bears these symmetrical wheels of pure, glistening white set off by the indigo-blue disk, the crimped petals revealing, where pinched-in, a glimpse of their inky reverse.*

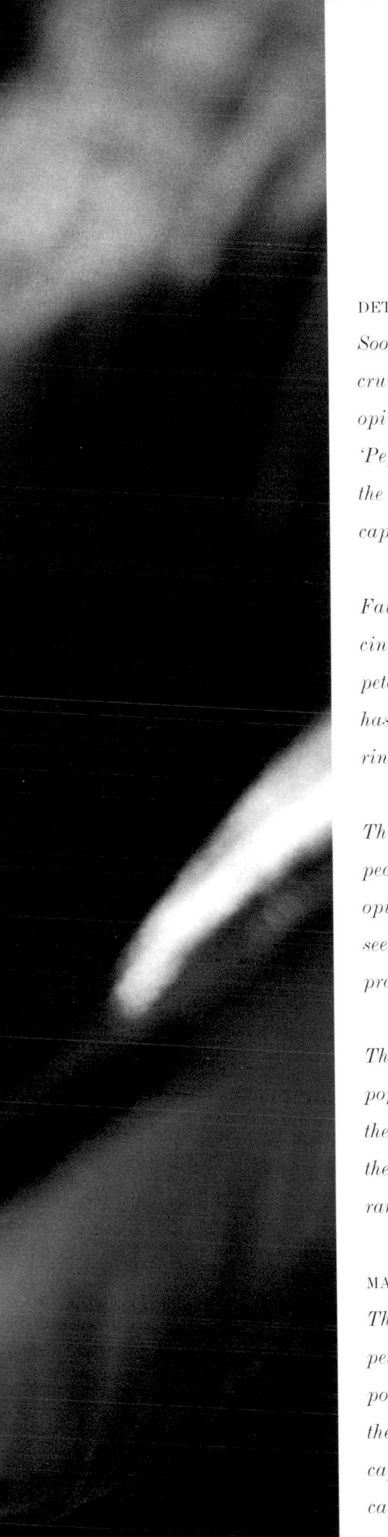

papaver
silken glories

DETAILS FROM TOP:
Soon after bud burst the crumpled petals of single opium poppies, such as 'Pepperbox', drop, leaving the glaucous-grey seed capsules.

Faintly smudged with cinnabar at the base of each petal, this Papaver oriental *has the typical shaggy, black ring of stamens.*

This frilled confection is a peony-flowered Series opium poppy, which will seed itself to leave countless progeny.

The petals of Shirley poppies seem to be made of the finest silk, endowing their glowing colours with a rare quality of translucence.

MAIN PICTURE:
These flaunting, silken petals of a single opium poppy will soon fall to leave the smooth globe and fluted cap of the poppy-seed capsule unadorned.

Papaver

perennials or annuals H 15–120cm/6in–4ft
early to high summer Z 3–7

Poppies are a delight on sunny summers' days, with their crumpled silken petals bursting from plump buds. They bask in full sun, in dry soil, poor rather than rich. Although the oriental poppies, *Papaver orientale*, are long-lived perennials, their hirsute green foliage dies away soon after midsummer; they are a glorious but fleeting incident in the early summer border. Their flowers are typically scarlet, with a maroon-black central blotch and shaggy indigo to black stamens surrounding the dark boss of the seed-capsule. The old vermilion, white and pink cultivars have been joined by a range of delicious colours: Turkish-delight pastels, strawberry-pink, melon, orange, salmon and plum, some with fringed or picotee petals. Most are single-flowered, displaying their black smudges; a few are blotchless; double-flowered cultivars are loose and full or quilled and pompon-like, as in the diminutive, orange-flowered *P.* 'Fireball'. All are increased by division or root cuttings.

The annual poppy of European cornfields, which bloomed in such scarlet profusion on the battlefields of Flanders, is *P. rhoeas*. In the 1880s, an English clergyman, the Revd. W. Wilks, discovered a white-edged corn poppy and from this produced the Shirley strain that encompasses white, pinks ranging from shell to mauve, slate-blues, and doubles in all these colours, always with the white base of the original.

Shirley poppies, so much daintier than the assertive opium poppies, come in delicious pastel shades, a far cry from the scarlet wildling of cornfields. Here, Queen Anne's lace is an airy companion.

The annual opium poppy, *P. somniferum*, comes in singles or powder-puff doubles, in shades of pink, lilac, white and cherry-red, set off by smooth, glaucous-grey foliage. The flowers are followed by blue-grey seed heads which are hardly less decorative; they shake their seeds out like pepper from a pot at a light breeze, and every seed seems to germinate where it lands.

P. commutatum, the ladybird poppy, is best raised singly in pots from an autumn sowing (wet conditions in winter may cause stem rot). Its clumps of finely-cut foliage are topped by intense scarlet flowers with a glossy black blotch at the base of each petal.

The castor oil plant, Ricinus communis, *is valued above all for its bold foliage, often richly tinted when young; but the spires of crimson bobble flowers are also handsome in their season.*

'Blepharophylla' means 'with eyelashed leaves', referring to the fine hairs along the margins of the leaves, but it is for its refulgent scarlet plush flowers that Salvia blepharophylla *is grown.*

Pulsatilla vulgaris

herbaceous perennial H 30cm/1ft S 30cm/1ft spring Z 4–9

Wandering among splendidly gothic rock formations in south western France, many years ago, I came upon a sunlit patch of grass, tucked among the rocks as if it were a courtyard in a ruined castle, in which pasque flowers grew by the hundred, lavender-blue and white and mauve, each silken-haired flower nodding over feathery leaves. But you do not need rocks for *Pulsatilla vulgaris* to grace your garden; merely a sunny corner and freely-draining soil. As well as the colours I found, there are deeper red-purples and near-pinks to be had, but none more beautiful, to my eye, than the pure whites with silvery hairs. The seeds ripen by midsummer and, sown fresh, are the best means of increase. Another method is root cuttings.

Ricinus communis

perennial grown as annual H 1.8–2.4m/6–8ft S 1.8–2.4m/6–8ft foliage Z 9–10

From seed sown in late spring, the seedlings kept moving in rich compost (and provided they are not checked by cool weather), the castor oil plant makes a grand foliage plant with bold, palmate leaves. *Ricinus communis* 'Carmencita' has rich bronze-purple foliage and red flowers and the new foliage of 'Impala' is mahogany-red, its flowers sulphur-yellow. All add a tropical lushness to border plantings, with cannas and bananas, as well as phormiums for contrast.

Salvia

herbaceous and evergreen perennials and shrubs H 45cm–1.8m/1½–6ft S 45–90cm/1½–3ft summer, autumn Z 8–10 [unless indicated]

From Mexico and Central and South America come a number of colourful sages which far outshine the scarlet salvia so widely grown for bedding, yet without any of its garishness. Some have flowers that might have been cut from plush velvet, others are as brilliantly blue as a gentian, and some form shrubs freely spangled with bright, dainty flowers. If scarlet appeals to you, the choice is between the low-growing *Salvia blepharophylla* [Z 9–10], with its large flowers on short stems and creeping roots, to the tall, velvety-furry *S. fulgens* [Z 9–10] and *S. gesneriiflora* [Z 9–10]. Of similar style to

S. blepharophylla, but with dark foliage and rich magenta-crimson, plush-textured flowers, is *S. buchananii* [Z 9–10]. Large flowers also belong to *S. patens*, which is easily raised from seed to produce its ultramarine-blue the same year. A less familiar blue, smaller of flower and more sprawling of habit, is *S. cacaliifolia* (see page 139) [Z 9–10]. The tall *S. guaranitica* [Z 7–10] comes in different styles, from plain royal blue to 'Black and Blue', in which the rich colouring is enhanced by black calyces, and mid-blue, green-calyxed 'Blue Enigma'. In *Salvia discolor* [Z 9–10] the flowers themselves are almost black, and are set off by white-felted foliage.

The narrow leaves of *S. leucantha* [Z 7–10] are grey, harmonizing with the long, slender, arching spikes of white and lilac, velvety flowers. *S. confertiflora* [Z 9–10] also has long, slender, furry spikes, but the effect is wholly different, for this tall plant with bold foliage, brownish beneath and with red stalks (and smelling nastily of burnt rubber when handled), holds its spikes tautly erect, and their colouring is unique, sienna brown in plush, cinnabar-red calyces. Another big, shrubby sage with large, pointed leaves is *S. involucrata*, in which the stout spikes of bright magenta-pink flowers are unusually fat-budded; 'Bethellii' is especially striking, with long spikes.

The slighter shrubs, *S. greggii* [Z 9–10] and *S. microphylla*, have foliage with the sweaty smell that earns some sages the politically-incorrect nickname 'hot housemaid'. The first has magenta-carmine flowers, varying to white in 'Alba', or to 'Peach' and 'Raspberry Royal'; the second has deep red flowers in dark calyces, and its var. *microphylla* (var. *neurepia*) has larger, paler green leaves with clear, soft scarlet flowers. In *S. elegans* 'Scarlet Pineapple' the slender, even anorexic crimson-scarlet flowers, often appearing in winter, are a secondary attraction compared with the delicious pineapple aroma of the foliage. Smelliest of the sages is *S. sclarea* var. *turkestanica*, the Vatican sage. But for this defect, it is a fine plant; of biennial habit, with sprays of papery flowers in lavender-blue or pink over a long summer season.

All these sages, large and small alike, do best in sunny places, in well-drained soil, and can be increased by cuttings; as noted, *S. patens* is best raised from seed, and those with creeping roots can be divided.

SCILLA

bulbous perennials
H 7.5–15cm/3–6in S 5cm/2in
early spring Z 2–10 [unless indicated]

Like the chionodoxas that they resemble (see page 146), the squills are easy and undemanding in any good, well-drained soil in sun or light shade, seeding themselves to make wide patches of blue. In *Scilla siberica* this is unusually pure in tone, without the faint lilac cast of the chionodoxas. 'Spring Beauty' is a fine selection, and there is also a white form. *S. bifolia* [Z 2–10] runs to mauve-pink, in 'Rosea', as well as the blue, which varies from ultramarine to lilac. Selected forms are increased by division of the clumps of bulbs.

There is a strange intensity to the blue-flowered bulbs of early spring, and in none more so than Scilla siberica *'Spring Beauty', here growing around half height daffodils,* Narcissus pseudonarcissus.

At the very end of the tulip season the exquisite flowers of Tulipa sprengeri *open. It is equally happy in the border or, as here, floating above ox-eye daisies growing in thin grass.*

Tulipa

bulbous perennials H 10–35cm/4–15in
S 10–15cm/4–6in spring Z 4–8 [unless indicated]

Everyone has their favourites among bedding tulips – the slender Darwins, elegant lily-flowered, frilled and goffered parrots, petticoated doubles, painted Rembrandts, all best lifted each year. The only one I offer you here – a personal favourite not seen enough in gardens – is 'Couleur Cardinal', a stocky, early-flowering tulip with square-shouldered flowers of unique colouring, oxblood red and cinnabar bloomed with plum-purple.

Among tulip species there are plenty of good things to enliven spring borders. And some are very lively indeed. *Tulipa praestans* 'Fusilier' bears several small, pointy-petalled flowers of vivid orange-vermilion on each stem (see page 141), while the smaller *T. linifolia* has brilliant scarlet flowers over narrow, crinkly, blue-grey leaves that spread out flat on the ground. The Batalinii Group (*T. batalinii*) is quieter, with the same pretty foliage setting off flowers of buff yellow, bronze or pale apricot with an olive-green central blotch. Whereas *T. praestans* will go on year after year without lifting, *T. linifolia* in all its manifestations is the better for being lifted and dried off each year.

The lady tulip, *T. clusiana* [Z 3–8] (see page 137), is as slender and graceful as her pet name suggests, with candle-flame petals of cream marked on the outside with crimson-pink on 30cm/12in stems; *T. clusiana* var. *chrysantha* has the same red stainings on a clear yellow ground . Such colours belong, too, to the waterlily tulip, *T. kaufmanniana*, its long, slim buds, pink- or red-washed outside, opening starry-wide in the sun to show their cream or yellow interior. The broad, greyish leaves are sometimes wavy-edged.

T. saxatilis, a Cretan native, has running roots, and given half a chance will run instead of flowering; but if you can confine it, by sinking slates vertically into the ground around its allotted patch perhaps, it will settle down to produce its bright lilac-pink, yellow-eyed flowers, opening rather later than those of the waterlily tulip. Last of all, in early summer, appears *T. sprengeri*, which if it likes you will naturalize in thin grass, in light shade or in sun, in damp soil or stodgy. It has slender flowers, satiny vermilion inside and matt orange-buff on the exterior. If you can obtain seed, it should produce flowering-sized bulbs within three years. The more usual method of propagation of tulips, however, is by division of the bulbs.

VERBENA

evergreen perennials H 15cm/6in
S 30–45cm/1–1½ft summer Z 6–9 [unless indicated]

The bedding verbenas that are perpetuated by cuttings, as distinct from seed strains, are invaluable for adding colour to the summer border; and, being sideways spreaders of some vigour, you need far fewer plants than of the seed strains to make a splash. Those with pink or lilac flowers are generally fragrant: 'Silver Anne' ('Pink Bouquet') in candy pink, 'Sissinghurst' in potent magenta. The diminutive *Verbena peruviana* [Z 9–10] is even more assertive in its vermilion-scarlet colouring; it also comes in pure white, 'Alba'. Autumn cuttings, overwintered in a frost-free place, will keep these verbenas going year after year in regions where the winters are too cold for them to survive.

VIOLA

perennials H 15cm/6in S 25cm/10in summer Z 5–7

Like verbenas, pansies, violas and violettas come in seed strains or as named cultivars kept going by cuttings. Seed catalogues are full of large-flowered pansies, with or without frowning faces, but my preference is for 'Maggie Mott', a famous old lavender-blue cultivar. If you appreciate odd colours, 'Irish Molly', in khaki and bronze, is sure to appeal. Specialist growers have scores of named cultivars, many of them highly desirable. In my experience, they need frequent renewal from cuttings; but it is never a problem to find a corner to tuck them into, preferably in light shade and cool soil. Treated thus, they will adorn the garden for weeks on months on end.

Verbena *'Silver Anne' displays a play of colours from shell to candy pink, while 'Sissinghurst' remains resolutely the same brilliant magenta from first opening. Behind are the white daisies of an* Argyranthemum.

ZIGADENUS ELEGANS

summer H 60cm/2ft S 23cm/9in bulbous perennial
Z 3–9

This discreet and slender plant is for those who value green flowers; more exactly, the little stars of *Zigadenus elegans* are ivory washed with green, and borne in airy spires on pale stems. It grows best in sun, in well-drained soil, and can be increased by division of the clumps of bulbs, or by seed.

Viola *'Maggie Mott' is an enduring favourite for her clarity of colour and easy temperament.*

The little alabaster-green stars of Zigadenus elegans *merit a close look, for they are marked with deeper green at the base of each segment, with the little central pointel lifting the stamens clear.*

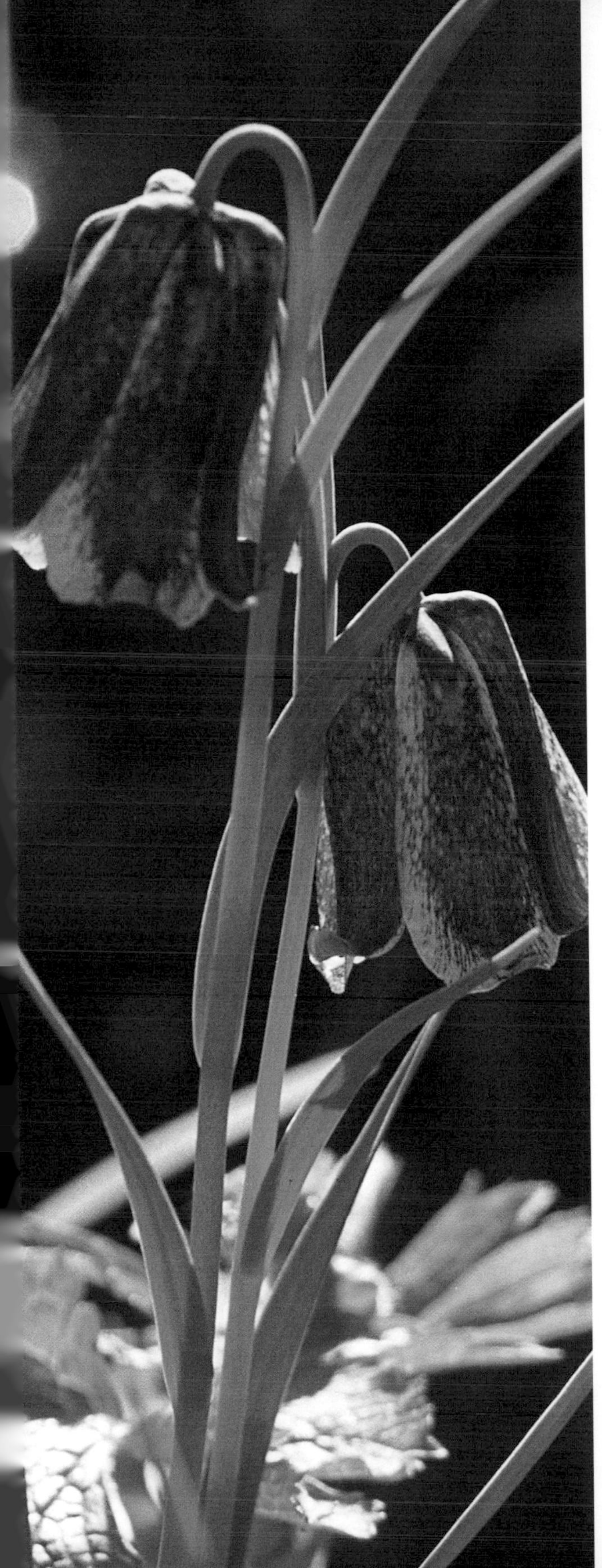

woodland & orchard

plants for shady & natural-looking areas

The fritillary of the Pyrenees, Fritillaria pyrenaica, *has hints of the chequered exterior familiar in the snake's head fritillary,* F. meleagris, *and the same high-shouldered, nodding bell-shape. But in the Pyrenean species the petal tips are flicked up, to reveal their greeny-gold reverse and the lemon margins of the inner segments.*

A single white-barked birch, an old nut tree, a rowan hung in autumn with scarlet berries – any one of these can create the ambience of a woodland in miniature in even the smallest garden. The leafy branches will filter the sun in summer and, even though bare, can mitigate winter's frosts; while all the year the shelter from wind creates a congenial home for some of nature's most appealing wildlings, the flowers of the forest floor and the fronds of ferns. Wood anemones and primroses, dog's tooth violets and trout lilies, wake robins and Lenten roses – the very names are a foretaste of their charms. Hydrangeas hold the stage in summer, ahead of the autumn pageant of baneberries and toad lilies, willow gentians, and the polished lapis-blue berries of dianellas. The winter woodland belongs to a few stalwart ferns, tiny cyclamen, and the marbled arum, beneath bare branches. In another mood, an old orchard, or even a single ancient, gnarled apple or pear tree growing in thin, shaded-out grass, may echo the meadow habitat of fritillaries, columbines, cuckoo flowers and cowslips – a primavera of flowers for spring and early summer.

woodland & orchard

The classic woodland garden is the rhododendron woodland, in which rhododendrons in all their diversity, with opulent bells or flights of airy flowers, the leaves of some backed with tawny or silver felt, others with lovely strokeable bark, are joined by a supporting cast of camellias, magnolias, pieris, and vacciniums.

BELOW LEFT *Hybrid deciduous azaleas derive their butterfly flowers and pure colours from a number of wild species, including* Rhododendron occidentale, *which has bequeathed its fragrance to the peach-pink 'Exquisitum'. The white azalea is 'Persil'. Overhead are the waxen, nodding blooms of* Magnolia sieboldii.

ABOVE *After fertilization the petals of* Helleborus orientalis *remain around the seed pods, shielding them from inclement weather.*

Even the smallest, one-tree woodland imposes its character on the plants that will find shelter and coolth in its compass. At its most informal, the woodland garden is barely distinct from a native copse, and the sensitive gardener will take care to include nothing that jars, while carefully managing the plantings so that delicate wildlings are not swamped by muscular weeds. Once admit that the world is your palette, however, and you begin to create an idealized woodland, an Eden in which plants from different continents co-exist. The potential both for harmonious compositions and for lapses of taste becomes much greater.

The great determinant, however, is soil. The classic woodland garden is the rhododendron woodland which can only be achieved on acid soil, either naturally leafy and moist, or – if thin and sandy – so conscientiously nourished with leafmould and

The epimediums are almost the perfect groundlings for woodland plantings. Epimedium × youngianum *is one of the prettiest of this tribe, with elegant foliage and flights of dancing flowers like tiny columbines.*

Vibrant, dark tones of foliage and flower are lit by the white beads of Muscari botryoides *'Album', the ivory foam of tiarella, and the sharp golden-green of feverfew. The dark-leaved double primrose is 'Captain Blood', the velvety crimson foliage to the right is that of* Euphorbia dulcis *'Chameleon'.*

mulched with autumn's fallen leaves each year that its deficiencies are made good. Between the noble shrubs that demand such conditions, the aristocrats of cool and leafy shade will flourish: trilliums, lapis-berried gaultherias and Himalayan blue poppies.

The most difficult soil for a would-be woodland gardener is thin, dry chalk. But an alkaline soil that has some body to it can grow many superb things beneath the noble, lime-tolerant shrubs – mahonias, many viburnums, some hydrangeas, osmanthus and the like – that can be picked out from the trees and shrubs in Chapter 1. Beneath them will grow winter aconites and snowdrops, epimediums and ferns, dicentras, martagon lilies and baneberries, pulmonarias and lily-of-the-valley. Whether acid-loving or lime-tolerant, most of these plants thrive where they are shielded not only from scorching sun, but also from wind, which desiccates their often thin-textured foliage, ill-adapted to moisture loss. Sheltering shrubs, as well as a spreading overhead canopy, may be needed to protect them, especially in spring, when their tender new growths are expanding and vulnerable to drying winds or a sudden spell of hot weather.

woodland & orchard

To western eyes, accustomed to scarlet poppies, the first sight of the fabled Himalayan blue poppy, Meconopsis betonicifolia, *is breathtaking. There is nothing to rival its pure tints of ultramarine and caerulean blue, and the poise of the silken petals around the central boss.*

In this woodland and water scene, Viburnum opulus *'Roseum' and the powerfully fragrant yellow* Rhododendron luteum *grow with shuttlecock ferns* (Matteuccia struthiopteris) *and rodgersias.*

Another kind of gardening beneath trees is what one may call orchard gardening. By this I mean, or imagine, growing plants in the grass beneath an old apple or pear tree, that may or may not yield much fruit, but is likely to have its own beauty of blossom and of outline and so to be worth retaining. Dancing columbines, cuckoo flowers, Lent lilies, the snake's head and Pyrenean fritillaries, cheerful cowslips and the more robust primroses, meadow geranium, and of course the ubiquitous daisy: all these will grow in thin grass among trees.

For fritillaries and Lent lilies – and true lilies such as the martagons and *Lilium pyrenaicum*, too – to naturalize in such conditions, they must be allowed to seed; and that means not cutting the grass too soon in summer, or at the very least steering the mower around the stems and ripening seedheads of your bulbs so that the seeds can mature and fall. Alternatively, you can save the seeds and sow them in trays, pricking out the tiny bulbs and growing them on until large enough to fend for themselves. The extra trouble is well repaid by the far more rapid increase in the size of your colonies, and is especially worthwhile if you want to make a drift of something special, such as white snake's head fritillaries.

The first cut of the season, then, is best made after midsummer, to allow for natural seeding. The next can be made in late summer, before autumn bulbs – colchicums, autumn-flowering crocuses – emerge; and in wet seasons a third, intermediate cut may be needed. It is best to take away the clippings and compost them; for if they are left to enrich the soil where they fall the coarser grasses will thrive at the expense of the finer ones and the bulbs and herbaceous perennials you want to encourage, and which will make a primavera meadow from your patch of orchard grass.

LEFT BELOW *The cerulean and ultramarine blues of lacecap hydrangeas,* H. macrophylla *'Lilacina', dance in the dappled sunlight of the now lush and leafy woodland, a cool refuge from summer's sultry heat.*

plants for shady & natural-looking areas

Did nature's hand, or that of a sensitive gardener, arrange this spring woodland scene? White wood anemones (Anemone nemorosa) *mingle with the ardent blue of* Scilla bifolia, *magenta-pink cyclamen, half-height yellow narcissus, and the marbled arrow-head leaves of* Arum italicum, *dappled with sunlight filtered through the canopy above.*

Actaea

herbaceous perennial H 90cm/3ft S 45cm/1½ft
autumn Z 3–9

Amid the gold and scarlet of autumn foliage and fruits, the pure white berries of Actaea alba *gleam in the shadows beneath the tree canopy.*

Unlike many woodlanders, the baneberries come into their own in autumn, when their spikes of berries ripen – the flowers that precede them are an unremarkable white fuzz, though the dissected leaves are decorative. In *Actaea rubra* the fruits are bright, shining scarlet, and in *A. alba* the smaller fruits are pure white and held in spikes on fleshy, scarlet stalks. Baneberries need a cool, leafy, fertile soil in a lightly shaded place, and can be increased by division or seed sown when ripe in autumn or early winter. A word of caution, suggested by the name: the berries are poisonous.

Adiantum

deciduous fern H 23cm/9in S 23cm/9in
summer foliage Z 3–8 [unless indicated]

Adiantum venustum is a dainty fern very like the tender maidenhair fern of greenhouses, with airy, lacy fronds slowly forming a neat carpet, admirable with miniature epimediums or hardy cyclamen. Another of similar character, though typically slightly taller, is *A. pedatum* [Z 3–8], which has wiry black stems to set off the green of its elegant fronds. Both need leafy, cool soil in a shady, sheltered spot, and can be increased by division or by sowing the spores on moist peat as soon as they begin to fall.

Anemone nemorosa

herbaceous perennials H 15cm/6in S 30cm/12in
spring Z 4–8

The starry, white or faintly pink-suffused *Anemone nemorosa* of Europe's copses and deciduous woodlands is enchanting in a mass; in the garden, though, it is the selected forms with fuller flowers, or in a range of tender colours, or with extra petals, that arouse the collector's urge. There is a double

Despite its dainty looks, Adiantum pedatum *is a tough little fern, well able to hold its own with the purple-leaved, free-spreading* Viola riviana *Purpurea Group* (V. labradorica) *and* Pleioblastus viridistriatus, *the golden-striped bamboo.*

white, 'Flore Pleno', and 'Rosea' is a mauve-pink single; but most appealing of all are the so-called blues, in reality gentle lavender and lilac, often with grey or fawn reverse: 'Robinsoniana', 'Allenii' and others. Of similar style to the wood anemone is *A.* × *lipsiensis* (*A. ranunculoides*), differing in its buttercup-yellow flowers. All these little anemones have dissected foliage and running roots that are happiest in cool, leafy soil; they are easily increased by division, every little scrap of root with a growing point willing to make a new plant. They are charming with choice primroses.

AQUILEGIA

herbaceous perennials H 23–90cm/9in–3ft
S 23–60cm/9in–2ft early summer Z 3–8

Among the tribe of columbines are two pretty miniatures for cool, lightly shaded places. *Aquilegia flabellata* var. *pumila* f. *alba*, living up to the rule of thumb that the smaller the plant, the longer the name it bears, is a compact little thing with smooth, grey-green leaves and tubby, ivory-cream flowers on short stems (*pumila* itself, like the full-sized *A. flabellata*, has milky blue flowers). In contrast, *A. viridiflora* has dissected leaves and discreet, fragrant, green and maroon flowers. In wider spaces, at woodland margins or in thin orchard grass, the much taller and more robust, cobalt-blue *A.* 'Hensol Harebell' should naturalize and seed itself; soft pink shades also crop up (see page 188), lovely with the dusty pink cow parsley, *Chaerophyllum hirsutum*. All these columbines can be grown from seed; although the taller kinds, especially the named ones, may not come true to type. If you have a strain that reliably produces good blues or smoky pink, count yourself lucky.

The white wood anemone, Anemone nemorosa, *grows here with the oxlip,* Primula elatior. *Both appreciate the leafy soil that forms beneath deciduous trees.*

Certain plants demand close scrutiny to reveal their charms; such is alabaster-green and maroon Aquilegia viridiflora, *subtle of colour and delicate of perfume.*

ARISAEMA

tuberous-rooted perennials H 30–45cm/1–1½ft S 30–45cm/1–1½ft spring, summer Z 5–8

These arum relatives are often bizarre, with their mottlings and stripings on leaf and spathe; at least two species are beautiful as well. *Arisaema sikokianum* has a slender-waisted, dark chocolate-brown spathe opening in spring before the leaves unfurl; it encloses an ivory-white, broad spadix which gleams pale against the dark, hooded spathe. Flowering later, at midsummer, is *A. candidissimum*. Its spathe is pure white striped with pale pink and is followed by broad leaves and a club of orange fruits, typical of the aroid family.

They deserve to stand alone, set off only by a mulch of dark leafmould. Both species can be raised from seed, and the rounded tubers also increase quite freely in moist, leafy soil.

In a genus that runs to subfusc brown and purple-green colourings, Arisaema candidissimum *stands out on account of its delicate pink, white-striped spathes, complemented by the broad, waxy textured leaves.*

The bold arrow-head, richly marbled leaves of Arum italicum *subsp.* italicum *'Marmoratum' would be handsome at any season; in winter, they are doubly precious. Here they accompany the double snowdrop,* Galanthus nivalis *'Flore Pleno'.*

ARUM ITALICUM *SUBSP.* ITALICUM *'MARMORATUM'*

tuberous-rooted winter-green perennial H 45cm/1½ft S 30cm/1ft spring Z 6–9

In this superior version of the hedgerow lords and ladies or cuckoo pint, the spathes that open in spring are unremarkable in greenish-white, and are followed by showy cylindrical spikes of orange-red berries in summer. But the leaves are what we grow them for. Emerging in autumn and lasting through the winter, they have an elegant, narrow spear-head outline, and their rich, glossy green is enhanced by conspicuous white marbling, as the name *Arum italicum* var. *italicum* 'Marmoratum' suggests (it may also be listed as *A. italicum pictum*). It makes a striking companion for a white-flowered *Daphne mezereum*, and for the spreading *Ribes laurifolium* with its leathery leaves and creamy-green winter flowers.

Any fertile soil is suitable for this undemanding plant, which can be increased by division as the leaves dies away.

ATHYRIUM NIPONICUM *VAR.* PICTUM

deciduous fern H 30cm/1ft S 45cm/1½ft
summer foliage Z 3–8

Athyrium niponicum var. *pictum* (*A. goeringianum* 'Pictum') has fronds of classic ferny laciness, but in place of the usual greenery it is subtly and unusually coloured in dove grey and pewter, flushed with rosy maroon, on burgundy-red stalks. Its subfusc tones are ideal with companions such as lilac-pink, coppery-leaved *Primula* 'Guinevere', *Helleborus lividus* which echoes its colouring and adds jade and celadon to the harmony, and *Anemonopsis macrophylla*, which has nodding, waxy flowers of slate-blue and white.

All appreciate cool, moist, leafy soil and a degree of shelter. The fern can be increased by division or from spores.

CARDAMINE

herbaceous prennials H 23–45cm/9in–1½ft
S 23–60cm/9in–2ft spring Z 4–9

The toothworts (formerly *Dentaria*) and cuckoo flowers are pretty spring flowers with a quality of freshness typified by the lady's smock, *Cardamine pratensis*, of damp high latitude and subalpine meadows, which spreads its fine lace of milky mauve generously over the grass. As well as the typical single there is a double-flowered variant, 'Flore Pleno'. The larger flowers of *C. pentaphyllos* (*Dentaria digitata*) are a more decided shade of mauve-pink, delightful with the cool yellow of cowslips.

Cool, moist soil and some shade are the preference of the toothworts and cuckoo flowers, which can be increased by division in autumn to make drifts of cool colour in the spring garden.

The double cuckoo flower, Cardamine pratensis *'Flore Pleno', is set off by the metallic purple foliage of a bugle* (Ajuga).

Uniquely among hardy ferns, Athyrium niponicum *var.* pictum *has silvered fronds with the midribs picked out in dove-pink, adding subtlety of colour to elegance of outline.*

If only a picture could capture the waxen texture of the bells of lily-of-the-valley, let alone its sweet perfume, the epitome of spring freshness and innocence. But who has not picked, or bought from a flower seller, a little bunch from which to inhale their fragrance?

Codonopsis

herbaceous perennials H 60cm–1.2m/2–4ft S 60cm–1.2m/2–4ft late summer Z 5–8

The larger species of *Codonopsis* are all inclined to sprawl or even decidedly to twine their way through neighbouring shrubs – something light and not too leafy, so that the codonopsis bells are not hidden from view, or peasticks if you thoughtfully supply them. In *C. convolvulacea* the wide-open bells are Spode blue, or white in *C. grey-wilsonii* 'Himal Snow' (*C. convolvulacea* 'Alba'). Charming though this is, it is not to be compared with the species with nodding, tubular bells, of which the most alluring is *C. clematidea*, in Wedgwood blue with inner scribblings and dabs of honey-gold and maroon, set off by greyish foliage. *C. ovata* is of similar style but less distinctly marked within.

Despite their delicate looks they are not difficult to establish in well-drained, leafy soil, in part shade and coolth; they can be increased from seed sown in autumn.

Convallaria majalis

herbaceous perennial H 23cm/9in S 30cm/12in late spring Z 2–9

Lily-of-the-valley or *muguet* is one of those unpredictable plants – like the winter aconite, *Eranthis hyemalis* – which spreads rapidly if it likes you, and sulks if it does not; it should be happiest in woodsy soil, but is just as likely to make the desired leafy carpet in the packed soil of an adjoining path or in stiff, soggy clay, while disdaining your carefully-prepared patch. The leaves are pleasant enough in their fresh greenery, but *Convallaria majalis* is loved above all for its sprays of waxy, white, delectably-perfumed bells. 'Fortin's Giant', larger in leaf and more ample in flower, blooms a week or ten days later than the type. The pink-flowered *Convallaria majalis* var. *rosea* is a frailer thing and its flowers have not the exquisite bell-shape of the white.

When starting a lily-of-the-valley planting from bare roots, lay the thongs horizontally and firm the soil around them. If you have access to an established patch you can simply spade out a square of soil complete with roots and plop it in elsewhere to start a new colony; the hole will quickly disappear if you fill it with fresh leafy soil.

CORYDALIS FLEXUOSA

herbaceous perennial H 23cm/9in S 23cm/9in
spring Z 5–8

A comparative newcomer to our gardens, *Corydalis flexuosa* has the delicate, filigree appeal of the genus, with the usual flights of small, spurred flowers, of the clear turquoise or opalescent blue that is so rare and so precious; yet unlike the temperamental *C. cashmeriana* it is an obliging plant, given cool, leafy soil. Several cultivars, named from wild-collected seed, are already available: pale 'China Blue', 'Père David' and 'Purple Leaf', with bronzed foliage to set off the azure flowers. The cool, pale yellow of primroses sets off to perfection the corydalis' opalescent tones, leavened perhaps with the fresh golden-green blades of Bowles' golden grass, *Milium effusum* 'Aureum'. Corydalis can be increased by division, and are well worth growing in drifts.

CYCLAMEN

tuberous perennials H 7.5cm/3in S 5–25cm/2–10in
late winter/early spring, autumn Z 5–9

From babyhood, when its translucent tubers, as small as seed pearls, bear a single marbled leaf, to maturity when a single tuber may be as large as a dinner plate, *Cyclamen hederifolium* is a long-lived plant that will thrive in that most difficult of positions, the rooty soil around the base of a tree, as well as in more congenial conditions between shrubs, in leafy soil. The ivy-shaped leaves are more or less heavily marbled with grey-green, emerging after the flights of ears-back, snub-nosed flowers and lasting into the following summer.

Although the flowers are typically pink, white seedlings often appear, sometimes in great quantity; in one of my gardens a couple of large, pink-flowered tubers, planted at the top of a slope beneath an old apple tree, had within five years produced enough progeny to carpet the entire slope, with a majority of the infants turning out to have pure white flowers. As the leaves last through the winter but die away with the plant's summer dormancy, this species can be planted among the tiny fern *Blechnum penna-marina* (following the example of Christopher Lloyd) which will cover the ground during summer when the cyclamen is leafless. The whites are enchanting with the black-leaved, grassy *Ophiopogon planiscapus* 'Nigrescens', which has black fruits in autumn.

Of the many other species of cyclamen that exist to tempt the collector, I shall mention only one more, equally willing to grow even in dry, rooty places beneath trees as well as in more congenial conditions of woodsy soil. At the turn of winter and spring the chubby flowers of *C. coum* open, their vivid magenta-rose a shout of defiance at the cold. There is also an adorable white form with a carmine 'nose'. The rounded leaves vary from plain dark green to green marbled with grey, the reverse green or deep burgundy-red.

Being so willing to increase by seeding themselves, these cyclamen can quickly be massed into a generous drift. If you start your colony with purchased tubers, buy them growing rather than dried, for they do not respond well to being treated like daffodil or tulip bulbs.

A relative newcomer to our gardens, Corydalis flexuosa *has won many admirers for its opalescent turquoise tints, set off here by the dark leaves that earn the name 'Purple Leaf'.*

Cyclamen hederifolium *seeds itself freely in leafy soil. The leaves that follow these flights of flower are beautiful too in their diversity of grey or jade marblings.*

DIANELLA

evergreen perennial H 1.2m/4ft S 45cm/1½ft
summer, autumn Z 9–10

The berries of Dianella *might have been carved from lapis lazuli and polished to a sheen by some loving hand, so smooth, symmetrical and intensely blue are they.*

The strong sword leaves of these southern hemisphere plants make good, weed-excluding clumps in moist, lime-free soil. Over them, in summer, hover airy sprays of small azure-blue, yellow-anthered flowers, pretty enough in themselves but only fully justifying their existence, to the gardener if not to the plant itself, when succeeded by large, polished, lapis-lazuli blue fruits. *Dianella tasmanica* is one of the tallest and easiest; other species are similar, and if your climate is remotely suitable all are amply worth garden space. They can be increased by division or seed.

There remains, on these fully developed fronds of Dryopteris erythrosora, *just a trace of the tawny pink tints of the unfurling croziers of spring.*

DRYOPTERIS

ferns H 60cm–1.5m/2–5ft S 60–90cm/2–3ft
summer foliage Z 4–8 [unless indicated]

The common male fern, *Dryopteris filix-mas*, is a handsome enough thing with its evergreen shuttle-cock fronds, and easy to grow in even uncongenial, dry places; but it cannot compete for beauty with *D. erythrosora* [Z 5–8], nor for magnificence with *D. wallichiana*. The first, which is deciduous, has thigh-high fronds, coral- and russet-tinted as they unfurl in spring and maturing to glossy green with red spore capsules on the reverse. When suited *D. wallichiana* may grow to shoulder height; the evergreen fronds are at first bright ochre, turning to deep green, on brown-furred stalks.

Both can be increased by division or from spores, and both deserve a place in fluffy, leafy, moist soil, sheltered from wind and sun, to keep the fronds in peak condition.

EOMECON CHIONANTHA

herbaceous perennial H 45cm/1½ft S 45cm/1½ft
spring Z 6–9

The dawn poppy, *Eomecon chionantha*, is one of a choice band of offbeat poppies that demand cool soil and dappled shade. Its nodding white flowers, enhanced by yellow stamens, are borne over beautiful large, rounded, bluish-glaucous leaves. The roots, which are filled with orange-red sap, run freely through loose soil, so the dawn poppy should be kept away from the tiny treasures of the woodland but allowed to spread unhindered among shrubs. It follows that propagation is a simple matter of division.

EPIMEDIUM

evergreen and deciduous perennials
H 15–45cm/6in–1½ft S 23–45cm/9in–1½ft spring
Z 4–8 [unless indicated]

Their flights of dainty flowers rather like tiny columbines (the likeness in some species even extending to the long spurs) are enchanting, but it is for their foliage that epimediums are valued as ground-cover. Best for this purpose are the evergreens, *Epimedium perralderianum* and its hybrid, *E.* × *perralchicum* [Z 5–8], with the semi-evergreen *E. pinnatum* subsp. *colchicum* [Z 5–8]. The first has almost spurless, bright yellow flowers over glossy, tooth-edged leaves; the hybrid is similar, but with the larger yellow flowers and smaller growth of the other parent. The foliage of *E. pinnatum* subsp. *colchicum* itself turns to rust and bronze in autumn and winter. Any of these yellow-flowered epimediums would assort well with other fresh spring tints.

The fully deciduous species tend to be of more modest growth; their foliage emerges in spring in pretty shades of apricot, terracotta, dusky pink and bronze and dies off in autumn in similar tints. One of the smaller is *E.* × *rubrum*, its flowers crimson with white spurs. In *E.* × *warleyense* the small flowers are tangerine over fresh green foliage, less dense than the others. The reddish colouring is probably inherited from its parent *E. alpinum*, a pretty creature with red and yellow flowers. Another hybrid of this, almost evergreen, is *E.* × *cantabrigiense*, with small red and yellow flowers. The blood of *E. pinnatum* subsp. *colchicum* gives *E.* × *versicolor* [Z 5–8] a range of pretty flower tints from pale yellow 'Sulphureum' to the more rarely seen pink-tinted 'Versicolor' (enchanting with small-flowered pink daffodils such as 'Foundling'). The soft tones of 'Sulphureum' are charming with ferns, the smaller Solomon's seals, white-variegated hostas and ivory-flowered *Pseudofumaria alba* (*Corydalis ochroleuca*). The other parent is *E. grandiflorum*, a species of great beauty with larger, long-spurred flowers, and flowers that may be pink ('Rose Queen) or white ('White Queen'). The smallest of epimediums is *E.* × *youngianum* and its variants, white 'Niveum' in which the flowers are set off by sulky purple young foliage, and 'Roseum' in which the flowers are lavender-coloured.

Epimediums are at their best in cool, shady places, in any fertile soil, but if planted at the margin of a pool of shade they will happily grow out into the sun and suffer no damage. They are increased by division. To display the flowers and the tinted new leaves at their best, trim away the foliage of all but the evergreen species in winter.

Pretty as the flowers of epimediums are, like tiny columbines, it is the leaves that earn them a place of honour in the woodland garden. The foliage of Epimedium × rubrum, *suffused with coppery-maroon, is here set off by the soft jade fans of* Alchemilla mollis *in which raindrops lie like pearls.*

erythronium

woodland wildlings

DETAILS FROM TOP:
Its mottled leaves are almost orchid-like, but Erythronium dens-canis *has the small, nodding lily-like flowers typical of the genus.*

The North American Erythronium revolutum *is more graceful than its European cousin, and no less easy-going in leafy soil.*

The nodding, pink flowers of Erythronium revolutum *seem poised to take flight, wings spread wide.*

The name of its cultivar hardly does justice to the exquisite purity of Erythronium californicum *'White Beauty', its swept-back petals enhanced by the protruding stamens.*

MAIN PICTURE:
The soft lemon-yellow flowers of Erythronium *'Pagoda' are washed with pale jade green on the exterior.*

ERYTHRONIUM

bulbous perennials H 10–23cm/4–9in S 10–15cm/4–6in
spring Z 4–8 [unless indicated]

The European dog's tooth violet, *Erythronium dens-canis* [Z 2–7], has smooth, maroon-blotched leaves and nodding flowers, which may be pink, purple or white. It will grow in the thin grass beneath trees; for collectors, there are several named cultivars, all of them desirable and worthy of a choice position in leafy soil, in dappled shade. The North American species betray more clearly their classification in the lily family, with their nodding flowers composed of reflexed, or sometimes starry, petals. Some have the palely marbled leaves that earn them the nickname trout lily. Of this type, one of the finest is 'White Beauty', a selection of *E. californicum* with recurving, ivory petals – *E. californicum* itself has cream or white flowers with tan markings around the yellow eye, over lightly bronzed leaves. 'Pagoda' is an outstanding hybrid, sulphur yellow with a tawny heart. Their colouring comes from the easy but less refined-looking *E. tuolumnense*, which has smallish, sharp yellow flowers over unmarbled leaves. In *E. revolutum* the flowers are pink, contrasting with the bronze-tinted leaves. For all these, as for the choicer selections of the dog's tooth violet, a cool, leafy soil, in dappled shade, is the recipe for success. The bulbs should not be allowed to dry out at any time, and as they spread, they can be divided to make new colonies.

Despite its ethereal looks, Erythronium *'Pagoda' is easy tempered; here it spreads its flighty flowers beneath hanging trails of the weeping cherry,* Prunus × yedoensis *'Shidare-yoshino'.*

FRITILLARIA

bulbous perennials H 23–90cm/9in–3ft
S 7.5–23cm/3–9in spring, early to midsummer
Z 5–8 [unless indicated]

Yet another genus that arouses the collector's instinct on account of their exquisite beauty and diversity, the fritillaries include a few species that thrive in cool, lightly shaded places. The snake's head lily, *Fritillaria meleagris* [Z 4–8], is one of the easiest, happy in the open in a grassy place that is not too dry, or in the thin grass beneath trees, as well as in the open ground among shrubs. Its hanging, squarish flowers are typically murrey-red with deeper chequering; darker or lighter red

The snake's head lily, Fritillaria meleagris, *grows in the wild in damp meadows. Modern cultivation methods have almost banished it from its native habitats, but where the old ways still prevail, it will grow in profusion. The grass in which it grows should remain uncut until the fritillary has ripened and let fall its seed, after midsummer. Thereafter a second cut, in late summer, will help to keep the grass fine; above all, avoid fertilizers, which will encourage coarse grass fit only to choke out the fritillaries and other choice meadow flowers.*

variants occur naturally, and about ten per cent of seedlings, in the wild, are ethereally beautiful in alabaster-white. Slightly taller than this, at 30cm/12in or so, is the exquisite, pale sulphur-yellow *F. pallidiflora*, its quite large nodding flowers shaped like angular tulips. Several species have green lantern- or bell-shaped flowers, sometimes marked with mahogany, as in *F. pontica*, which is green with chocolate tips, or the taller *F. acmopetala* [Z 6–8], jade-green with sienna-brown inner segments. In *F. pyrenaica* the flared bells are gleaming gold with brown markings within, and mahogany-brown outside (see page169). Last to flower, at midsummer, is *F. camtschatcensis* [Z 3–8], a Japanese woodland and subalpine meadow plant with whorls of bright green leaves above which hang near-black bells.

Fritillaries can be propagated by division of the bulbs, or by seed; the snake's head lily, in particular, can be very rapidly increased if every seed is saved and sown in moist compost when ripe, in summer, to be grown on past babyhood before planting out in the open ground.

GENTIANA ASCLEPIADEA

herbaceous perennial H 90cm/3ft S 60cm/2ft
autumn Z 5–8

The willow gentian, *Gentiana asclepiadea*, unlike some of its smaller cousins cherished in rock gardens, is an easy-going woodlander with arching, leafy stems, set with sheaves of pure blue trumpets; there is also a lovely albino touched with ivory and jade in the throat, and pale sky-blues sometimes appear. The white is exquisite with baneberries, especially the white-berried *Actaea alba*; the blues with yellow-fruited *Coriaria terminalis* var. *xanthocarpa* or with the more vigorous toad lilies.

A cool, leafy soil in light shade suits the willow gentian, which can be increased from seed and, once settled in its quarters, asks only to be left alone to spread into ample clumps.

HACQUETIA EPIPACTIS

herbaceous perennial H 10cm/4in S 15cm/6in
early spring Z 5–8

This little plant looks, at first casual glance, something like a winter aconite; but *Hacquetia epipactis* merits a closer look, for it is an umbellifer, a tiny relative of cow parsley, with lime-yellow flowers set in a little green ruff, opening at ground level in early spring and gradually emerging on a lengthening stem as the divided leaves unfurl.

It has extremely deep roots which dislike disturbance and do not divide readily; seed is a better method of increase. A fertile, cool soil in light shade suits it best.

The acid green ruffs of Hacquetia epipactis *offer an early foretaste of spring as they push through the wintry soil.*

The exquisite but sometimes temperamental gentians of high alpine slopes have an undemanding counterpart in the willow gentian, Gentiana asclepiadea. *Its flowers are no less beautiful than theirs, fluted trumpets of ultramarine or aqua or alabaster.*

helleborus

winter grace

DETAILS FROM TOP:

The flowers of Lenten roses last long in beauty, for even after fertilization the petals do not fall but remain to protect the ripening seed capsules.

After the jade cups of Helleborus argutifolius *have yielded to ripe seed, the stems that bore them die and should be cut away.*

Lenten roses with outward-facing flowers are especially valued when they reveal the rich freckling of Helleborus orientalis *subsp.* guttatus.

The red-flushed stems of Helleborus foetidus *Wester Flisk Group set off deeply fingered leaves of black-green suffused with a steely haze around jade bells.*

MAIN PICTURE:

The sultry maroon forms of Lenten roses, Helleborus orientalis, *are lit by the creamy stamens at their heart, which fall after pollination, leaving the unadorned calyx.*

HELLEBORUS

evergreen perennials h: 30–45cm/1–1½ft s: 30–45cm/1–1½ft
winter to spring z 5–9 [unless indicated]

Indispensable for shady and woodland gardens, the genus *Helleborus* includes the white-flowered Christmas rose, *H. niger* [z 4–7], and several green-flowered species. The shade-loving stinking hellebore, *H. foetidus* [z 4–9], has darkest green, deeply fingered leaves topped in winter by a sheaf of maroon-rimmed jade bells. Occasionally offered, the fragrant form spills its sweet perfume on the cold air. The Wester Flisk Group is a fine selection with reddish stems. All make bold contrasts with the broad paddle leaves of bergenias. The semi-woody stems of *H. argutifolius* (*H. corsicus*) [z 6–8] bear, in their first year, sub-prickly leaves of celadon green netted with grey veins; in the second, a stout cluster of pale green buds opens to nodding jade cups that last for weeks. Any fertile, well-drained soil, in sun or part shade, suits the Corsican hellebore, which, like the stinking hellebore, is increased by seed – a job it normally accomplishes for itself.

The Lenten rose, *H. orientalis*, flowers in late winter and early spring, beginning with the deep plum-purple *H. orientalis* Early Purple Group . *H. orientalis* subsp. *guttatus* has white flowers heavily spotted with blood-red. Selective breeding has produced a range of colours from white and greenish-primrose through shades of dusky pink, to slate-blue and near-black, and of flower forms from the outward-facing saucer – most sought-after in the freckled forms – to a more elegant nodding, flared outline. The smaller, daintier *H. torquatus* has slaty-purple flowers; it has given rise to double-flowered forms in the full range of Lenten rose colours.

If the old leaves of Lenten roses are looking tatty by flowering time, it does no harm to cut them off. The Lenten rose types can be seed-raised. The sterile Early Purple Group, and any named or special form that is to be increased vegetatively, can be divided just after (or even during) flowering. These hellebores thrive in fertile, moist soil among shrubs or beneath trees, with snowdrops perhaps, or in part-shady borders, where they look well with herbaceous peonies, whose mahogany young shoots echo plum-red hellebores.

The collector's instinct is aroused by named forms of the exquisite Helleborus torquatus; *this is 'Dido'.*

The big hydrangeas belonging to Hydrangea aspera *subsp.* sargentiana *are quality plants, with their large, rough-velvety leaves and domed flowerheads encircled by the showy sterile florets.*

Hepatica

evergreen perennials H 15cm/6in S 30cm/12in
spring Z 4–7

The hepaticas have cool lavender-blue anemone-flowers and lobed leaves, blunt-ended in *Hepatica nobilis* and more pointed in *H. acutiloba*. The first also comes in white, pink and cyclamen-crimson, but none is lovelier than the blues. Give them all a cool, shady place in woodsy soil, and increase them by division as the leaves die away.

Soft pink × Heucherella alba *'Rosalie' is accompanied by flights of pink and blush columbines in this charming woodland scene.*

x Heucherella

evergreen perennials H 45cm/1½ft S 45cm/1½ft
late spring Z 4–8

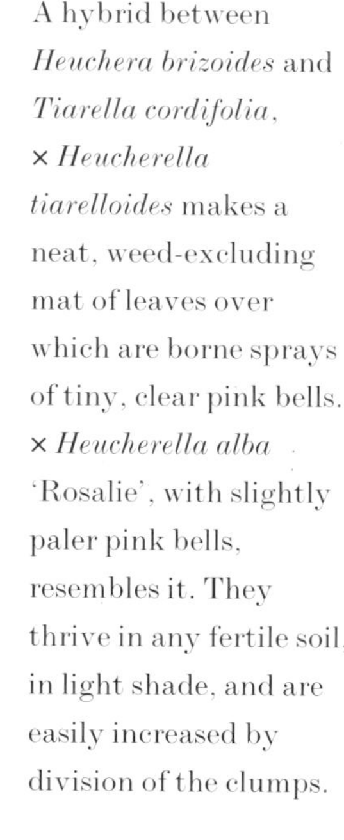

A hybrid between *Heuchera brizoides* and *Tiarella cordifolia*, × *Heucherella tiarelloides* makes a neat, weed-excluding mat of leaves over which are borne sprays of tiny, clear pink bells. × *Heucherella alba* 'Rosalie', with slightly paler pink bells, resembles it. They thrive in any fertile soil, in light shade, and are easily increased by division of the clumps.

Hydrangea

deciduous shrub H 1–2.4/3½–8ft S 1–1.8m/3½–6ft
summer to autumn Z 6–9

The big hydrangea of the *Hydrangea aspera* Villosa Group, or *H. villosa*, as it was simply called when I first came to know it, is a fine shrub for dappled shade, in a place sheltered from wind and spring frosts, both of which it dislikes. Often described as blue-flowered in all soils, whether acid or chalky, it is neither blue nor does it need such apologetics, for its lacecap flowers are composed of warm lilac ray-florets around tiny fertile florets which lean towards blue-mauve but certainly do not reach true blue. The pointed leaves are hairy. Little or no pruning is needed except to remove weak or frost-damaged growths; the shrub should be allowed to develop a permanent framework of branches and given enough space to do so. It can be propagated by cuttings taken in summer.

The lacecap forms of *H. macrophylla* and *H. serrata* also make charming woodland shrubs. To *H. serrata* belong several pretty lacecaps, such as 'Bluebird', and 'Grayswood', with flowers that open white and, regardless of soil pH, gradually age through pink to ruby-crimson. The larger, more muscular *H. macrophylla* also offers some fine lacecaps: 'Lanarth White', large-growing 'White Wave', 'Mariesii Perfecta' (better known as 'Blue Wave' – which despite this name is rather reluctant to turn blue even in acid soils), soft-toned 'Lilacina' (see page 172) and deep red 'Geoffrey Chadbund'.

As already noted, hydrangeas are easily distressed by drought, whether at the root or caused by desiccating winds. The serratas are more demanding of shade than the macrophyllas, but lacecap forms of both generally look better in informal, woodland settings, thriving in leafy soil with shelter from wind. They are easily propagated by cuttings taken in summer or autumn.

HYLOMECON JAPONICA

herbaceous perennial H 30cm/12in S 23cm/9in spring Z 6–8

Clear yellow poppies, rather like those of the Welsh poppy (*Meconopsis cambrica*) but more refined, float over a tuffet of fresh green, divided leaves. *Hylomecon japonica* lacks also the over-enthusiastically free-seeding ways of the Welsh poppy, and is increased by division; the clumps increase slowly in cool, leafy soil.

LEUCOTHOE

evergreen shrubs H 60–90cm/2–3ft S 90cm–1.2m/3–4ft spring Z 5–8

The leucothoes are fine weed-excluders for dappled shade, in lime-free, leafy soil, in which they make luxuriant, dense thickets. *Leucothoe walteri* (*L. fontanesiana*) has long-pointed, glossy foliage, burnished to shades of copper and mahogany in winter, on arching stems from which hang clusters of small, white urn-shaped flowers in spring. Its popular variegated cultivar, 'Rainbow', is endowed with leaves marbled cream, yellow and pink on green, again intensifying to shades of oxblood and copper in winter. Although preferring a soil that does not dry out, both the type and its jazzy derivative tolerate moderately droughty conditions. The neat little *L. keiskei*, only half the height, is more insistent on constant moisture; it has reddish, zigzag stems bearing, at every angle, a polished, dark green, pointed leaf; the white pitcher flowers are larger, and open later, after midsummer. Neither should need pruning, and both can be increased by cuttings.

The gracefully arching stems of Leucothoe keiskei *bear clusters of white urns in summer, set off by the rich red stems. Red suffuses the leaves, too, where they are touched by the sun.*

MATTEUCCIA STRUTHIOPTERIS

deciduous fern H 90cm/3ft S 60cm/2ft spring and summer foliage Z 2–8

The ostrich plume fern enjoys moist soils, where it will quickly spread at the root to form colonies of handsome, fresh green shuttlecocks of much-divided fronds on short stems. They look their best when each plume stands clear of its neighbours. It is worth, therefore, clearing from time to time to remove cluttering crowns. For the same reason, choose low-growing companion plants, but not too frail and choice lest the fern crowd them out.

So much does it enjoy dampness at the root that it might have gone into the chapter on the waterside, but for its dislike of drying winds, from which woodland conditions offer protection. It is perfectly frost-hardy and is easily increased by division as growth starts in spring.

By mid spring the fronds of the ostrich plume fern, Matteuccia struthiopteris, *have unfurled to their characteristic shuttlecock outline, with the tips still curled inwards. Their upright posture is set off by the modestly nodding erythroniums.*

The camera does not lie: Meconopsis grandis *really does have poppy flowers of this intense electric blue, emerging from furred buds over a rosette of hairy leaves.*

RIGHT *The common name, Virginian cowslip, conveys the form and nodding grace that characterize the flowers of* Mertensia pulmonarioides; *but no cowslip ever came in this tender, cool blue, touched with lilac in the bud.*

MECONOPSIS

perennials H 45cm/1.2m/1½–4ft S 30–60cm/1–2ft spring, summer Z 6–8

This is the genus that embraces the Himalayan blue poppies, those most tantalizing and, when suited, most beautiful of flowers, their petals of crumpled, silken texture ranging from purest azure and turquoise to ultramarine and electric blue. To achieve this, a moist lime-free soil and a humid atmosphere are needed; less than ideal conditions may give you a more commonplace off-blue colouring, if the plants grow for you at all.

Meconopsis betonicifolia (see page 172) is one of the least challenging; not always long-lived, but easy from seed, sown when fresh. As well as sky-blue, it comes in alabaster-white, both with yellow stamens, emerging from furry buds that open from the top of the spike downwards. More imposing than this is *M. grandis*, which may grow to shoulder height, with correspondingly large blooms, somewhat cupped and nodding. This too can be raised from seed, or increased by division – this latter the only method of ensuring that named cultivars are true to type.

MERTENSIA PULMONARIOIDES

herbaceous perennial H 45cm/1½ft S 23cm/9in spring Z 5–9

The Virginian cowslip, *Mertensia pulmonarioides* (*M. virginica*), is of a different quality of blue from the Himalayan poppies, but the cool colouring, just touched with lilac, of its nodding, tubular bells is perfectly in tune with the grey-green of its smooth

leaves. The Virginian cowslip is in no sense a carpeting plant. These die down by midsummer. A woodlander by nature, it needs garden conditions to remind it of the shady, leafy places it inhabits. It can be increased by division, seed or root cuttings.

MILIUM EFFUSUM *'AUREUM'*

deciduous grass H 60cm/2ft S 30cm/1ft summer foliage Z 5–8

Even as a child I loved the wood millet, *Milium effusum*, because of the soft, strokable texture and gentle green tone of its leaf-blades. In the garden, however, it is Mr Bowles' golden grass, *M. effusum* 'Aureum', that is the one to grow. In spring its clear yellow blades emerge, to be topped after a few weeks by dainty, airy flower sprays of the same tender colouring. It seeds itself generously and true in the woodsy soil and shade it prefers, so you can quickly have a haze of pale gold among shrubs or to accompany lacy ferns or the broad blades of hostas.

NARCISSUS

bulbous perennials H 7.5–45cm/3–18in S 7.5cm/3in spring Z 4–9 [unless indicated]

As well as the so-familiar yellow trumpet daffodils and other more or less over-blown confections on offer from bulb merchants, there are almost as many enchanting small narcissi for the lightly shaded margins of your miniature woodland or copse, or to spread in the grass amid orchard trees. The Lent lily, *Narcissus pseudonarcissus* [Z 6–9], a native of southern England, is a perfect little trumpet daffodil in soft yellow with paler, rather twisted perianth segments. Later, right at the end of the narcissus season, it is the turn of the pheasant's eye narcissus, *N. poeticus* 'Recurvus', which has a tiny yellow cup margined with orange, set in elegantly back-swept white perianth segments, and a tremendous fragrance. Early in the year the tiny *N. cyclamineus* opens its bright lemon yellow flowers, with their slender trumpets and fully reflexed perianth segments. In *N. bulbocodium* [Z 6–9], another slender species though rather taller than *N. cyclamineus*, the perianth segments are reduced to mere wisps around the crinoline-skirted cup which gives the species its nickname of hoop petticoat daffodil. As well as the typical clear yellow, there is a form of richer colouring, var. *conspicuus*, and an irresistible, but sadly hard to obtain, palest lemon form, var. *citrinus*. All these I have found to be perfectly happy in light shade and leafy soil, as in thin grass where the soil does not dry out. They are increased by seed or division.

PAROCHETUS COMMUNIS

perennial H 7.5cm/3in S 30cm/1ft summer Z 9–10

In the moist, warm shade that it loves, *Parochetus communis* will quickly spread a carpet of its shamrock-like leaves, above which hover bright turquoise-blue pea-flowers over a long season. It will even grow at the water's edge if you have a streamlet in the woodland patch of your garden. It is just the thing to scuttle around a clump of *Dianella*, foreshadowing the spires of lapis-blue berries of that iris-relative. Increase is a simple matter of division.

Bowles' golden grass, Milium effusum *'Aureum', lights up shady corners with its chartreuse blades and the shimmer of its fresh, clear yellow inflorescence.*

Among the tiniest of daffodils, Narcissus cyclamineus *will, if suited, spread into generous drifts in mossy, cool soil or moist meadows where the surrounding grass does not grow too lushly.*

This Pieris *'Forest Flame' is growing in ideal conditions, shaded and sheltered enough for its tender, brilliant scarlet spring foliage to emerge untouched by frost, searing winds or sudden hot sun, yet back-lit to glow with the richness of a ruby.*

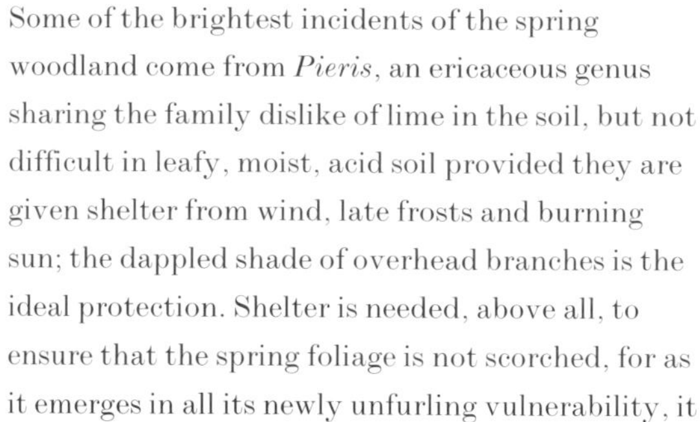

Pieris

evergreen shrubs H 90cm–3m/3–10ft
S 90cm–2.1m/3–7ft spring Z 5–8 [unless indicated]

Some of the brightest incidents of the spring woodland come from *Pieris*, an ericaceous genus sharing the family dislike of lime in the soil, but not difficult in leafy, moist, acid soil provided they are given shelter from wind, late frosts and burning sun; the dappled shade of overhead branches is the ideal protection. Shelter is needed, above all, to ensure that the spring foliage is not scorched, for as it emerges in all its newly unfurling vulnerability, it is as brilliant a scarlet as any flower could be. Pieris flowers are not to be scorned either, for the little urns, typically white but sometimes pink or claret, are borne in ample, graceful sprays. One of the best is 'Forest Flame', in which the scarlet young growths gradually fade through shrimp and clotted cream to the green of summer. It is generally considered hardier than *P. formosa* var. *forrestii* [Z 5–7], which is of similar colouring; 'Wakehurst' is a fine cultivar of this, with vivid scarlet young foliage fading through coral and lemon to green, sometimes with a paler encore in late summer.

The species which has given us the widest range of cultivars is *P. japonica*. For leaf colour, there are 'Mountain Fire' and, if you must, those with variegated foliage, as well as the more subtle 'Grayswood', which has bronzed young foliage and long, elegant flower sprays opening from sepia buds. Another that is especially good in flower is 'Purity', with upright, rather than drooping, flower sprays on a shrub of compact growth. But *P. japonica* is also the source of cultivars with flowers that depart from the typical white: 'Christmas Cheer' among them. The genes that provide its clear pink must also have given *P.* 'Flamingo' its curious colouring, burgundy in bud opening to the colour of red wine that has been diluted with water for midday drinking.

Pierises are stylish shrubs, and deserve equally classy companions: snake-bark maples, the tiered, open-habited *Enkianthus campanulatus* with hanging, coral and cream bells, squatty evergreen azaleas with white flowers, or the soft tangerine of *kaempferi* azaleas perhaps. They can be increased by half ripe autumn cuttings. Little or no pruning is needed – unless to remove frost-damaged wood – until, with age, they become large enough to arborize, when the lower branches can be trimmed to leave clear stems and allow for under-planting. Pieris also respond well to hard pruning to keep them compact, if that is your preference. This is best done in spring as the flowers fade.

Podophyllum

herbaceous perennial H 45cm/1½ft S 30cm/1ft
spring Z 5–8

The nickname of this curiously appealing genus is umbrella leaf, which conveys the image of the unfurling foliage, folded from the top of the stem and gradually expanding. The deeply-lobed leaves of *Podophyllum hexandrum* (*P. emodi*) are glossy, mottled brownish-green, and almost conceal the nodding, white flowers, which are followed by fruits the size and shape of a plum tomato, and of the same polished bright red. *P. hexandrum* var. *chinense* has larger, pink flowers, and its leaves are more deeply cut.

Both can be increased by seed or division, and are happiest in cool shade, in moist soil.

Polygonatum

herbaceous perennials H 30cm–1.2m/1–4ft S 30–60cm/1–2ft spring Z 4–8

The Solomon's seals are characterized by arching stems set with horizontally-poised leaves of fresh green, more or less broad or pointed according to species, beneath which hang little ivory or greenish-white bells. They range from the tall, freely-spreading *Polygonatum biflorum* (*P. giganteum*), through the mid-sized familiar robust *P.* × *hybridum* (*P. multiflorum*), to neat little *P. falcatum*, most appealing in its manifestation known as 'Variegatum', which has leaves margined with white tinged pink. Another variegated Solomon's seal is less discreet; the ivory-striped form of *P. odoratum*, a species characterized by its angular stems. Both *P. odoratum* and *P.* × *hybridum* have double-flowered forms. Whichever you choose, the ideal companions are ferns.

Solomon's seals are easy to grow in woodsy soil, in shade, with one caveat: the leaves can be stripped down to the midrib by sawfly caterpillars in early summer. They can be increased by division, or by seed from the indigo-black fruits that may follow the flowers.

Polypodium

evergreen fern H 30cm/1ft S 30cm/1ft foliage Z 5–8

The common polypody, *Polypodium vulgare*, is an attractive fern, adaptable enough to make a carpet of divided, rather narrow fronds in leafy soil, or to perch on mossy branches, in shade or sun. Far finer than this, however, is the Cornish polypody, *P. interjectum* 'Cornubiense', with more finely divided fronds; like those of the common polypody, they are spring-fresh in late summer, lasting in beauty through the winter but tatty by late spring when they can be cut down. The polypody spreads itself around by spores, and selected forms such as the Cornish polypody can be increased by division.

Though tolerant of quite dry soils, the Cornish polypody, Polypodium interjectum *'Cornubiense' deserves the best of leafy blends, to ensure its fronds last in immaculate freshness throughout winter.*

The stems of Solomon's seal (Polygonatum × hybridum) *seem poised to take flight, with their leaves raised to display the hanging, green-tipped bells ranked beneath.*

The sweetly scented yellow bells of cowslips, Primula veris, *are set off by the dark foliage and jade green bells of* Helleborus foetidus, *with the broad blades of hostas in the foreground.*

The elegant, lacy symmetry that characterizes so many ferns finds expression in a softness of visual texture in the soft shield fern, Polystichum setiferum*; the one seen here is in the Plumosodivisilobum Group.*

Polystichum

evergreen ferns
H 60cm–1.2m/2–4ft
S 60–90cm/2–3ft
Z 5–8 [unless indicated]

The shield ferns are among the most elegant of their tribe. The soft shield fern, *Polystichum setiferum*, is particularly beautiful, its lacy, mossy fronds piled one upon the other. It reaches its acme of ruffled luxuriance in the Divisilobum and Plumosodivisilobum Groups. Scarcely less fetching are the Acutilobum Group, in which the feathery fronds spiral around the crown; bulbils form along the stem, which if pegged down will quickly give you plenty of youngsters. Surprisingly for such luxuriant-seeming ferns, they tolerate quite dry soils, except in spring when the new fronds are unfurling, and are at their best when sheltered from drying winds. As secondary crowns form, they can be divided, both for increase and to maintain the uncluttered outline which shows off the fronds to best advantage. The hard shield fern, *P. aculeatum* [Z 4–8], is of equal elegance, with its long, filigree fronds, unfurling in sharp acid green and aging to glossy deep green. It can be propagated by division or spores.

Primula

perennials H 7.5–20cm/3–8in S 7.5–20cm/3–8in spring Z 5–8 [unless indicated]

The genus *Primula* is so diverse that almost any corner of the garden might boast at least one, and the woodland is no exception. A native of Europe, where it grows at the margins of deciduous woodland, is the oxlip, *P. elatior* (see page 175), with its loosely bunched heads of pale yellow flowers, more open than those of the cowslip, *P. veris* [Z 3–8]. It is the perfect companion for the lilac flowers of the cuckoo flower, *Cardamine pratensis*. The common primrose, *P. vulgaris*, needs no description; as well as the moon-pale type, it comes in white, or in the clear lavender-mauve of subsp. *sibthorpii*. Primroses with the blood of *P. juliae* in them (the julianas) tend to have smaller, neater leaves; typical is 'Wanda', in potent magenta. Among many seed strains of primrose and polyanthus, the dark-leaved Cowichans are characterized by their 'eyeless' flowers, which gives their velvety colourings – cinnabar, crimson, royal purple, garnet – an extra depth. They assort well with the coppery foliage of *Heuchera americana*. In the Gold Laced polyanthus the deep garnet ground colour is enhanced by the fine yellow rim to the petals, extending down to meet the golden eye so as to give the impression of a double ration of narrow petals. In the Silver Laced polyanthus the margin is white on a deep crimson ground.

Primroses do best in enriched soil that does not dry out, in a lightly shaded, sheltered place. Named cultivars need regular division and replanting or they may dwindle away; seed strains are of variable longevity but easily maintained by regular sowings.

Pulmonaria

evergreen and deciduous perennials
H 15–30cm/6–12in S 45–60cm/1½–2ft spring
Z 4–8

The lungworts make excellent cover among shrubs, in shady places where the soil remains moist. Most are evergreen, the exception being the lowly *Pulmonaria angustifolia*, which has unspotted, dark green leaves opening with the first flowers. These are pink in bud, opening to pure blue, at its most intense in subsp. *azurea*. The common lungwort, *P. officinalis*, is the 'soldiers and sailors' or 'Joseph and Mary' of cottage gardens, and pretty enough with its spotted leaves and pink and blue flowers, or white in 'Sissinghurst White'; but far finer foliage is borne by *P. saccharata* Argentea Group and by *P. vallarsae* 'Margery Fish', both of them more substantial plants in which the leaves are so heavily spotted as to have an almost uniform platinum finish; the flowers are pink at first turning to blue. The muscular *P. rubra* has plain, rather pale green leaves and coral-red flowers in late winter or very early spring. Latest to flower is *P. longifolia*, in late spring, when its heads of ultramarine blue flowers are held over long, narrow, heavily silver-spotted leaves.

In dry seasons the pulmonarias are apt to suffer from mildew, and the leaves often look rather tatty after flowering; the remedy is to cut them off, give the plants a good watering and a feed if the soil is poor, and wait for new, lush foliage to cover the plants for the rest of the season. They can be increased by division.

Ranunculus ficaria

herbaceous perennials H 5–8cm/2–3in
S 7.5–15cm/3–6in early spring Z 4–8

The lesser celandine, *Ranunculus ficaria*, is a fast-spreading wildling with starry, lemon-yellow flowers, increasing by seed and by the brittle clusters of little tubers, any scrap of which seems to make a new plant. As such, it is suitable only for the wilder corners of the garden, among shrubs. Choice forms, however, can be trusted in polite company, as it might be with the select forms of the wood anemone, or even in shady corners of the dell garden. 'Brazen Hussy' has the vivid lemon flowers of the wildling allied to deepest bronze-black foliage, and there is a citron, green-eyed double, with little pompom flowers that as yet has no botanical name.

These cute little collectables are worth cosseting in leafy, cool soil, and can easily be increased by division of the tiny tubers. If only they would spread a tenth as fast as the energetic wildling.

The vivid blue flowers of Pulmonaria angustifolia, *ranging from the ultramarine of this* P. angustifolia *subsp.* azurea *to violet, are one of the joys of early spring in the woodland garden, ideally set off by pale primroses or white wood anemones.*

Ranunculus ficaria flore-pleno *and other choice forms of celandine do not spread with the same relentless vigour as their wildling progenitor, but make neat little clumps dying away by midsummer.*

Though several of the hardier rhododendron hybrids will grow in open places, they never look so well as in the dappled shade beneath a high tree canopy, where their paler tones gleam in the half-light and the more assertive crimsons and magentas are softened.

RHODODENDRON

evergreen shrubs H 60cm–2.4m/2–8ft
S 60cm–2.4m/2–8ft spring Z 7–8 [unless indicated]

The flowers of the blood root, Sanguinaria canadensis, *emerge before the foliage, but as the stems lengthen so the broad leaves begin to expand, their sombre grey-green the ideal foil for the pure white pompons.*

The protean genus *Rhododendron* has much to offer the fortunate gardener with acid soil and dappled shade. Some species are almost azalea-like in their grace and butterfly blooms; among these are *R. augustinii* [Z 6–8], which ranges in colour from lavender and soft violet to slate-blue, never quite reaching true blue – Electra Group, in violet with a lime-green flash, is especially good – and *R. lutescens*, which is equally tall and slender in habit, with small, dainty blooms of clear citron to primrose early in the year, and narrow leaves of coppery-red tint. Azaleas themselves, especially the deciduous kinds with flights of often fragrant flowers, bring another range of colour to the woodland – not just pink and crimson, but true yellow and all the dawn and sunset tints. *R. ciliatum* is another species that flowers early enough in spring to be at risk of late frosts if not protected by an overhead canopy of branches; it is of rounded outline, with nodding pink bells.

In late spring and early summer it is the turn of the lapageria-flowered rhododendrons. Formerly considered distinct species, the following are now all deemed to belong to *R. cinnabarinum*, and are known respectively as *R. cinnabarinum*, *R. cinnabarinum* subsp. *xanthocodon*, and *R. cinnabarinum* subsp. × Concatenans Group. All are desirable, none perhaps more so than the blue-leaved, ochre-belled Concatenans Group. Only their susceptibility to powdery mildew counts against them.

Rich scarlet is the colour of the *R. forrestii* Repens Group, characterized by its creeping habit; 'Carmen' is a fine hybrid of this, freer of flower, with dark foliage and waxy, blood-red bells. A dwarf species of very distinct character, only half-heartedly evergreen, is *R. lepidostylum* [Z 6–8], which has intensely blue-glaucous, bristly leaves and citron-yellow, funnel-shaped flowers in late spring and early summer.

At the other end of the scale come the big-leaved rhododendrons such as *R. macabeanum* [Z 8–9], one of a group of species which need sheltered woodland conditions to develop to their full magnificence. The leaves of Macabe, as rhododendron buffs are apt affectionately to call this species, are huge paddles up to 30cm/12in long, dark glossy green above and grey or silvery-white beneath; they emerge in spring, as pale as platinum, from scarlet bud scales. The flowers are stout, waxy, squarish bells, cream to primrose to citron, marked with plum-crimson stains at the base where the nectaries lie. If you grow a batch of *R. macabeanum* seedlings, select and keep those with the boldest, whitest-backed leaves, as they are likely to have the finest flowers as well.

For the amateur, layers are the most satisfactory method of propagating these choice rhododendrons. Seed is another possibility, but anything may result – a mongrel, or a potential prize winner. None needs pruning, but it is worth removing the spent flowers both for aesthetic reasons and to save the energies that would otherwise go into ripening seed.

ROSCOEA

herbaceous perennials H 30–45cm/1–1½ft
S 30–45cm/1–1½ft summer
Z 6–9 [unless indicated]

Remarkably frost-hardy members of the ginger family, the roscoeas have intriguing, hooded flowers held in a sheaf of polished, sword-shaped leaves. *Roscoea cautleoides* has soft yellow flowers in early summer, at which time also flowers *R. humeana* in purple. *R. purpurea* [Z 5–9] follows on in late summer; it has narrow leaves and royal purple flowers.

All need a leafy, moist soil, when they will make good compact clumps in sun or light shade They can be increased by seed or division.

SANGUINARIA CANADENSIS 'PLENA'

rhizomatous perennial H 15cm/6in S 45cm/1½ft
spring Z 3–8

The single-flowered blood root is pretty but fleeting; the double-flowered *Sanguinaria canadensis* 'Plena' is the one to go for, with its pure white rosettes and waxy, pale leaves expanding as the flower stems lengthen and, as the flowers fade, remaining in beauty for weeks, surprising in their size and substance. The roots bleed orange sap when cut – hence the common name.

Give the blood root a leafy, moist soil in a sheltered, shady place, and increase it by careful division if you must.

SAXIFRAGA

herbaceous perennial H 45cm/1½ft S 30cm/1ft
autumn Z 6–8

Right at the end of the season the delicate fountains of starry white flowers of *Saxifraga fortunei* make their appearance; but even before they open, the broad, glossy leaves have paid generous rent, especially when, as in *S.* 'Wada', they are burnished mahogany with burgundy reverse. The type has green leaves with the same red backs. Cool woodsy soil and sheltered shade make for unblemished leaves and flowers that will be spared autumn's frosts. The species can be increased by seed or division, cultivars by division.

Mingling with the veined leaves and foamy white flowers of Tiarella cordifolia *are the glossy leaves of* Saxifraga fortunei, *the nodding creamy blooms of* Erythronium californicum *'White Beauty' and the pink lockets and grey-green foliage of* Dicentra formosa.

Tiarella wherryi is even frothier in flower than the foam flower T. cordifolia (see previous page), its fuzzy spires palest blush white over lobed leaves.

Smilacina racemosa is seen here in full sail, its wide-spread leaves a foil for the starbursts of white, fragrant flowers at the stem tips.

SMILACINA RACEMOSA

herbaceous perennial H 75cm/2½ft S 45cm/1½ft spring Z 4–9

The false spikenard, *Smilacina racemosa*, is related to Solomon's seal and, in foliage at least, is very like it, making a good clump of fresh green leaves on arching stems, lovely with ferns and the coppery-tinted leaves of epimediums. The flowers, however, are erect spikes of ivory, fragrant froth borne at the ends of the stems. Shade and leafy soil, preferably lime-free, suit it; it can be increased from seed or by division.

STYLOPHORUM DIPHYLLUM

herbaceous perennial H 45cm/1½ft S 30cm/1ft spring to summer Z 4–8

The celandine poppy, *Stylophorum diphyllum*, is one of those offbeat poppies that I find irresistible. It has crinkled, somewhat hairy, pale jade leaves somewhat like those of the greater celandine, and clear yellow poppies over a long season, succeeded by blue-green seed pods, from the contents of which more plants can be raised. Sadly it does not self-sow as freely as its cousin *Meconopsis cambrica*. Cool, leafy soil suit it best, in dappled shade.

TIARELLA

evergreen perennials H 23cm/9in S 30cm/12in spring Z 3–8

The tiarellas are pretty and easy-tempered weed-excluders for shady places, among shrubs or in garden woodland, where the soil is cool and leafy. The foam flower, *Tiarella cordifolia* (see page 197), has lobed, hairy leaves, bronzed in winter, and frothy sprays of creamy flowers. It is more vigorous than *T. wherryi*, which has taller flower-plumes tinged with pink; in *T. polyphylla* the pink tints are more marked still, and the leaves are conspicuously purple-veined. All can be increased by division.

TRICYRTIS

herbaceous perennials H 45–90cm/1½–3ft S 45–60cm/1½–2ft summer, autumn Z 5–9

The toad lilies earn their nickname from the blotches and freckles that decorate the flowers and leaves of several species; the flowers are intricately constructed and very alluring. First to bloom, in summer, is ochre-yellow, maroon-mottled *Tricyrtis latifolia*, which also has blotched foliage. The autumn-flowering *T. formosana* has shining, dark green leaves and branching stems bearing glossy brown buds opening to star-shaped flowers of mauve-buff colour heavily freckled with deeper mauve around a yellow throat. The Stolonifera Group run freely at the root in the cool, leafy, moist soil all toad lilies prefer. The tall *T. hirta* bears its flowers not in sprays above the leaves but in the leaf axils; each flower is larger than those of *T. formosana*, in white mottled and blotched with lilac-purple, or all-white in *T. hirta alba*, which has pink stamens. Another exquisite white toad lily is 'White Towers', which has softly furry foliage and large flowers on rather shorter stems. Most irresistible of all, however, is the one with soft yellow, waxy, shuttlecock flowers on sheaves of green-leafy, arching stems: *T. macrantha* subsp. *macranthopsis*. All the toad lilies can be increased by seed or division.

Trillium

tuberous-rooted perennials H 15–60cm/6in–2ft S 15–30cm/6in–1ft spring Z 4–9

Trilliums are so-called because all their parts are in threes: three-petalled flowers are held on short stems over, or emerging stemless from, a ruff of three usually broad and often marbled leaves. The wake robin, *Trillium grandiflorum*, has arching stems bearing pure white flowers over plain green leaves; it has a highly desirable fully double-flowered form, *flore-pleno*, and a subtle pink, f. *roseum*. *T. cernuum* is also white, with a purple heart and anthers, aging to pink; the flowers nod so modestly as almost to hide themselves among the broad green leaves. Of those with erect petals that seem to erupt from the heart of the leaves, *T. chloropetalum* is handsome and easy in maroon, pink or white, and *T. sessile* is similar in deep maroon, with marbled leaves. The fine *T. erectum* also ranges from dusky maroon to white (f. *albiflorum*) and greenish-yellow (f. *luteum*). If yellow is the colour you seek, *T. luteum* varies from lemon to butter yellow over marbled leaves. Much smaller than these is *T. rivale*, which has white to blush-pink flowers flecked at the heart with maroon.

The recipe for success with trilliums, as with so many of the plants in this chapter, is a cool, leafy soil in part-shade. They can be increased by division or seed.

The wake robin, Trillium grandiflorum, *is more usually seen in vestal white, but the pink form growing here is no less beautiful.*

Dark red stems and maroon, hairy buds frame the curiously-structured, blotched and mottled flowers of the toad lily, Tricyrtis formosana. *Like the baneberries, this is one of those precious woodlanders that are at their best late in the season.*

UVULARIA

herbaceous perennials H 30–60cm/1–2ft
S 23–30cm/9–12in spring Z 4–9

Hanging from arching stems clad with modestly downcast, fresh green foliage, the slender flowers of the merrybells, Uvularia perfoliata, *echo the colour of spring sunshine.*

The merrybells are related to the Solomon's seals, and have something of the same poise and grace, with their arching stems and hanging bells in spring. *Uvularia grandiflora*, the big merrybells, has fresh green foliage and slightly flared, soft yellow flowers; *U. perfoliata* is smaller in growth, and the paler flowers open later, held above the leaves where those of the big merrybells hang beneath the foliage. Both need the same leafy soil and shady conditions that suit the Solomon's seals, and can be increased by division while dormant.

VACCINIUM

evergreen shrubs H 90cm–2.4m/3–8ft
S 1.2–2.4m/4–8ft early summer, late summer
Z 7–9

Bilberries, blueberries, whortleberries and cranberries – shrubs of the open heath or peat moorland, with delicious edible fruits – all belong to the genus *Vaccinium*, which also boasts some fine, if not showy, shrubs for sheltered, shady places, in leafy, lime-free soil. In *V. ovatum* the neat foliage – which lasts well when cut – is at first coppery-red, maturing to polished dark green, set in stylishly patterned sprays on the arching branches; the tiny urn-shaped flowers are blush-white to pink and give way to red fruits which ripen to black. It can be increased by half-ripe autumn cuttings, and needs no pruning unless to keep it in bounds – best done in spring, or when you need lovely leaves in the house, at any time of the year.

VIOLA

perennials H 7.5–30cm/3–12in S:15–60cm/6in–2ft
spring, early to late summer
Z 4–8 [unless indicated]

The sweet violet, *Viola odorata*, is as much a flower of a northern European spring as the primrose, its blue-violet or milk-white flowers nestling in hedgerows and at woodland edges. They have the curious property of anaesthetizing the sense of smell, so that after a few sniffs they seem to have lost their characteristic perfume; leave them alone for a while and your olfactory nerves will recover. Selections of the sweet violet, all with the same meandering habit, include violet-purple 'Czar', and buff, amber-eyed 'Sulphurea'. A clumping or tufted habit characterizes the bright yellow, unperfumed *V. biflora*, a free self-seeder. Also scentless, with wide, butterfly flowers, are the fully herbaceous *V. cucullata* (*V. obliqua*) and *V. sororia* (*V. papilionacea*); 'Freckles' (a *sororia* selection) is white heavily flecked with blue-mauve.

Of similar style in flower to the sweet violets, but of clumpier habit, are the scentless dog violets: sulky pink, green-leaved *V. rupestris rosea* and purple-leaved, pale purple-flowered *V. riviniana* Purpurea Group (*V. labradorica*) [z 3–8] (see page 155), very appealing in combination with the silvered lamiums such as white-flowered *Lamium maculatum* 'White Nancy' or rosy-pink flowered 'Beacon Silver', or as a carpet for snowdrops. It develops the most intense leaf colour in an open place, but is equally at home in light shade. Of very different style is the horned pansy, *V. cornuta* [z 6–9], which forms loose mounds of fresh green foliage and even sends out insinuating stems so that its perky flowers peer out amid neighbouring plants. Typically soft mauve, it also comes in white (Alba Group, see page 119). After the first flush of flowers is over, they can be encouraged to a repeat performance if the foliage is clipped over, removing all the straggly stems, and the plants given a generous liquid feed. They can be increased by division or cuttings.

In early summer it is the turn of something very different, and much less frost-resistant: the chinless *V. hederacea* [z 7–9], a little carpeter over which float white and violet flowers on long stems. Like the other species, it can be increased by seed, or by division, and enjoys a fertile soil in light shade.

Viola sororia *'Freckles' is aptly named, for its plump little violets are thickly flecked with violet-mauve on white.*

WOODWARDIA RADICANS

evergreen fern H 90cm/3ft S 90cm/3ft foliage
Z 9–10

A grand fern for warm shade, the Japanese *Woodwardia radicans* has large, arching fronds of fresh green, much divided, which have the curious characteristic of rooting from the bud at the tip if held down in moist and woodsy soil. In this way is will walk over quite a large area if space permits. It is a grand companion for *Dianella*.

ZENOBIA PULVERULENTA

deciduous shrub H 90cm/3ft S 90cm/3ft
early summer Z 6–9

Imagine flowers like those of lily-of-the-valley, but twice as large, on a shrub of which stems and leaves alike are bloomed with white, and you have an image of *Zenobia pulverulenta*. It lacks the delicious fragrance of lily-of-the-valley, but has instead an aniseed aroma. To keep the shrub looking its best and whitest, cut back the flowered stems to strong new shoots each year in summer, after the flowers have faded. New plants can be raised from seed. Lime-free soil in dappled shade is a must for this exquisite creature.

Woodwardia radicans *is a big fern, and the bold simplicity of its fronds is heightened by the glossy texture of the upper surface.*

pond, stream & bog

moisture-loving plants

The music of water, the play of fountains or the calmness of still pools, are enhanced by the plants that revel in coolness and moisture. Here is the chance to make lush, leafy plantings in which the imagination can wander as if in a jungle, with the bold shuttlecocks of royal fern, the web-footed foliage of rodgersias and the great jagged leaves of ornamental rhubarb, or to make in little a flowery water meadow with drifts of candelabra primulas, meadowsweet and globe flower, gold-pencilled irises and yellow flags, bachelor's buttons and plumy astilbes. A soggy patch of soil need never again be a nightmare squelch of weeds, whether in earliest spring, when the elegant spathes of bog arums emerge from the muddy soil, or lit with summer's byzantine blends of orange daisies and lobelias in scarlet, garnet and purple, and the cool contrast of ferns and sedges, the sheeny kaffir lilies of autumn and bright willow wands giving the lie to winter's ice and snow.

In autumn the bold fronds of the moisture-loving royal fern, Osmunda regalis, *adopt harlequin tints of rust and lemon, reflected more sombrely in the dark water to give double value.*

pond, stream & bog

Calm water yields double returns to these delights, with its surface reflections and its still, mysterious depths. One moment it gives back the sky and the clouds; the next it is limpid and clear, sparkling, or darkly shadowed.

Water plays a triple illusion, the reflected branches of a Japanese maple seeming to wear once again its own fallen leaves that float on the calm surface, beneath which other leaves, earlier fallen, are slowly submerging.

Inspired breeding has produced, of late, a range of spectacular arum lily (Zantedeschia) *hybrids in glowing colours.*

The season of moisture-loving plants opens with yellow and white bog arums (*Lysichiton*), drumstick primulas and the shocking pink *Primula rosea*, soon to be followed by globe flowers in clear pale yellow and the first of the great tribe of candelabra primulas, set off by the unfurling, richly-coloured, finely-dissected astilbe foliage. By now a diversity of foliage plants – *Rheum palmatum*, rodgersias with their web-footed or horse-chestnut leaves, the pale dinner-plates of *Astilboides tabularis*, the glossy-backed maroon discs of *Ligularia dentata* 'Othello' – are in full leaf, set off by the arching rapier blades of sedges, the strong spears of iris, and the fingered fronds of the sensitive and the royal fern. Amid this profuse growth the airy plumes of astilbes and the pink or cream fuzz of meadowsweet and queen of the prairies (species of *Filipendula*) make soft outlines in contrast to the clean-cut lines of iris blooms. Only as high summer's ligularias and lobelias yield to autumn's kaffir lilies and the white wands of cimicifuga, and frost touches the fern fronds to russet death, does this abundance begin to give way to winter's bare soil.

Moisture-gardening is all about profusion, abundance, growth; this is no place for stifled restraint. Nature will not allow it; if you attempt to control her, she will have the last laugh, for if your ligularias and rodgersias do not grow lush and luxuriant, she will fill the space with weeds instead, and you will have all sorts of trouble extracting them without bringing up a squelch of soil with each one. Go along with the old lady, however, and indulge her whims by making a jungle of growth – of your choosing, not hers – and you will have understood the art of gardening in wet places.

If you have natural water in the garden, in the shape of a stream or pool, you will also have naturally moist soil alongside it, and will be able to grow bog plants and marginals, water plants and those that merely enjoy a soil that never dries out. A surprising number of such plants will also submit to growing under water, and this is a good way of protecting those that are a little tender, their crowns vulnerable to winter frost in the moist soils that they demand and which are especially apt to lie cold and inimical in winter.

Among such plants are kaffir lilies (*Schizostylis coccinea*) and arum lilies (*Zantedeschia*), neither of which are true lilies at all. So long as they are growing in water just deep enough for their crowns not to freeze, they may survive quite bitter winters that would kill them outright in the open border. Both would lend

In damp soil, foliage grows lush and opulent. Here, a swathe of bronzed Rodgersia podophylla *contrasts with upright spears of* Iris pseudacorus, *the fronds of* Dryopteris, *rounded glossy leaves of* Caltha palustris *(the kingcup or marsh marigold) and the rasp-textured leaves of* Gunnera manicata, *which will become far larger still with age. Flowery incidents are provided by yellow* Lysimachia nummularia *and, later, orange-daisied* Ligularia dentata.

themselves to decorating a formal, stone-edged pool, though the kaffir lilies would need regular lifting and replanting, spreading fast if they are suited.

And that leads me to another potential difficulty. The soil around an artificial pool is not likely to be naturally moist, so that if you want your *pièce d'eau* to be surrounded with moisture-loving plants, you will need to create an artificial bog as well, by lining the planting areas with plastic sheeting, pierced here and there so that water does not lie stagnant, but not so much that it all simply drains away as freely as if the plastic were not there. Once made and planted, a

Primula pulverulenta is one of the finest candelabra primulas, its widely spread whorls of brilliant magenta flowers set off by the white-bloomed stems that give it its specific name. Here it grows among the yellow fleur de lis and green spears of Iris pseudacorus, with the bold fronds of Osmunda regalis in their green summer garb.

The magenta plumes of Astilbe chinensis var. aquetii *'Superba' soar above the handsome, divided foliage. The arching blades of golden sedge and the drooping, creamy plumes of aruncus soften the military bearing of the astilbe. Behind are tawny daylilies and the orange-gold daisies of* Ligularia dentata.

moisture bed can look entirely natural. It is worth the little trouble, for nothing looks more miserable than a wilting ligularia or an astilbe with its foliage crisped by drought.

And a final word about the choice of plants. It is not always easy to persuade plants into the neat categories of chapters, and several that are in the chapter on borders could equally well have appeared here: notably *Persicaria*, hostas, *Cimicifuga*, certain euphorbias (such as *Euphorbia schillingii*), and the short-growing, golden-striped bamboo, *Pleioblastus auricomus*.

Primula florindae *(foreground right) is known as the giant Himalayan cowslip, and its soft yellow bells, on stems that may be waist-high, are endowed with all the fragrance of the little cowslip of European meadows. Alongside it, the boldly jagged leaves of* Ligularia przewalskii *form a plinth for its narrow steeples of golden daisies. Hostas, ferns, bamboos and a white-plumed astilbe add cool grace notes in the shadows beyond.*

ABOVE Astilbe *'Sprite' is one of a group of enchanting small hybrids deriving from* A. simplicifolia, *all with dainty flower sprays in varying shades of pink or white over a plinth of finely dissected foliage.*

OPPOSITE, LEFT Carex elata *'Aurea', its slender, arching golden blades finely edged in green, is here thrown into relief by the broad, blue-glaucous paddles of* Hosta sieboldiana *var.* elegans.

Astilbe

herbaceous perennials H 45cm–1.2m/1½–4ft S 60–90cm/2–3ft summer Z 4–8 [unless indicated]

Handsome in flower and often colourful in leaf, the astilbes are indispensable plants for damp or boggy soils. A size up from the tiny *Astilbe simplicifolia* are a group of its hybrids typified by 'Bronce Elegans', which has finely dissected, bronzed foliage and arching, airy sprays of peach-pink flowers. 'Sprite' is shell pink and 'Praecox Alba' is white; richer colouring belongs to salmon-pink 'Dunkellachs', and 'Willie Buchanan'; allies ivory flowers to coppery-crimson foliage. Try them with smallish hostas: the 'blues', such as 'Halcyon', with pink astilbes or the white-variegated *Hosta undulata* var. *undulata* with white ones. Another short-growing astilbe is *A. chinensis* var. *pumila*, very different in its tight, nubbly buds opening to stiff, fuzzy spikes of bright mauve flowers shot with scarlet, borne in late summer over freely spreading carpets of ferny foliage. Its tall cousin, *A. chinensis* var. *taquetii* 'Superba', is of much the same eye-wiping magenta colouring; it has bold, dark-toned foliage and is more tolerant of dry soils than most.

The astilbes collectively known as *A.* × *arendsii* [Z 5–8] are a group of mid-sized hybrids with crisply dissected foliage and foamy plumes of flower, held boldly upright or, in a few choice cultivars, gracefully arching. They range in colour from white through shades of palest to deep pink, mauve and a range of reds from fiery near-scarlet to garnet-crimson. As a general rule the whites and palest pinks have green foliage, the deeper pinks tend to coppery tones and the reds are generally endowed with rich mahogany tints, especially when first unfurling in spring.

Astilbes are increased by division of the roots. They need no staking. A place in the sun is best, but if the soil is on the dry side, fleeting or part shade helps to compensate for the lack of moisture.

Astilboides tabularis

herbaceous perennial H 90cm/3ft S 90cm/3ft summer Z 5–7

Formerly known as *Rodgersia tabularis*, this fine plant is now infelicitously named, for nothing could be less like the dissected leaves of astilbes than the circular, flat, dinner plate-sized, light green leaves with their shallow marginal lobing. Perhaps the likeness is supposed to be found in the tall plumes of creamy-white flowers that tower over the leaves in summer; but with such splendid foliage, who needs flowers? For a green harmony, plant it with the dark green, arching blades and cylindrical green flowers of the great drooping sedge, *Carex pendula*, or the lettuce-green, broadly-fingered fronds of the sensitive fern, *Onoclea sensibilis*, in a damp or even wet place in sun or light shade. Increase is by division or seed.

CAREX ELATA *'AUREA'*

sedge H 60cm/2ft S 45cm/1½ft summer Z 5-9

More modest in size than the great drooping sedge, Bowles' golden sedge, *Carex elata* (*C. stricta*) 'Aurea', has narrow, arching blades, almost entirely bright yellow with only the suggestion of green striping, at their most vivid in late spring and early summer. The flowers are a kind of non-colour topped by chocolate-brown spikelets. Slow to settle, the golden sedge makes a good clump in time, and can be increased by division in spring.

CIMICIFUGA SIMPLEX

herbaceous perennial H 1.2–2.1m/4–7ft S 60cm–1.2m/2–4ft autumn Z 3–8 [unless indicated]

The finest of the bugbanes, *Cimicifuga simplex* brings a spring-like note of freshness to the autumn garden, with its tall, white bottlebrush wands of flower over deeply dissected foliage. It reaches its greatest size in *C.* var. *simplex* 'Prichard's Giant' (*C. ramosa*) [Z 4–8], which makes an ample pile of foliage beneath the branching flower spikes. *C. simplex* var. *matsumurae* 'Elstead', latest to flower, is distinguished by its purple stems and buds opening to ivory flowers with pink stamens. Purple suffuses even the foliage of the *C.* var. *simplex* Atropurpurea Group, which must be grown in an open position in full light if the metallic bronze-purple tones are not to fade to a dirty green.

With this caveat, all bugbanes will grow and flower with reasonable abandon in light shade; moist soil is a must. Their wiry stems need no staking. The plants can be increased by division or seed; purple-leaved parents breed reasonably true and the best seedlings can be selected.

FILIPENDULA

herbaceous perennials H 90cm–1.8m/3–6ft S 60cm–1.2m/2–4ft summer Z 3–9

The meadowsweets have flat, fluffy heads of tiny flowers, cream or pink or cerise-crimson, over jagged foliage. The European queen of the meadows, *Filipendula ulmaria*, is pretty enough with its cream flowers, but in the garden its selected cultivar 'Aurea' is the one to choose, on account of its bright lime to chartreuse yellow foliage which fades to sulphur where touched by the sun. It must have plenty of light if it is not to fade to off-green, and a moist soil, lest the sunkisses turn to brown scorch; and the flowers should be removed, for they divert the plant's energies from its foliage, and anyway seedlings come plain green.

Among pink-flowered species, *F. purpurea* is first to show its wide heads of countless glowing cerise flowers, followed in a week or so by the paler pink *F. palmata*, of which 'Elegantissima' and 'Rosea' are fine selections. The queen of the prairies, *F. rubra*, is a whopping plant, fast-spreading in moist soil, with big leaves and huge flat heads of washy pink flowers; in 'Venusta' the colour most nearly approaches a decided pink.

The meadowsweets can all be increased by division. Despite the size of their flower heads, even the tallest are unlikely to need staking.

ABOVE Filipendula palmata *'Rosea' is a richly-coloured selection of the pink meadowsweet, its candy-pink, bubbly buds and the froth of the open florets floating light and airy above the boldly jagged green leaves.*

iris
heraldic symbols

DETAILS FROM TOP:

In Iris sibirica *'Limeheart', the breeders art has produced a flower of unusual charm and poise.*

The gold pencillings of Iris chrysographes *invite close inspection, while from a distance the near-black forms are strikingly distinct.*

Iris ensata *has given rise to a range of cultivars with such wide, flat flowers that they seem more like a clematis than an iris.*

The common name of Iris pseudacorus *is yellow flag, a reminder that the flowers of irises have been stylized into the heraldic symbol known as the* fleur de lis.

MAIN PICTURE:

Iris sibirica, *like every other iris, is beautiful at every stage, from scrolled bud to full flaunting petal-spread.*

IRIS

herbaceous perennials H 30–90cm/1–3ft
S 30–45cm/1–1½ft summer Z 4–9 [unless indicated]

The season of moisture-loving irises opens in early summer with *Iris chrysographes* [Z 6–9], which is at its most beautiful in its so-called black forms, velvety-dark of petal to contrast with the fine gold scribblings described in the botanical name. The flowers reach knee-high or a little more, over narrow, grassy foliage. The yellow flag, *I. pseudacorus* [Z 5–9], has a striking cultivar known as 'Variegata', of which the sword leaves emerge brightly striped with primrose and butter yellow in spring, turning, after the yellow flowers fade at midsummer, to plain green. Be sure to remove the seedheads before they ripen, as this is a free-seeding beast and all the young come green-leaved. Also flowering in early summer is *I. sibirica*, of similar style to *I. chrysographes* but taller, and ranging in colour from the violet-blue of the type to rich purple and claret, Cambridge blue and white; named cultivars of merit include 'Perry's Blue' and paler 'Ottawa', rich blue 'Flight of Butterflies' which has white, blue-veined falls, blue 'Papillon' and yellow-hearted 'White Swirl', plum-red 'Helen Astor', and sultry 'Tropic Night'.

In Iris laevigata *'Variegata', the light green broadsword leaves are striped with ivory and cream.*

The flowers of the Japanese water irises, *I. ensata* (*I. kaempferi*) [Z 5–9] and *I. laevigata*, are far more exuberant confections than the dainty flights of the Siberian iris. Colours range from white and ice-lavender to rich violet, and from mauve to royal purple. *I. ensata* 'Rose Queen' is a fine cultivar in the old style with drooping falls, in dusky lilac-pink. *I. laevigata*, which will even grow in shallow water, comes in lavender or white; the light green leaves are striped, in 'Variegata', with cream.

The least demanding of moisture among these irises is *I. sibirica*, though it will do just as well in a boggy patch as in good border soil; all the others must have abundant moisture, and *I. ensata* demands, in addition, a soil free of lime. They all flower most freely in sunny places but will tolerate light shade. Cultivars must be increased by division; seed of some species, notably *I. chrysographes*, is worth sowing.

Few yellow-daisied plants have more quality than the substantial Ligularia dentata *'Othello', its yolk-yellow tones set off by their dark stems and by the maroon reverse to the bold, kidney-shaped leaves.*

The rich blue of Lobelia siphilitica*'s alert-seeming flowers is enhanced by the white flash at the base of each pointy petal.*

Ligularia

herbaceous perennials H 1.2–1.8m/4–6ft
s 60–90cm/2–3ft summer Z 4-8

The flaunting yellow or burnt orange daisies and spires of ligularias light up high to late summer. Alluring to butterflies, they are big leafy plants revelling in soggy soil in a sunny place. In the well-known *Ligularia dentata* 'Othello' and 'Desdemona' the colour-schemes of the flowers are further heightened by the rich mahogany-crimson reverse to the bronze-green, kidney-shaped leaves. Their saffron daisies are borne in wide, flattish clusters. The taller 'Gregynog Gold' has heart-shaped green leaves and broad spires of golden-orange daisies. The narrower spikes of yolk-yellow daisies of *L. veitchiana* are held over very large, almost circular leaves; in fluffy, pale seed the spikes remain attractive, if less colourful. The rich coloring of ligularias calls for assertive companions, such as scarlet *Lobelia* 'Queen Victoria' or purple *Lobelia × gerardii* 'Vedrariensis'.

The cultivars should be increased by division; species can be seed-raised or divided to make more.

Lobelia

herbaceous perennials H 90cm–1.2m/3–4ft
s 30cm/1ft summer Z 3–9 [unless indicated]

The moisture-loving lobelias are completely unlike the lowly blue lobelia of bedding schemes; instead, they bear upright spikes of lipped flowers in a range of colours that includes not only blue but also, more commonly, fuliginous scarlet, together with cerise and garnet, royal purple and shocking pink. The scarlet shades derive from the cardinal flower, *Lobelia cardinalis*, which has green foliage. In the enduring old hybrid 'Queen Victoria' vivid scarlet flowers are allied with rich beetroot-purple foliage, derived from the more tender *L. fulgens* [Z 8–9]. A bright pink, somewhat too leafy for my taste, is 'Pink Flamingo'. Hybrids bred for greater hardiness include cerise 'Cherry Ripe', and velvety garnet, dark-leaved 'Dark Crusader'. *L. × gerardii* 'Vedrariensis' [Z 5–8] is crimson-purple, and *L. siphilitica* [Z 4–8] comes in blue or white.

All these lobelias, hardy or no, are vulnerable to slug damage in early spring, so it is worth lifting a few of the rosettes and wintering them in slug-proof, frost-free, moist peat, while also guarding from slugs any rosettes that you leave in the open ground. Propagation is by division or by two-node cuttings of the flowering stems after the flowers fade, overwintered in a frost-free place; the species can also be seed-raised, and 'Vedrariensis' is reputed to come reasonably true from seed also.

Lysichiton

herbaceous perennials H 90cm–1.2m/3–4ft
s 90cm–1.8m/3–6ft early spring Z 7–9

The bog arums need plenty of space in a bog or even in shallow, flowing water, for their leaves, especially those of *Lysichiton americanus*, are huge, clear green, soap-smooth paddles up to 1.2m/4ft long. At flowering time, it seems restrained enough, with its pointed, clear yellow spathes, smelling curiously like cheap instant coffee (the fruits that follow smell distinctly nasty). White-flowered *L. camtschatcensis* is a little smaller; hybrids between the two come in alluring shades of primrose or ivory. All are beautiful in flower, with the elegant lines common to most arums; in early spring when there is little else in flower, they are doubly welcome. Both species sow themselves freely in wet soil. Unwanted seedlings should be removed when still small; big plants have big roots, calling for something nearer to a mechanical digger than a spade.

Onoclea sensibilis

deciduous fern H 60cm/2ft S 90cm/3ft foliage Z 3–8

The sensitive fern has arching, fresh green fronds divided into broad, finger-like pinnae, retaining a spring-like freshness of tint until, at the first touch of frost they turn to a warm russet tint. Beautiful in cool foliage schemes, the sensitive fern also makes a graceful setting for the flowery moisture-lovers such as primulas, iris or lobelias. The running roots thrive in wet soils, and can easily be divided if you want to start another colony.

Osmunda regalis

deciduous fern H 1.2m/4ft S 90cm/3ft foliage Z 4–9

The royal fern is well named, for it is a grand thing at all stages from the moment, in spring, when the tan-brown croziers unfurl, through the summer maturity of its tall, rich green fronds to its dying autumn harmonies of lemon and rust-red (see page 203). Like the sensitive fern, it revels in marshy soils. It can be divided, but you will need a sharp spade and plenty of muscle to cut through the solid mat of roots. Alternatively, you can sow the dust-fine spores that form on the reverse of the fronds. When suited, ferns will often sow themselves.

Framed against the still, dark waters of a pool, the clear yellow spathes of Lysichiton americanus *glow in the spring sunshine.*

The spring-fresh green of the sensitive fern, Onoclea sensibilis, *gives full value to the rich royal purple* Iris sibirica *on its proud, stiff stems. Behind,* Geranium endressi *makes a weed-excluding carpet.*

The strong magenta of Primula beesiana, *one of the most obliging of the candelabra primulas, is here cooled by glaucous-blue hostas against a background of fern fronds.*

PRIMULA

herbaceous perennials H 15–90cm/6in–3ft
S 30–60cm/1–2ft spring, early summer
Z 6–8 [unless indicated]

Primulas are among the most alluring of flowering plants for damp places, to which the candelabras, in particular, bring a range of vivid or subtle colours. The cowslip-like Sikkimensis primulas are also deliciously fragrant. One of the earliest flowers in the bog garden is *Primula rosea* [Z 5–8], a diminutive creature with shocking-pink flowers opening at the first hint of the unfurling, red-bronze leaves, at first snug at ground level and gradually lengthening their stems. It spreads fast when happy. The drumstick primula, *P. denticulata* [Z 4–7], is almost as early, bearing its rounded heads on strong stems before the long, narrow leaves; the usual colour is soft lavender, and pure white is also common, but it also comes in purple, rose and ruby shades, increased by root cuttings to be sure of maintaining the colour – seed gives varying colours. In late spring it is the turn of the first of the candelabra primulas, the stocky *P. japonica* [Z 4–8], which has the typical candelabra whorls of outward-facing flowers, more closely-packed than its taller, later cousins, in crimson-purple or white ('Postford White' which comes more or less true from seed, sometimes with a pink eye), as well as the purer red of 'Miller's Crimson', or pink shades. Following *P. japonica*, in early summer, comes the taller *P. pulverulenta* [Z 5–8], its name derived from the mealy white stems on which are borne rich crimson-magenta flowers (see page 206); or pale shell to coral pink, in the Bartley hybrids. Another with rosy-magenta flowers is yellow-eyed *P. beesiana* [Z 5–8]. By now the candelabra season is in full swing, and the potential for horrible colour clashes is considerable. The tall *P. bulleyana* has clear orange flowers, and similar colours belong to a pair of species of modest dimensions, *P. chungensis* with red-budded flowers and the dainty, tangerine-orange *P. cockburniana* [Z 5–8]. Brighter still, and much bigger, is 'Inverewe', a sterile hybrid that must be increased by division; just a few stems of its assertive vermilion-orange flowers may be enough, cooled by white-variegated hostas or flaunting among lime and chartreuse foliage and the sultry dark leaves and burnt orange bracts of *Euphorbia griffithii* in the wonderful form named 'Dixter'. There is a grand yellow-flowered candelabra primula too, *P. prolifera* [Z 5–8], with orange buds opening to bright yellow flowers and a sweet fragrance.

The most delicious fragrance belongs to the cowslip-like Sikkimensis primulas, with their nodding bells in early summer. The group is named for *P. sikkimensis* itself, a charmer with mealy-white stems and sulphur-yellow bells, exquisite with the velvety black forms of *Iris chrysographes*. *P. alpicola* comes in ivory, primrose or lavender-grey. Much taller than these, with broad rather than narrow leaves, is the giant Tibetan cowslip, *P. florindae* [Z 5–8], with hanging, soft yellow, white-dusted bells and the true cowslip fragrance. It seeds itself freely, but is sometimes tainted with alien blood to produce a range of seedlings in art shades, copper and tangerine and cinnabar.

The poker-flowered *P. vialii* [Z 6–7] is very different from these, with its dense, tapering poker spikes, at their most bizarre at the half-way stage when the upper portion of the spike is still in tight scarlet bud and the lower fully expanded into a cylinder of mauve-violet. I have never found it reliably perennial, but suspect that losses are as often due to theft as to slugs or senescence. In late summer and autumn, comes *P. capitata* [Z 5–8]. Like a refined *P. denticulata*, it has dense rounded heads of violet flowers over a rosette of white-backed leaves.

These primulas are increased by division, for identical offspring, or seed, for fun and maybe something new and exciting.

RHEUM

herbaceous perennial H 1.8m/6ft S 1.8m/6ft
early summer Z 5–9

The massive *Rheum palmatum* 'Atrosanguineum' and 'Bowles' Crimson' have large jagged leaves, crimson as they emerge and remaining red-bronzed above and burgundy on the reverse until the tall spires of bright crimson-red flowers open in early summer. There are few more handsome foliage plants than the ornamental rhubarb, where space allows it to reach its full potential. They need moist, rich soil, though not an out-and-out bog; some say, indeed, that permanently soggy soil may rot the crown, though my 'Atrosanguineum' for years survived being submerged under feet of cold water for days on end in winter.

The great metallic purple leaves of Rheum palmatum *'Bowles' Crimson' unfurl from crimson-scarlet leaf buds and eventually fade to bronzed red above and rich maroon beneath.*

Touched to coppery-bronze by the sun, the bold leaves of Rodgersia aesculifolia *are thrown into relief by the foam of pink astilbe spikes beyond.*

Originally known only in its crimson-scarlet form, the satin-petalled kaffir lily, Schizostylis coccinea, *is now available in the full range from white through to crimson. One of the finest pink cultivars is 'Sunrise', ample of petal and abundant in bloom.*

Rodgersia

herbaceous perennials H 90cm–1.2m/3–4ft
S 60–90cm/2–3ft summer Z 5–7

Handsome foliage of a different order belongs to the rodgersias: *Rodgersia aesculifolia* with leaves like a horse chestnut's only larger, bronzed where the light touches them; dark-leaved *R. pinnata* 'Superba'; and *R. podophylla*, with leaves like a big webbed foot, copper-tinted at first turning to bronzed green in summer and metallic, burnished bronze in autumn. The first has tall plumes of ivory or creamy-pink flowers, the second rich pink spires. I have never seen a flower on *R. podophylla*, but the leaves are ample compensation. All can be increased by division, or seed when it is formed.

Salix

deciduous shrubs H 1.8–2.4m/6–8ft S 1.8–2.4m/6–8ft
foliage and bark Z 3–8 [unless indicated]

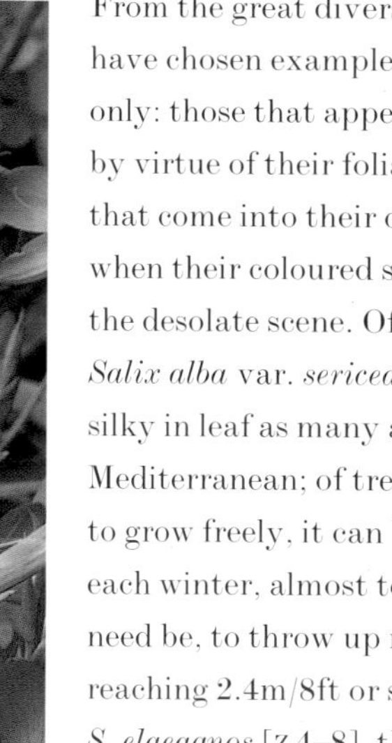

From the great diversity of willows I have chosen examples of two groups only: those that appeal in summer, by virtue of their foliage, and those that come into their own in winter, when their coloured stems light up the desolate scene. Of the former, *Salix alba* var. *sericea* is as silvery-silky in leaf as many a sun-loving Mediterranean; of tree stature if left to grow freely, it can be hard-pruned each winter, almost to the ground if need be, to throw up new stems reaching 2.4m/8ft or so. In *S. elaeagnos* [Z 4–8], the hoary willow, the leaves are needle-slender, grey on the upper surface and white beneath, on slender, dark maroon stems; the shrub forms a rounded dome, head-high or more, and is especially appealing when a breeze ruffles its feathers to make a play of pewter and platinum tints. The slender and dainty *S. purpurea* 'Pendula' has leaves almost as narrow, of dark sea-green, on whip-fine, drooping stems. The willows with coloured winter stems include those with plum-purple, white-bloomed stems, such as *S. irrorata* (a lovely name, meaning 'bedewed'), [Z 5–8] and the brighter *S. alba* var. *vitellina* in yolk-yellow and *S. alba* var. *vitellina* 'Britzensis' in orange-scarlet. As with the silvered white willow, hard pruning – in early spring, so as not to lose the winter display – keeps them compact and ensures a fresh annual supply of young growths, which have the best colour.

Willows are easily increased by hardwood cuttings, which can be simply stuck in the ground, at any time during autumn or winter, where a new plant is required.

Schizostylis coccinea

herbaceous perennial H 60cm/2ft S 30cm/1ft
autumn Z 6–9

The kaffir lilies are among the last flowers of the season, their satiny, crimson-scarlet, pink or white flowers – which are not very much like lilies at all, for these are iris relatives – opening from early to late autumn or even in winter. *Schizostylis coccinea*, typically scarlet-crimson, has given rise to cultivars which extend the season over three or four months, from pale pink 'Mrs Hegarty' to the bright, clear pink 'Sunrise'.

In moist soil, or even shallow water, kaffir lilies increase fast at the root to make a thicket of grassy blades, and can easily be divided to make a generous colony in little time. A single potful from a reputable nursery could make a dozen divisions right away, and quickly grow into a drift.

TROLLIUS

herbaceous perennials H 60–90cm/2–3ft
S 30–45cm/1–1½ft spring/summer Z 3–7

The globe flower of damp, subalpine meadows, *Trollius europaeus*, is one of the delights of spring, with its clear citron, cupped flowers. Hybrid cultivars known collectively as *T.* × *cultorum* are bigger and often brighter, but no lovelier, in shades of primrose ('Earliest of All'), lemon ('Lemon Queen') and buttercup ('Canary Bird'), corn-gold and tangerine ('Orange Princess'). The warmer shades may come from the blood of *T. chinensis*, which has a bowl of outer petals around a central cluster of petaloid stamens; 'Golden Queen' is a fine cultivar, though to my eye with less charm than the globe flower. Later, in early summer, it is the turn of *T. yunnanensis*, which has wide-open saucer flowers of gleaming yellow with green reverse.

The globe flowers need a moist to boggy soil and can be increased by seed, or by division of named cultivars.

There are bolder, brighter cultivars of the globe flower, but none can rival the beauty of the wild species, Trollius europaeus, *which illumines damp subalpine meadows with its cupped lemon-yellow blooms.*

ZANTEDESCHIA

herbaceous perennials H 60cm–1.2m/2–4ft
S 45–60cm/1½–2ft summer Z 9–10

Though it looks so exotic, the most frost-resistant of arum lilies is the lily of the Nile, *Zantedeschia aethiopica*, which has bold, broad spear-head leaves of shining green to set off its great white spathes with the golden candle of the spadix at their hearts. 'Green Goddess' is a curiosity with green, not white spathes. Planted in water deep enough to keep their crowns from freezing, they will survive quite severe winters; in the open ground a good mulch is advisable where frost may threaten them. The coloured arum lilies are more tender: *Z. elliottiana* in clear yellow, with white-flecked leaves, and *Z. rehmannii* in soft pink, narrower of both spathe and leaf. A range of coloured hybrids has recently become available, including yellow with black heart, shades of pure yellow to tangerine (see page 204), dusky pinks and mauves and magnolia-purples. Cultivars must be divided to keep true to type; species can be seed-raised.

The leaves of the white arum lily, Zantedeschia aethiopica, *are handsome, broad spearheads of dark, bloomy green, amid which arise elegant spathes enfolding a rich yellow spadix. In 'Green Goddess' the pure white of the spathes is suffused with peridot green at the tips.*

index

Figures in bold type refer to main entries, figures in *italics* refer to illustrations and captions

acknowledgments

The publisher thanks the photographers and organizations for their kind permission to reproduce the photographs on the following pages:

1 Andrew Lawson; 2-5 Marijke Heuff; 6-7 Andrew Lawson; 8 S & O Mathews; 10-11 Marijke Heuff/Mrs L Goosenaerts, Holland; 12-13 S & O Mathews/RHS garden, Wisley; 14 Marijke Heuff/ Hidcote; 15 left S & O Mathews; 15 above right Marijke Heuff/Noailles, France; 15 below right Marijke Heuff/ Mrs L Goosenaerts, Holland; 16 Marijke Heuff; 17 above Marijke Heuff/Family Lenshoek; 17 below left Marijke Heuff/Mr & Mrs Poley, Holland; 17 below right Andrew Lawson; 18 left Marijke Heuff/Mrs L Goosenaerts, Holland; 18 right Marijke Heuff/Arcade Kalmthout, Belgium; 19 below Marijke Heuff/Mrs M van Bennekom, Holland; 20 John Glover; 21 Andrew Lawson; 22 top Andrew Lawson; 22 above John Glover; 22 below S & O Mathews; 22 bottom Anne Hyde; 22-23 Marijke Heuff; 23 Andrew Lawson; 24 above Jane Taylor; 24 below Andrew Lawson; 25 Andrew Lawson; 26 S & O Mathews; 27 left Harry Smith Collection; 27 right Andrew Lawson; 28 Marijke Heuff; 29 Marijke Heuff/La Casella, France; 30 above S & O Mathews; 30 below S & O Mathews; 31 Neil Campbell-Sharp; 32 Eric Crichton; 33 above Eric Crichton; 33 below S & O Mathews; 34 top & above Marijke Heuff; 34 below S & O Mathews; 34 bottom Oxford Scientific Films/Deni Bown; 34-35 Marijke Heuff; 35 Michèle Lamontagne; 36 above John Fielding Slide Library; 36 below Marijke Heuff/ Mr & Mrs Gentis, Holland; 37 left Eric Crichton; 37 right Andrew Lawson; 38 above Marijke Heuff/Mrs M van Bennekom, Holland; 38 below Neil Campbell-Sharp; 39 above Marijke Heuff/ Mr & Mrs Poley, Holland; 39 below Andrew Lawson; 40 above Andrew Lawson; 40 below Jane Taylor; 41 S & O Mathews; 42 top & below Marijke Heuff; 42 above Marijke Heuff; 42 bottom John Glover; 42-43 Marijke Heuff; 43 Marijke Heuff; 44 above Andrew Lawson; 44 below Harry Smith Collection; 45 Andrew Lawson; 46 top, above & below Marijke Heuff; 46 bottom S & O Mathews; 46-47 Marijke Heuff; 47 Marijke Heuff; 48 above Andrew Lawson; 48 below Neil Campbell-Sharp; 49 Marijke Heuff; 50 S & O Mathews; 51 left Eric Crichton; 51 right Marijke Heuff; 52 Andrew Lawson; 53 left John Glover; 53 right S & O Mathews; 54 top Michèle Lamontagne; 54 above Garden Picture Library/John Glover; 54 below Marijke Heuff; 54 bottom Eric Crichton; 54-55 A-Z Botanical/Anthony Seinet; 55 Oxford Scientific Films/Deni Bown; 56 above John Glover; 56 below Royal Botanc Garden, Edinburgh; 57 Garden Picture Library/Gary Rogers; 58 top S & O Mathews; 58 above & below Marijke Heuff; 58 bottom Andrew Lawson; 58-59 Marijke Heuff; 59 Andrew Lawson; 60 top & below Andrew Lawson; 60 above & bottom Marijke Heuff; 61 Marijke Heuff; 62 Andrew Lawson; 63 above John Glover; 63 below S & O Mathews; 64 Clive Nichols; 65 Andrew Lawson; 66-67 Marijke Heuff; 68-69 Marijke Heuff/La Casella, France; 70 left S & O Mathews; 70 right Andrew Lawson; 71 Marijke Heuff; 72 left Marijke Heuff/ Mrs L Goosenaerts, Holland; 72 centre Marijke Heuff/designer Piet Oudolf, Holland, 72 right Marijke Heuff/Old Rectory, Burghfield; 73 Marijke Heuff; 74 top & above Marijke Heuff; 74 below & bottom S & O Mathews; 74-75 Marijke Heuff; 75 Marijke Heuff; 76 top & below Marijke Heuff; 76 above & bottom Andrew Lawson; 77 Clive Nichols; 78 above S & O Mathews; 78 below Andrew Lawson; 79 Marijke Heuff/Mrs L Goosenaerts, Holland; 80 above S & O Mathews; 80 below John Glover; 81 Andrew Lawson; 82 Eric Crichton; 83 left S & O Mathews; 83 right Marijke Heuff/ Old Rectory, Burghfield; 86 above John Glover; 86 below Eric Crichton; 87 Jane Taylor; 88 Andrew Lawson; 89 Marijke Heuff/Ilnacullin, Ireland (on Garnish Island); 90-91 Marijke Heuff/ garden designer Piet Oudolf, Holland; 92 Marijke Heuff/Mrs G Lauxtermann, Holland; 93 above Marijke Heuff/The Priona gardens, Holland; 93 below Marijke Heuff; 94 above Marijke Heuff; 94 below Andrew Lawson; 95 Marijke Heuff/La Casella, France; 96 above Oxford Scientific Films/Deni Bown; 96 below Marijke Heuff/Mrs G Lauxtermann, Holland; 97 S & O Mathews; 98 Marijke Heuff/Mr & Mrs Helsen, Holland; 99 above Andrew Lawson; 99 below S & O Mathews; 100 left Jerry Harpur/Great Dixter, North Iam, East Sussex; 100 right S & O Mathews; 101 Marijke Heuff; 102-103 S & O Mathews; 104 Andrew Lawson; 105 Marijke Heuff; 106 Marijke Heuff/Els de Boer, Holland; 107 Andrew Lawson; 108 top Harry Smith Collection; 108 above Noel Kavanagh; 108 below & bottom S & O Mathews; 108-109 S & O Mathews; 109 S & O Mathews; 110 top S & O Mathews; 110 above Andrew Lawson; 110 below A-Z Botanical/Mrs P S Baker; 110 bottom John Glover; 111 left Andrew Lawson; 111 right A-Z Botanical/'The Picture Source'; 112 above John Glover; 112 below S & O Mathews; 113 Marijke Heuff/Mrs M van Bennekom, Holland; 114 top Clive Nichols; 114 above Anne Hyde; 114 below Marijke Heuff; 114 bottom Andrew Lawson; 114-115 Neil Campbell-Sharp; 115 Marijke Heuff; 116 John Glover; 117 Andrew Lawson; 118 Andrew Lawson; 119 above Charles Mann; 119 below Andrew Lawson; 120 left Jerry Harpur/Great Dixter, North Iam, East Sussex; 120 right Andrew Lawson/ credit Sticky Wicket Dorchester, Dorset; 121 above Derek Gould; 121 below John Glover; 122 Eric Crichton; 123 left Jerry Harpur; 123 right Andrew Lawson; 124 John Fielding Slide Library; 125 above Clive Nichols; 125 below Marijke Heuff; 126 S & O Mathews; 127 above Marijke Heuff; 127 below Neil Campbell-Sharp; 128 Marijke Heuff/Mr & Mrs Torringa, Holland, 129 above Jerry Harpur/Iden Croft Herbs, Kent; 129 below Marijke Heuff/garden designer Jean Mus, France; 130 Marijke Heuff/ Brookwell, Surrey; 131 above John Glover; 131 below Jerry Harpur/Beth Chatto; 132 Marijke Heuff/ Mrs L Goosenaerts, Holland; 133 S & O Mathews/Saling Hall; 134-135 Andrew Lawson; 136 Marijke Heuff/ Tonter Linden; 137 Marijke Heuff; 138 S & O Mathews; 139 above John Glover; 139 below left Andrew Lawson; 139 below right Andrew Lawson; 140 left Marijke Heuff/The Priona garden, Holland; 140 right Marijke Heuff/ Helmingham House, Suffolk; 141 Marijke Heuff; 142 top & below Marijke Heuff; 142 above Andrew Lawson; 142 bottom Neil Campbell-Sharp; 142-143 Marijke Heuff; 143 Andrew Lawson; 144 S & O Mathews; 145 above John Glover; 145 below Andrew Lawson; 146 above Marijke Heuff; 146 below John Fielding Slide Library; 147 Marijke Heuff; 148 above John Glover; 148 below Andrew Lawson; 149 Andrew Lawson; 150 Andrew Lawson; 151 above S & O Mathews; 151 below Neil Campbell-Sharp; 152 above Clive Nichols; 152 below Neil Campbell-Sharp; 153 John Fielding Slide Library; 154 Derek Gould; 155 Clive Nichols; 156-157 Marijke Heuff; 158 A-Z Botanical/ Terence Exley; 159 Marijke Heuff/Mrs L Goosenaerts, Holland; 160 Andrew Lawson; 161 above S & O Mathews; 161 below Andrew Lawson; 162 top Marijke Heuff; 162 above & below Andrew Lawson; 162 bottom S & O Mathews; 162-163 Marijke Heuff; 163 Marijke Heuff; 164 above S & O Mathews; 164 below Andrew Lawson; 165 Neil Campbell-Sharp; 166 Marijke Heuff/ Mrs L Goosenaerts, Holland; 166 left Andrew Lawson; 167 right Marijke Heuff; 168-169 Andrew Lawson; 170 left Marijke Heuff/Mrs L Goosenaerts, Holland; 170 right Marijke Heuff; 171 left Andrew Lawson/Bosvigo garden; 171 right Marijke Heuff; 172 above left Marijke Heuff; 172 below left Marijke Heuff; 173 right Andrew Lawson; 174 above Andrew Lawson; 174 below John Glover; 175 above Marijke Heuff; 175 below Andrew Lawson; 176 left Andrew Lawson; 176 right John Glover; 177 S & O Mathews; 178 S & O Mathews/ Hambledon House; 179 above Andrew Lawson; 179 below John Glover; 180 above Jane Taylor; 180 below S & O Mathews; 181 Marijke Heuff; 182 top & below John Glover; 182 above Eric Crichton; 182 bottom S & O Mathews; 182-183 Marijke Heuff; 183 Andrew Lawson; 184 Marijke Heuff; 185 above Eric Crichton; 185 below Jane Taylor; 186 top Andrew Lawson; 186 above & bottom S & O Mathews; 186 below MarijkeHeuff; 186-187 Marijke Heuff; 187 Andrew Lawson; 188 above Marijke Heuff; 188 below Marijke Heuff/Mrs L Goosenaerts, Holland; 189 left S & O Mathews; 189 right Andrew Lawson; 190 above Marijke Heuff; 190 below John Glover; 191 above Clive Nichols; 191 below Andrew Lawson; 192 S & O Mathews; 193 above Oxford Scientific Films/Deni Bown; 193 below S & O Mathews; 194 left Marijke Heuff; 194 right John Glover; 195 above Andrew Lawson; 195 below S & O Mathews; 196 above A-Z Botanical/Anthony Seinet; 196 below S & O Mathews; 197 Andrew Lawson; 198 above John Glover; 198 below Marijke Heuff; 199 above S & O Mathews; 199 below John Glover; 200 S & O Mathews; 201 above Neil Campbell-Sharp; 201 below S & O Mathews; 202-203 John Glover; 204 above Marijke Heuff/Mrs L Goosenaerts, Holland; 204 below Michèle Lamontagne; 205 Marijke Heuff/Bordehill, Sussex; 206 Andrew Lawson; 206 below Andrew Lawson; 207 Andrew Lawson; 208 Jane Taylor; 209 left Andrew Lawson; 209 right Clive Nichols; 210 top & below S & O Mathews; 210 above & bottom Marijke Heuff; 210-211 Marijke Heuff; 211 Marijke Heuff; 212 above Andrew Lawson; 212 below Marijke Heuff; 213 above Andrew Lawson; 213 below Eric Crichton; 214 S & O Mathews/RHS Garden, Wisley; 215 S & O Mathews; 216 above John Glover; 216 below S & O Mathews; 217 Andrew Lawson.

hardiness zones

The hardines zones given for each plant are an indication of the minimum temperatures that a plant will tolerate. Hardiness depends a many factors, including the depth of a plant's roots, the rate at which temperatures drop, the duration of the cold weather and the temperatures during the preceding summer. The zone ratings are based on those devised by the United States Department of Agriculture. Zones are allocated to plants according to their tolerance of winter cold in Western Europe. In climates with hotter and/or drier summers, such as in Australasia, some plants will survive colder temperatures and their hardiness in these countries may be a zone lower than quoted.

°CELSIUS	ZONES	°FAHRENHEIT
below -45	1	below -50
-45 to -40	2	-50 to -40
-40 to -34	3	-40 to -30
-34 to -29	4	-30 to -20
-29 to -23	5	-20 to -10
-23 to -18	6	-10 to 0
-18 to -12	7	0 to 10
-12 to -7	8	10 to 20
-7 to -1	9	20 to 30
-1 to 4	10	30 to 40
above 4	11	above 40